Another Promised Land

Paulette Jones

Onwards and Upwards Publishers

Berkeley House, 11 Nightingale Crescent, Leatherhead,
Surrey, KT24 6PD.

www.onwardsandupwards.org

Printed in the UK.

ISBN: 978-1-910197-12-7
Typeface: Sabon LT
Graphic design: LM Graphic Design

About the Author

Paulette Jones lives in south-west France with her husband, where they run a rest & recuperation project called Joie de Vie for current military personnel, veterans and those who work closely with our Armed Forces. Their son and daughter are fervent city professionals back in Blighty, but happy to swap a few weeks of the year for the calm of rural France.

Paulette has no French family connections; her mother chose her French name simply for its appeal. As a small child she scribbled stories and attempted to illustrate her own little paperbacks – the highlight being to be able to borrow her father's stapler to fashion a smart book spine! As an adult she had absolutely no intention of writing a book until someone very mighty kept telling her to get on with it!

She is a keen long-distance walker, a volunteer case worker for SSAFA France Lifelong support for the Forces, a supporter of the Royal Air Force Association Sud-Ouest France branch and, much to her astonishment, in March 2014 became a councillor in the French Local Government Elections.

Endorsements

If you want to be assured that Jesus Christ is alive and interested in His people, read this delightful and heart-warming story. Throughout the time Paulette and her husband were preparing 'Joie de Vie' my wife and I had the privilege, together with others, of praying for each phase of the process. Moreover, having ourselves founded a Christian Conference Centre for the Armed Forces, we know that what is described in this inspiring book is only the half of it, and I was struck again by the greatness of the God we serve – a God who is able to take what is offered, no matter how weak or ill-equipped and make something wonderful out of it.

We have already experienced the warmth and sheer delight of visiting St. Fort sur le Né. So, to any Serviceman or woman considering a break, I'd say, "Go!" You will encounter a right royal welcome in an enchanting, healing and peaceful setting.

Wing Commander Dan Gleed E P Cert FCMI RAF (Ret'd)

Paulette is one of those people for whom hard work, guts and determination are a way of life. This attitude is so much of a part of her that I doubt whether she realises what a powerful example she sets to us all, which shows clearly in her book. There is no doubt that it is a record of her faith and how she has overcome the challenges to it along the way. It would have been easy for her to fall into the trap of writing something that sought to enlist our sympathy, but this she has not done. In a paradoxical way her book is always upbeat, even at those times when she describes herself as lonely, in pain and scared during the treatment for her ailment. I was reminded of St Paul's attitude to his 'thorn in the flesh'. Her commitment to prayer is clear and a fine example to us all. The book is worth reading for that alone.

I have had the privilege of staying with the Joneses at their home in France, and I can vouch that despite all the energy around Paulette it is an oasis of peace and tranquillity. The Joie de Vie project, which she so lovingly describes, has turned out to be everything she and her husband wanted it to be, and I have no doubt that this book will be an inspiration to many.

Tony Gilbert
Team Rector of the Three Valleys Benefice
Former RAF Chaplain

Paulette tells her story in a very humble manner that is inspiring, honest and easy to read. It left me rejoicing at God's work in her life and how He is using her in France today. I am delighted that she has written this book so that others can be encouraged that God does heal today.

Frances Cunningham
Retired military wife

Paulette tells her remarkable story with honesty and clarity. How does an independent-minded and self-reliant coper deal with being stripped bare like a peeled orange? Her experience of suffering chronic pain whilst still attempting to be a good mother and an exemplary military wife leaves her feeling overwhelmed by fear, despair and depression. From the wreckage of her well-constructed dreams there emerges a growing recognition of God's love for her. The Pied-Piper storyteller figure of her childhood, Jesus, draws alongside as a new, unchangeable friend. As she learns to lean on him rather than her own resources the story she tells is one of healing and re-building as she allows herself to be led on an adventure far more fulfilling and purposeful than she had ever imagined.

This is a story to lift and encourage anyone who is struggling to cope; anyone who cries out, "Why me?" Paulette's story allows us to dare to hold on to hope and to dare to trust there will be light at the end of the tunnel.

Rev'd Diana Rees-Jones
Former Curate of St. Firmin's Thurlby
Former Assistant Chaplain, Oundle School

Paulette's testimony illustrates that despite her trials and difficulties she remained convinced that her afflictions were working towards her restoration, and a life beyond her expectations. Her secret was that she had an encounter with Jesus which made all the difference. It led to her spending time prayerfully looking into the Scriptures with an openness of heart and mind. As result, her passion for Jesus and France has brought joy and blessing to the lives of many of her fellow travellers.

Squadron Leader Bob Abbott (Ret'd) MBE

After spending much of her life striving to be a capable military wife and mother whilst also studying and working, Paulette spurns spiritual guidance, preferring to believe that her life is full of "spookily fluky" coincidences! But discovering that nothing has occurred by accident, Paulette finds that her life is a navigator's chart inscribed by a Supreme hand with markers, routes, targets and a safe path home. Whether or not you believe in the Almighty, Paulette's journey is beautifully written in a gently amusing and engaging manner. You will want to turn the page to read on and find out what twists and turns her life holds. From a childhood passion for making little 'paperbacks' to a book of a life well lived – now that's a journey to Another Promised Land!

Squadron Leader Beryl Dennett-Stannard RAF (Ret'd)
Chairman, RAF Association Sud-Ouest France

Author's Note

All royalties received by the author will be donated to:

Armed Forces Christian Union
– Interdenominational tri-service all ranks fellowship for
serving, retired and associate members

Havelock House
Barrack Road
Aldershot
GU11 3NP

– and –

Combat Stress
– The Veteran's Mental Health Charity

Tyrwhitt House
Oaklawn Road
Leatherhead
KT22 0BX

Foreword by Jonathan Chaffey

There are three reasons why it is a delight for me to write this foreword: firstly, because I had the pleasure of sharing in part of Paulette's journey, during Phil's tour at RAF Waddington and their membership of the Station's church community; secondly, it is always a joy to highlight the wonderful touch of Jesus Christ on someone's life, the way that he meets us where we are and leads us along pathways that may be both familiar and somewhat adventurous; and finally, because any work in support of our Armed Forces personnel, their families and veterans should be applauded and given the widest possible circulation.

Paulette offers a story that will resonate with a broad audience. Some will simply enjoy a remarkable tale of adventure, starting with a romance that had its roots at school, through a very eventful journey to life and work in France. Military readers will recognise the sharing of her husband's dream to be a RAF pilot, with his subsequent tours on fast jet, tanker, training and reconnaissance aircraft. They will appreciate the graphic portrayal of the 'ups and downs' of Service life, the spice of flying display duties, the fun of the Mess and the rewarding nature of operational duties, juxtaposed with the trials of ejection and an uncertain future, with yet another house move impacting on a spouse's work and children's education.

Throw in a chronic and debilitating illness and you can imagine a highly stressed and potentially unsustainable situation. This is where the reader is treated to a description of the transformative power of Christian faith. Paulette discovered that Jesus is always available to meet us at our point of need. As she turned her heart, body and mind towards him, responding to his love and call, she received cleansing, healing and new direction. In the strategic purposes of God, so Phil also changed course and, together, they received an unexpected posting notice!

They stand as evidence that the 'God of Surprises' is able to take our gifts and histories, develop our passions and resource our projects in ways that will benefit others greatly. Joie de Vie is a timely and generous gift of 'R&R' to the Armed Forces community, both serving and retired. Following 25 years of continual operations in the Gulf, the Balkans and Afghanistan, there exists an unknown number of sailors, soldiers and airmen suffering cumulative strain from their service; some of this may be hidden while others carry more openly the physical and mental scars of their experience. Since its inception in 2011, the Armed Forces Covenant has articulated the contract between the UK and its military personnel, recognising the debt of honour that is owed to those who put their lives on the line as a 'force for good' and working to ensure fairness at a policy level. Nonetheless, the work of Joie de Vie at ground level, alongside agencies such as SSAFA and Combat Stress, remains crucial in connecting individuals with the support that they need.

Paulette's account of her journey with Phil, written with honesty and humour, is a really good read. More importantly, being full of hope, it invites the reader to trust for the future and especially in the God of hope who knows each of our unique stories.

Venerable Jonathan Chaffey
Chaplain-in-Chief, RAF
July 2014

CHAPTER ONE

Man is a mere phantom as he goes to and fro;
He bustles about, but only in vain...

Psalm 39:6

I was lying on a hard operating table and aware of many faces peering down; concerned eyes made more prominent by their tight blue masks. Huge lights, unnaturally bright overhead, sterile square ceiling tiles, strange equipment in my periphery... and suddenly a soft voice spoke matter-of-factly: "Now Paulette, you've got to think of somewhere really peaceful, calm and tranquil."

Sheer panic set in. I had been compliant and brave up to now, but this request unnerved me completely.

Time was of the essence.

Quick... think of something... quick... quick... think.

But I couldn't. Where had I known peace? Calm? Where? Where? A tranquil place? How do you grab such moments with two young children?

Another voice, sounding seriously efficient: "We are about to inject something in the cannula to put you to sleep."

Further panic set in because of not having done as first requested. I needed more time. I wasn't ready. My mind a whirl of questions and far from remaining calm. My brain seemed to have seized up. Was thinking of somewhere peaceful really important? Was it the difference between getting through the operation or not?

All of a sudden a tall majestic palm tree with beautiful waving branches came into my mind, and all I could do was mouth to myself... palm tree... peace... palm tree... peace... p...

Many hours later I was cocooned in the High Dependency Unit of the City Hospital, Nottingham beginning the first stage of recovery, having had a benign tumour known as a neurofibroma removed – a large tumour consisting of a mass of nerves, attached to an intercostal muscle, in the wall of my chest. I remember being seriously frightened, feeling totally out of control and fearing the different machines beside me as they omitted their ominous beeps. Any noise in the room seemed magnified and I couldn't shut out the noise or the fear. I desperately wanted to be able to fall asleep, to disappear from it all and ironically savour peace, calm and tranquillity.

Then the reality of the situation struck home: I had cheated death and had survived! Thank you, palm tree! I wanted to punch the air, but felt utterly exhausted to even lift a finger as my whole body felt very, very peculiar.

As my environment came more into focus I soon realised that I had two nurses personally caring for me who were disturbingly busy all around me. I remember feeling very annoyed about them constantly bustling around the bed, lifting the bed cover and letting the cold air rush in, lifting my limbs and peering too close to my face. They were much too much in my comfort zone, and I kept trying to turn my head to get away from them. On top of this, just when I thought I might slip into sleep they kept bothering me with ridiculous questions, as if I didn't know who I was or where I was.

Then yet another question: "What job do you do?" *For crying out loud,* I thought, *don't you realise that I've just had a lengthy major operation, I feel really terrible – and you want to know what job I do? (Surely, surely, it's in my notes!)*

With all the strength I could muster, I declared as loudly as possible, "I'm an astronaut!"

They both chuckled out loud with evident relief. "Now you are going to be alright!" one nurse said, and either they ceased to bother me quite as much or at long, long last I fell asleep.

This major operation had brought the reality of death far too close for my liking, and it had frightened me much more than I was willing to admit. It had brought me up really sharp. Life could be momentary and death could be quick. I don't think I spent too much time wondering about the actual meaning of life, but simply knew that I was far too young to die.

The skills of a great medical team had saved me and had given me the encouragement that normal life could resume where I had left off, if I did as they advised. Therefore any morbid contemplations and 'what ifs' had to be pushed aside as the most important thing now was to deal with the battle of recovery. I had to fix my sight ahead, with no time allowed for brooding, melancholy or pessimism in considering what might have been. All my efforts concentrated on just breathing, controlling pain, moving and eating. Convalescence and rehabilitation were going to be my next challenge, and I vowed that I would overcome everything easily just from my own strength of character. My 'soul' purpose was going to be mind over matter, and my inner resourcefulness would inspire me to keep on track. After all, what else was there to get through life other than inner strength? And I had often heard people say, "The only person who can do it is you." The medical team had given me another chance to triumph in this world and I wasn't going to disappoint them or my family, but foremost I was going to succeed for myself.

I wanted to be away from the hospital as soon as possible and to be back with my husband, Phil, and children, Rob (aged five) and Amy (aged three), and after eight days in hospital I felt back in the game of life; keen, upbeat, enthusiastic and doggedly determined to win the race of recovery.

Perhaps, at that moment, it was just as well that I had absolutely no idea that game, set and match would endure for fifteen long years and, more significantly, I was totally clueless of how I needed God in my life to be healed.

CHAPTER TWO

And he took the children in his arms,
put his hands on them and blessed them.

Mark 10:16

I was born on Good Friday, 1958 – history in the making on three counts: firstly, for the Bowey family, as I was so much yearned for by my parents; secondly the first march of ten thousand protesters took place from Trafalgar Square, London to Aldermaston, Berkshire as part of the Campaign for Nuclear disarmament; and thirdly it was the first time Good Friday had fallen on 4th April during the Twentieth Century. In fact I had to wait until1969 before my birth date aligned with Good Friday again, a further wait until 1980 and then the unbelievable discovery that such an alignment will not occur again until I am eighty-four in 2042! History indeed!

The significance of Good Friday being a religious holiday passed me by as a small child, because I was far more interested in the significance of how many Easter eggs might brighten up our sideboard by Easter Sunday. I do remember colouring bright Easter pictures at infant school, mostly of downy chicks sitting happily in spiky straw, but then really only comprehending that the date was special because it was a school holiday.

With the same school I can remember a particularly exciting afternoon, when we were lined up, hand in hand, to visit Crowthorne Parish Church to celebrate Harvest Festival. So much of that autumn day remains so vivid in my mind: the snake of children, holding hands tightly, walking in a long line; the teachers constantly keeping us in check; the clarity of the bright coloured leaves underfoot and the fat squirming worms on the pavement too; and finally being ushered up a path through the graves to a dark, foreboding church. I remember being a little nervous about going inside, not really knowing what to expect. I'd probably been into a church before, for a family christening or wedding perhaps, but I have no recollection of doing so until this one memorable time and being astonished at its immense size and of being nervous in having to sit so hushed and still.

I'm not sure whether it was in this church or elsewhere in school where I first saw a picture of Jesus comforting a group of very beautiful looking children. I can still visualise the dull brown frame around the picture, which hung askance on a yellowing wall, yet the bright pigments of colour in the picture were such a striking contrast. The little children seemed so perfect in every way – lovely curly blond locks, unblemished skin, pretty vibrant clothes and clearly all wanting to clamber on to the lap to get as close as possible to this foreign looking man with his long, dark beard. His gentle eyes stared out of the frame, but he wasn't like anyone I had seen before – at home, at school or shopping with my mother and brother in the High Street.

In time, as Jesus' name became more familiar with the telling of the parables in primary school, he became merely a figure of story-telling, alongside Gulliver and the Pied Piper. Jesus was never illustrated exactly in the same way in the books I looked at, and he was often described in different ways too by various teachers – some even said he was black – so he lacked significance through the inconsistent descriptions of his appearance.

There was, however, one very consistent fact about Jesus: he had been born at Christmas and no one seemed to dispute that fact – parents, teachers, neighbours, children, shopkeepers, Blue Peter. Unlike today, baby Jesus was an ever present figure on Advent calendars and Christmas cards.

As young children we knew the whole Nativity story off by heart and also many of the shorter Christmas carols too. There was much excitement and consternation around the production of the school Nativity play. The girls all wanted to be Mary and nurse the baby doll, whilst the boys fought to be kings rather than shepherds, or at the very least to have the part of the nasty innkeeper rather than just carry the cardboard star around the stage.

Through the Nativity, Jesus became an accepted figure in primary school. We learned he had escaped with his parents from the extremely evil Herod, lived in poverty, worked as a simple carpenter, later walked along the shore of Galilee to find good fishermen to help him do good work. Then because he was different he ran into trouble with the people in charge, who nailed him on a cross, so that he died in time for Easter.

When I went on to secondary school in East Sussex, Religious Education (R.E.) featured twice on the weekly school timetable, and I soon realised that I was going to have to fill in many gaps in my biblical knowledge if I was going to pass the frequent tests and end of year exams!

School assemblies were very different too from primary school. Much more serious. Formal times where pupils' discipline, good behaviour and silence were the order of the day, unless of course when having to sing hymns, when everyone was expected to turn up the volume big time in the featureless school hall. In one such assembly the new intake were handed a red Gideon New Testament Bible, and I remember feeling quite proud to walk up on to the stage and receive something formally, but other than flicking through a few pages and carrying it around in my school bag for a short while, it was stowed in the back of my wardrobe, never again to see the light of day. At a later date, when it was the time to make my O Level choices, I was really pleased and thankful to be able to give up R.E. It was a great relief to push aside what seemed a very dry subject with nothing seemingly relevant for everyday modern teenage life.

School life was very enjoyable and out-of-school life fun too. Sport was high on the agenda as well as going to the Teen 'n' Twenty Youth Club in Crowborough on Friday nights. The club was run in a lovely modern church hall, with room for volleyball and table tennis, as well as a snack bar. It was a safe place to go, run by the curate of All Saints Church, and it was a good feeling to be part of a nice group of youngsters from other schools and to mix with older members too. I loved the friendly atmosphere so much that it was only natural to want to attend the Easter holiday schemes they ran too. It was a really welcome opportunity to get out of the house and be with friends, even if that meant attending church really early before our shared breakfasts.

All Saints is a very different church today from the church I knew in the 1970's. In those days the main part of the church was very austere, dark and dingy with narrow, uncomfortable pews, and it always seemed so very cold inside, regardless of the air temperature outside. Not very conducive for encouraging young people to worship, but the ministry team were keen to involve us and I was introduced to a Bible Study group through their constant urging. I remember feeling very out of my depth and wishing I had taken more notice of those rather dull R.E. lessons! I don't remember participating much in the discussion, but was keen to listen to what others had to say, although in truth much seemed very deep, abstract and confusing. Why on earth would God want to have his only son killed on the cross? If he was such a great God could he not have saved Jesus? Still, the friendship and camaraderie were super so I could leave the rest of the nitty gritty to wash over me.

I left school in the summer of '76 and it was a tremendous feeling to finally leave. I'd lost the impetus to succeed at the beginning of the year. Most of my friends were making plans to go to university or college, but I couldn't get interested in their intentions. I couldn't see the point of doing further study. It was such a turn off. I just wanted to leave home and do something different. I wanted to get involved with the real world, not students or tutors, to begin living life for real, not delaying any further seeking employment. I certainly had no help or direction as to which way to turn, which left me further in turmoil, and it was only through reading advertisements in The Lady magazine that I was inspired to apply for an Assistant Matron's position at a preparatory school in Hampshire. It is ironic really that in trying to escape education I ended up back in a school situation – but it was a very different type of culture from my secondary school.

The job involved looking after the health and well-being of the boarding pupils and getting very involved in many aspects of school life. It introduced me to a completely different world. I had to attend chapel in the mornings as we were expected to be a good example to the boys, but the services didn't particularly inspire me and if it was possible I would find an excuse to miss the service.

As the school year continued, the formal and solemn surroundings of the chapel made me question if there was any relevance in my going to church. I found it dull, and any curiosity regarding religion that might have once had a chance to develop in my youth was now utterly quenched. A few months later I left that job and I was very relieved not to have to go to another chapel service. The death knoll had tolled and I gladly hammered securely the final nail in the coffin labelled 'church' – and how good it felt in having done so.

CHAPTER THREE

If a man has recently married,
he must not be sent to war or have any other duty laid on him.
For one year he is to be free to stay at home
and bring happiness to the wife he has married.

Deuteronomy 24:5

I don't suppose for a moment that I am the first wife to have first encountered her husband-to-be at primary school in Crowborough, but it still astonishes me that the writing was on the wall in our early years. Phil did a couple of terms in the class above mine, before going on to grammar school. The most vivid early impression I have of him is during the following Autumn Term when he came back to visit his class teacher, sporting his grey short trousers and over-sized duffle coat. His kindness, politeness and quiet way was very noticeable at that age as he chatted to the class teacher while we all tried to get on with our work.

Our paths were to cross on several occasions throughout our teenage years, including his being part of the group of friends at Teen 'n' Twenty. As is typical, he was very humble about his achievements, but his passionate interest in all things to do with flying was most evident. I was certainly enormously impressed when I learnt he had gained his Private Pilot's Licence before even having passed his driving test. Those facts certainly made my own achievements to date seem pretty uneventful and dull.

Phil went up to Oxford for four years to study Chemistry at New College, having gained another string to his bow by being awarded a scholarship from the Royal Air Force. He will be the first to admit that his main love of student life was the holy ground of the Oxford University Air Squadron, where he continued his flying experience. We started 'going out' in March 1979, and we knew from the start that our relationship was very special. We were separated by distance and commitments of study and work. I was teaching in a residential school near Crowborough, as a keen but unqualified teacher, and the miles further increased as Phil began his Officer Training at RAF Cranwell, Lincolnshire the following September, adding the challenge of military life and commitment to the equation. Another whole new world opened up before me of spit and polish, rules and regulations, pomp and parade, rank and uniform, security and red tape, RAF jargon and abbreviations, Mess custom and formal dinners, cocktail parties and jolly japes, ball dresses, hand-tied bow ties and patent shoes. To name but a few! There were procedures and protocol to learn, excellent entertainment to enjoy, military history to grasp and a realisation of the tremendous importance of the 'military family'. It was a steep learning curve but it was so much fun that new ways were just accepted without any rationalisation. Once he had graduated as an officer, Phil began his Basic Flying training at Cranwell and each step drew us deeper into the Armed Forces way of life.

It seemed as if this pleasant lifestyle would continue forever, but I began to be dogged by unexplained stomach pain. I didn't heed much attention to my occasional ill health at first as I had known similar problems over the past few years as a result of contracting Hepatitis A whilst on holiday in Brittany. I had eaten contaminated shellfish fresh off the beach and coupled with glandular fever suffered impaired liver function, with a very long recovery afterwards. I often felt bilious anyway as a legacy in recovering from the Hepatitis but my stomach pain felt like something new. I remember travelling back on the Inter-city train from Lincolnshire to Seaford on the South Coast, where I was working at the time in a school for the partially-sighted, watching those endless cereal crops rush past and thinking how very unjust it seemed that in the few weekends Phil and I could timetable off together I was more often than not ruining our plans by being unwell.

Eventually I had to seek specialist help, and life continued to appear unfair as medical examination after examination and glass upon glass of barium meal revealed absolutely nothing in the way of a positive diagnosis. It was such a frustrating time, because I was certain that there was something seriously wrong with me, but none of my symptoms seemed to add up to my GP or consultant. Eventually, having been taken back into hospital yet again, an exploratory operation was planned, which resulted in the removal of my appendix.

Afterwards, the surgeon came to see me on the ward, with a big grin on his face. He sat on the edge of my bed, clearly excited, and explained how my unusually long appendix had wrapped itself around the bowel to cause all the mysterious pain. I really couldn't share in his enthusiasm, and certainly the last thing I was interested in was the gory detail. I rather unkindly suggested perhaps he might like to frame my appendix and hang it on his wall. Not very generous of me at all after all he had done! But all I could do at the time was think of all the wasted months of hassle and bother I had spent convincing doctors something was wrong, the time spent off sick from work and the precious weekends I had missed seeing Phil. Unfortunately I had an allergic reaction to a pain-relief drug I was given which further lengthened my recovery time in hospital. I left hospital after a fortnight and enjoyed three weeks of much needed recuperation at home with my parents before I returned to my work as a Matron in the residential school.

Life was back on track, and I was eager to get back to the good times, but such pleasure was drastically short lived. After a mere three weeks, on 8th May, 1980, a Jet Provost T.5A aircraft from No.3 Flying Training School, RAF Cranwell, crashed ninety-one metres from the A46 road at Swinderby, near Newark, with a flying instructor and his flying student, Phil, having ejected. The plane had failed to recover from a spinning manoeuvre exercise, and after parachuting safely they were both taken by ambulance to RAF Nocton Hall near Cranwell – a hospital treating military personnel and civilians. Phil and his instructor had suffered compression of the spine, as a result of the ejector-seat action thrusting them upwards and out through the jettisoned aircraft canopy, for which the treatment consisted of twelve weeks' bed rest under traction, physiotherapy, gym work and exercise. Phil lost a couple of centimetres in height through the compression of a couple of his lower vertebrae, but this seemed a small price to pay for having had his life saved by the acclaimed Martin-Baker ejector seat.

I was very shocked in learning about the incident, knowing I had come so close to losing Phil. A kind colleague swapped her weekend off with mine, and my equally kind father agreed to drive me up to Nocton so that I could visit Phil without the difficulties of using public transport on a Sunday. It was tremendous to see Phil on the ward and verify that in time he would be able to return to his pilot training at Cranwell, albeit having to join a later scheduled course with a different set of flying comrades. I was relieved to discover that the problem bothering him the most was boredom from lying completely flat and thus not being able to read a book easily!

Our return journey to East Sussex turned out not to be without incident either, because we had only driven five miles from the hospital when the car began to behave oddly and we realised that the petrol tank had run dry. Fortunately we were not in open countryside, having just come into the outskirts of Scopwick village. We pulled my mother's mini up just before a junction, rather disheartened that there was not a soul in sight, got out of the car, walked down to the junction to get our bearings, and couldn't believe our luck as we spotted a small car repair garage with petrol pumps a hundred meters up the road. Although the garage was clearly closed, Dad went to investigate and soon came back cheerfully swinging a full petrol can. What amazing luck – and what is even more astonishing about this incident is that sixteen years later we actually bought a house in Kirkby Green, the hamlet adjoining the village of Scopwick, and used the services of that same garage for ten years!

The weeks of Phil's recovery dragged for both of us, and he was eventually sent to RAF Headley Court, a Grade II mansion located near Leatherhead, Surrey which specialised in treating RAF injured aircrew.[1] I remember Phil was very struck by the beauty of the location, the fine building and its gardens, and I'm sure after all that he had been through, the location must have been a very comfortable, rejuvenating experience for him.

After completing his Basic Flying Training, Phil qualified as a pilot and was posted to RAF Valley, Anglesey in April 1981 to commence his Advanced Training on the Hawk T.1. With each step of his training the distance in miles between us became greater. I couldn't bear to be so far away from Phil and decided to give up work on the south coast and move to Holyhead, just a short drive away from Valley. With what seemed an accidental stroke of luck I found a job with an upholsterer and a cheap B&B just around the corner, and even more of a fluke occurred a few days later in the bar

---

[1] It is now known as the Defence Medical Rehabilitation Unit, Headley Court, which treats all ranks of military personnel, from all sections of the Armed Forces.

at RAF Valley when I met a lovely lady air traffic controller who happened to be looking for a flatmate. The following week I moved in with her, into a modern flat in the beautiful location of Trearddur Bay. Having come from living by the sea in Seaford to be living right by the sea again, on an island off the coast of Wales, was thrilling. I couldn't believe my good fortune and was utterly convinced I had made the right decision in moving north, although I really wasn't cut out for the upholstery job and quickly sought work instead in working with children. I was soon employed by the County Council to care for vulnerable adolescents, but the job did not match my previous experience and only lasted a couple of months as I struggled to be accepted as part of the team. I believe this was mainly because I was English; the staff chose to speak a lot of the time in Welsh, and I felt very isolated and lonely in my work.

Fortunately, by December we were moving on to pastures new, as Phil had been posted to RAF Chivenor, near Barnstaple in North Devon to do his Tactical Weapons Training, flying the BAE Hawk T.1, better known to me as the Red Arrows jet. Phil sought permission from the Station Commander to 'live out', and we rented a bungalow in Croyde Bay just up from Jones' Hill, which seemed a good omen. We put in place our plans to marry in the following April, which would coincide with the end of Phil's flying course. We loved the local area, finding time to explore the countryside and the stunning beaches in between Phil's studies.

It was a very happy social time too with new friends and we enjoyed some tremendous fancy dress parties in the Mess, although Phil and I were never greatly successful at choosing fancy dress outfits! One big faux pas we made was choosing to wear our wetsuits for the theme 'What you were wearing when the boat went down'. We were very impressed with this choice at first as it involved very little thought or organisation, just a case of putting on the wetsuits at the last minute. Yet we couldn't have been more wrong in our choice: we had to leave the party hours early from the sheer exhaustion of dancing in those heavy sweaty suits and because of not having taken anything else to change into! In fact, although we soon cooled off in the car, once home it was a great challenge to get out of the suits, which was almost as exhausting as trying to dance in them!

Another time the fancy dress called for us to 'Dress as an under-8', as it was celebrating the imminent end of '8' Course's training. I put my long hair in pigtails and dressed appropriately as a sweet little girl, but Phil and his best-man-to-be dressed simply as babies, wearing towels for nappies, knitted bonnets (sourced from a charity shop) tightly stretched over their heads, popped dummies in their mouths, and carried cute teddies. All very plausible and fitting, but possibly a step too far as the car broke down in Braunton, a few miles short of the party at RAF Chivenor! The guys decided that they simply daren't get out of the car dressed as they were and due to the fact that it was it bitterly cold outside. Instead they chose to hail a group of tough looking lads hanging around outside a shop to give us a push, winding up the windows extremely fast as the lads approached. Fortunately, with our hearts in our mouths, the lads got on with the job, the push worked, the engine caught and we were off once again, with tears streaming down our faces from hysterics. Phil and his best man definitely looked the part a couple of weeks later at our wedding, all spruced up in their RAF uniforms. Fancy dress, yes, but not a dummy in sight!

We purposefully chose a Registry office ceremony as we felt that marriage in church would be hypocrisy as we were not churchgoers and we preferred a simple, civil commitment for our vows. That easy decision turned out to be the least simple of all our wedding arrangements, mostly due to the action of Registrars at the time who, because of industrial action, were not carrying out marriage ceremonies on Saturdays. Therefore we were married late on the Friday afternoon, on 16th April, 1982, in Crowborough, but with our wedding reception going ahead as planned on the Saturday lunchtime. Presumably I wasn't the only bride that weekend who gladly wore her wedding dress twice in twenty-four hours.

Our gradual immersion into all things military even extended to our wedding, with our three-tier cake expertly iced with RAF insignia and with many guests in uniform, including my brother who sailed soon afterwards as part of the Naval Task Force to the Falkland Islands. For him the weekend was a honeymoon period, but for us we had to delay our honeymoon and make the long journey back to North Devon for Phil to complete his course and learn where he would be posted next. I had a strange feeling of apprehension at the time, not knowing the exact location of our next home and, I suppose, the fact that someone else was making that decision for us. However I was quickly introduced to the lark of last minute posting notices, the rushed process of obtaining quotes for removals, man-handling large flat-packed boxes and expert wrapping techniques for our few treasured possessions. Over the years moving house would become an education in itself and the ability of master-minding, motivating, organising and prioritising removals would seem worthy of adding to the management skills section in my curriculum vitae. In fact I have had as many jobs, paid or voluntary, as we have had house moves: seventeen!

CHAPTER FOUR

He says to himself, "Nothing will shake me;
I'll always be happy and never have trouble."

Psalm 10:6

Phil was assigned to fly the F-4 Phantom later that year, but in the interim he was posted to RAF Kemble to fulfil a role as a 'ferry pilot' for their Maintenance Unit, making use of his Jet Provost and Hawk aircraft experience. We spent an idyllic three months living in Bisley, Gloucestershire, a lovely village consisting of pretty Cotswold stone cottages and fine houses with wonderful views of the surrounding valley. We rented The Lodge at Jaynes Court with kind permission to enjoy the tennis court alongside, and we were really delighted with our good fortune. The well-manicured grounds were extremely attractive, and it was a simply wonderful summer notwithstanding the persistent nuisance of noisy, hissing geese at the back door. Their snapping beaks were determined to undermine my confidence as I tried to hang washing out on the long line stretched across the courtyard, and they persistently blocked my way back into the house. Apparently they were perfect 'guards' for the property and very revered by their owner so any complaint about them being such an inconvenience to us was clearly out of the question. With all the skiddy mess they left in their wake, I failed to see anything charming about them!

In August 1982 we moved north to Tattershall in Lincolnshire, close to RAF Coningsby. Phil began his Operational Conversion course to fly the Phantom in the Air Defence role, and we took up residence in our first RAF quarter. Our living accommodation was a stark contrast to our previous cosy rental property: a semi-detached, plain, dull-red brick house with a low wire fencing bordering a featureless garden and devoid of any plants. A bare view except for an out of condition, lumpy lawn and a drab telephone exchange building beyond – but no geese. The local countryside was a real disappointment too: flat fen land, uninspiring sugar beet fields, deep dykes and so few trees to enjoy after the expanses of mixed deciduous woodland in the Cotswolds. I felt as if I was living in the middle of nowhere, except for the oasis of nearby Woodhall Spa. It felt a bit of a comedown from the Cotswold estate surroundings and rather unsettling knowing that this was the promise of things to come – limited choice in the future in choosing where we would live or the type of housing. The sudden disheartening awareness was not helped by the temperamental solid fuel boiler which went out or broke down with increasing regularity, nor the wondrous, bright orange coloured carpet which graced our quarter! However, acquiring new friends, re-acquainting with others, passing my driving test in Boston (the first attempt in Eastbourne but fortunately difficult to find a place to carry out a hill start in Boston), the continued fun of social life, and a variety of leisure and sport pursuits were sufficient to fulfil and satisfy any qualms we had about Phil having a career in the Armed Forces.

The six months of Phil's course flew by incredibly fast, and we were soon packing up again to make the move into a mercifully modern quarter at RAF Leuchars with reliable electric heating. We were thrilled to be living once again in a beautiful area with the advantage this time of not just rolling hills but forests, pretty coastal and harbour scenery, and the joy of having the immense mountains of Scotland so easily accessible. We decided to make a leap into the housing market and bought our first house in Gauldry, a small village with views over the Tay to Dundee, where we felt very welcomed by our neighbours, had few stresses and strains to put up with, pleased ourselves as we wished, and felt completely satisfied with the way our lives were mapping out.

I worked as a care assistant in a nursing home for the elderly in St. Andrew's. It was such a pleasure to have a job again, especially as Phil was often away overnight on duty for Quick Reaction Alert, which involved him sleeping in the QRA building on the airfield in a constant state of readiness, in case of being scrambled to provide air defence for the north of the UK. He was often away on detachments, and time spent apart became more the norm rather than the exception; however, we adapted to each separation in our own way and I became more used to coping alone.

Naturally there was a great deal of disappointment and some heartache when a particular social occasion with friends or family had to be missed because of his absence. Instead I often went to events alone convincing myself from the start that it certainly wasn't worth wasting my time by being miserable. This was military life and I had to deal with it in a fighting spirit, being stoical and taking it for granted.

I decided that distraction was the key to beating any doldrums and took up various crafts, busied away landscaping the garden, grew a lot of produce on an allotment and spent hours preserving the fruits of my labour, went to evening classes and aerobics, cycled and did voluntary work with the elderly living in their own homes. Not much time to think about being alone with that timetable! I was convinced that nothing was insurmountable. I just had to push forward, not give in and prove to myself and others that I was quite capable of holding my own. In fact I was very content to be an RAF wife, supporting Phil in his chosen career and simply accepted the role as part of our commitment to all things military.

It seemed as if life couldn't get any better, until one morning opening up the local St. Andrew's Citizen newspaper I discovered Dundee College of Further Education were advertising a two-year diploma course to gain a Social Work qualification. I had a spine tingling moment and just knew that this was an unequivocal opportunity to consolidate all my care work experiences into one qualification. Phil had no hesitation in agreeing to me doing the course, even though it was possible that he would be posted before I graduated. I applied, and in September 1983, after a successful application process, began my studies at Broughty Ferry College of Education (now part of the University of Dundee). It was such an enjoyable course, and I have so many wonderful memories of the children, adolescents and staff I encountered during three long work placements as well as my fellow students and staff on the course itself.

The last placement in 1985 of three months was at a school near Prestwick on the west coast of Scotland, which virtually coincided exactly with Phil's detachment to RAF Mount Pleasant in the Falklands. The squadron had a commitment in the Falklands as part of the government's role to deter further Argentinean invasion, and it was Phil's turn to do his bit for Queen and country 12,700 kilometres away. I quickly had to find accommodation in Ayrshire in order to be able to work long shifts and unsociable hours at the school, and by some incredible chance my air traffic controller friend from our

Valley days now had a house in Prestwick. I moved in with her, driving back to Gauldry as often as possible to check up on our house and garden when my shifts allowed enough time to do so.

At the time it seemed quite extraordinary how these various circumstances had evolved and how much in our life was spookily fluky. Phil's stroke of luck was that his 'turn down south' took place in a Falklands summer, although the down side of his four month detachment was that we had to spend Christmas apart for the first time – yet the timing of both 'work commitments' for us both could not have worked out better. On his return from the Falklands in the third week in January we celebrated in true festive style with the house completely decorated for Christmas: all the cards up on the wall and a large Christmas tree with twinkling lights, a roast turkey dinner and the next evening our neighbours joining us for Christmas drinks. One kind soul even struggled through the door with a huge Clootie dumpling – a steamed fruit pudding traditionally enjoyed in Scotland at Christmas – to help the celebrations go with a truly festive swing.

As expected, Phil was indeed posted before the end of my college course and he joined 29 Squadron back at RAF Coningsby in February 1986 to continue to fly the Phantom. I was busy completing the final stages of coursework before exams and graduation, and organising our house sale, and we both spent a lot of time travelling on the East Coast line at the weekends to be with one another, Phil's detachments permitting.

Unfortunately, on May 9th that year, virtually six years to the day Phil had ejected, he had an incident on landing at Gibraltar, which resulted in him ceasing to fly the Phantom the following month. Just when we thought everything was going swimmingly well too.

Meanwhile the house sold in Scotland and we moved our furniture into a married quarter in Tattershall. Phil worked as an Operations Officer for the Station, whilst awaiting the long ramifications of his Board of Enquiry. I quickly made friends and through one contact was introduced to an RAF Chaplain who was masterminding a 'Listening Ear' confidential telephone service for all ranks. With my past experience and recent qualification I was invited to join the steering group. I thought the service was an excellent idea, as it was difficult for military personnel to discuss their problems confidentially and privately without going down the normal chain of command route. I spent many weeks helping to put a training programme together for the prospective volunteers who would be manning the telephone line, and it was great to get my teeth into the project.

To work alongside a chaplain was very interesting too. I was aware of chaplains saying grace before formal dining in the Mess and I had seen them on parade occasions, but was clueless to the fact there was a church on every RAF station. Oddly I really cannot recall seeing any church facade at any one of Phil's previous stations, and yet I know now that they were in very prominent places. I seem to have been completely blinded to their existence, including the fact that there are three different denominational churches within ninety metres of each other at RAF Cranwell! I really cannot fathom how I missed them in the year Phil was doing his officer and flying training at Cranwell. I learnt that chaplains existed in all three services of the Armed Forces and that, as well as leading worship, they had a care role for the military community and an education role in imparting a moral understanding of military action.

Finally a decision was made to transfer Phil away from a fighter pilot role to the multi-engine pilot role (even though he was ultimately not found negligent) and he was given a forward date to begin that training. The past six months had been a stressful time, but I was, and remain, extremely proud of the way Phil conducted himself throughout that period – calmly and honestly – for which many of much higher rank afforded him a great deal of respect. We didn't have the slightest clue at the time how this particular decision of flying role change would open so very many doors in the future, although we did very much realise that we had been given a wonderful sweetener for any stress endured over the past months: we were expecting our first child.

CHAPTER FIVE

I have seen something else under the sun:
The race is not to the swift or the battle to the strong,
nor does food come to the wise or wealth to the brilliant
or favour to the learned;
but time and chance happen to them all.

Ecclesiastes 9:11

In January 1987 we moved to RAF Finningly, now Robin Hood Doncaster Sheffield airport, for Phil to undertake his multi-engine ground school training. Then in the first week of April he commenced dual-pilot flying training in a turbo-prop Jetstream T.1. We were totally thrilled when our son, Rob, was born three weeks later by caesarean section. Phil made the medical team laugh aloud as he joined me in the operating theatre, gowned, masked and well scrubbed, looking every bit the part but with a book about Concorde under his arm! After I had spent a week in hospital we brought Rob home. Whilst Phil slept like a baby each night, courtesy of a pair of highly efficient ear plugs, I got to grips with recovering from the operation, being a mother, sleepless nights and the demands of a continually hungry son (no change to this day)!

On top of those early daunting days I found myself preparing to move house and once more packing up boxes as we moved south to RAF Brize Norton, Oxfordshire, seven weeks after Rob's birth. We moved into a quarter at Brize where Phil would eventually be flying the VC-10 transport aeroplane, but first he had to serve as an Admin Officer at RAF St. Athan, South Wales for their forthcoming Airshow. Phil's interim posting was not long enough for him to qualify for a quarter at St. Athan, but to be offered a quarter early at Brize meant that he could commute back home easily at weekends. We were equally delighted to be on the edge of the Cotswolds as we loved the charm of the familiar honey-coloured villages from our time in Bisley. We began an immediate search for a house to purchase, soon realising that the sale price of our home in Gauldry wouldn't even provide sufficient funds to purchase a garage in Oxfordshire let alone a house to go with it! We discovered the reality of the north-south divide yet once we got over the shock of the house prices we sought out a nearly new home on an estate on the outskirts of Witney. It seemed the perfect choice for meeting other young families. Our neighbours were lovely people, and much later the estate proved to be a popular location for a quick sale.

We decided against having Rob christened, not being churchgoers, and thought that in all honesty such an event would just be an expensive day with little meaning for us and certainly no meaning for our baby son. I am sure that many friends thought this a very unusual decision and our parents were similarly disappointed, but we have never regretted having made that decision. Meanwhile I existed in our married quarter for several months, surrounded by the paraphernalia of baby accessories and mostly unopened packing cases – having only unpacked the absolute necessities – whilst Phil had busy weeks and then made the 341 kilometre round trip home every weekend. Not a very normal start to parenthood, but we just got on with whatever tasks we had to face.

By September 1988 we were able to move into our house, and the following March Phil had completed ground school and flying training on the VC-10 at Brize. Looking through Phil's flying log book I notice that someone has written, "Welcome aboard," before his first operational flight – a nice sentiment, and indeed for the first time in Phil's flying career he experienced a fine welcome. He was immediately plunged into the air transport role flying to Bermuda and Belize, whilst I had to face the fact that having taken on the role of CEO in our household for what I had thought might be short-term whilst Phil had been away in St. Athan was now going to become a long-term occupation. Phil was going to be away much more than I had at first imagined and one of us had to be consistently responsible for all the errands and tasks to guarantee the smooth running of our home and family life... so that had better be me! I'm sure Phil was very glad and relieved that I was a born organiser, saving him any distracting concern about how his family were coping in his absence.

Phil was delighted and excited to be flying to various locations around the world: west to the USA, east to Hong Kong and Australia, south to Nairobi, as well as ticking off many European locations. He particularly favoured working with an all rank crew and enjoyed meeting a variety of passengers: serving personnel, families, as well as civilians. We had a happy eighteen months, with the icing on the cake being the birth of our daughter, Amy, in October 1989. We enjoyed some lovely holidays too as we took advantage of several concessionary scheme 'indulgence flights', particularly to Washington and Seattle to meet up with Oxford university friends even though it meant that I sometimes travelled across the Atlantic by myself with our young children. According to regulations, if Phil was a crew member we were not able to travel on the same flight together; however, we were amazingly lucky that each time our 'indulgence' holiday plans worked like clockwork. It was a wonderful opportunity to keep up with good friends living in the USA, and such opportunities were a real tonic and a welcome appeasement, which helped to make up for the rougher side of the coin of me feeling the stress of being a 'sole' parent.

The old adage of mind over matter was a powerful force in my capacity to cope, and we made the best of every opportunity to lead a fulfilling life. We were determined too that the young minds of our children would not be tainted by their father's absence and they would phone him as often as possible so that they could hear his voice. We also had an enormous world map on the kitchen wall with a photo of Phil smiling broadly affixed by blue tack, and we would move Phil's photo around the map as he reached various destinations. The children soon learnt which part of the map was 'home' and they would become very excited as I moved him closer to home. This idea also resulted in them having a very early spatial awareness of the world and its continents, learning the names of countries and very many capital cities.

As he was enjoying his airline role so much, Phil began to consider leaving the RAF. He had an option coming up in the following year (1991) at thirty-four years of age, and it seemed the perfect opportunity in time to move into 'civvy street' as a pilot. In preparation for a move to the south-east to be near Gatwick, we sold our Witney house and moved into a married quarter in Carterton, which is literally a stone's throw from the Brize Norton airfield. Changing jobs also seemed an attractive idea as it coincided with economic sanctions having been actioned against Iraq following the invasion of Kuwait by Iraqi troops in August 1990 and the media talked continually of an imminent war. We were delighted when Phil was successful in being offered a job with the charter airline Air Europe and the paperwork was put in place for him to leave the RAF in spring 1991. We found a property perfectly located in East Sussex; an ideal distance for Phil to travel to Gatwick Airport, close to grandparents and close to friends.

Then in one fell swoop our luck ran out.

The onset of war seemed very likely as a UN-authorised coalition force was set up, and Phil was immediately moved across to 101 Sqn at Brize to fly VC-10 re-fuelling tankers. At New Year we said an emotional goodbye to Phil as he flew off to Saudi Arabia to take part in Operation Desert Storm[2], which finally expelled Iraqi troops from Kuwait. During this time financial problems were escalating for Air Europe, and rumours ran in the media regarding their possible bankruptcy, which greatly concerned us. We immediately made the decision to pull out of our house purchase in Sussex; and from the Gulf, Phil put in a request to the RAF regarding the possibility of him retracting his application to leave and for their consideration of his 'staying on' in the RAF. He received no immediate answer to that conundrum and we just had to get on with our lives as best we could in the circumstances.

I continued to meet up with friends from around the Witney area and had little contact with my RAF neighbours, mostly because our quarter was located off base, and being the first one in the cul-de-sac I had no reason to go down our road; also because my social circle from Witney was already large enough not to get involved with RAF social events. I continued doing volunteer work with Social Services and also with a local volunteer bureau. I rarely went on to the RAF station or attended anything organised by other wives for families with a parent detached, because it didn't seem emotionally healthy to surround myself with others in the same boat. I needed to get away from the worry and constant military conversation and lead as normal a life as possible, and I was extremely lucky with supportive friends and family.

Having isolated myself from the military I am sure that this is the reason why I reacted very badly one day as I opened the front door to an RAF chaplain standing on the doorstep, with a deadly serious look on his face. My mind went into overdrive and I was immediately convinced that something terrible had happened to Phil. The shock

---

[2] 17.01.91 - 28.02.91

was awful. To give the padre his due, he did explain to me that if that had been the case he would not have been alone but two RAF personnel would have been standing on the doorstep! I am not sure whether at that moment I was more cross with him or with Phil for not explaining this well-known fact, but at any rate I couldn't think for the life of me why on earth a chaplain would want to visit me. I was uncommunicative, and after a couple of moments of small talk he left, with much relief on my part and most likely a great deal on his part too! I don't suppose he had a clue that his untimely visit had been my first conversation with an RAF chaplain in four years or that his innocent social visit had made me vow it would also be my last encounter with such men from the church!

As expected, Air Europe went bankrupt at the beginning of March, and finally in the following week Phil returned home to a rapturous welcome, kindly organised by the Squadron, so that we could meet Phil right on the taxiway at Brize. We were so excited, emotions brimming to the full, and it was wonderful to share the excitement of all the other families meeting their loved ones too. Sharing in the beautiful, warm, sunny day, the emotion seized us all as the planes touched down on the tarmac and taxied towards us; the sheer delight on everyone's faces as they hugged one another for the first time in ages was truly magical and carved in stone in my memory. It was a wonderful time of reunion and one which I find hard to reconcile with the repatriations we have since watched on the television news at exactly the same location.

How happy we were to be together again, and a couple of months later our good fortune was further credited as Phil received the good news that he would be allowed to remain in the RAF with the proviso that he would become a qualified flying instructor. Although we were disappointed that Phil would not be able to continue the airline-type flying role at Brize, the hand of chance had been placed face up on the table, and with no option to play the hand any other way he accepted the job of preparing pilot aircrew for basic fast jet training – final posting destination unknown.

CHAPTER SIX

In everything set them an example by doing what is good.
In your teaching show integrity...

Titus 2:7

Phil moved to RAF Scampton, north of Lincoln, to undergo his instructor training, resulting in yet another period of prolonged separation to come to terms with, and once again the duration of his course was too short in length for him to qualify for a married quarter. Phil got back into the habit of being a 'bean stealer' (a married man living in single mess quarters) for five months and driving yet another lengthy round trip to home every weekend. All hankerings of living an ordinary life had been completely erased, and we had to become resigned to the military lifestyle continuing to dominate our lives – our short taste of possible escape into the outside world having turned sour. However, determined and not deterred we purchased a terraced property in a popular student rental location in Oxford, to allow us to remain in the Oxfordshire / south of England housing market, whilst letting the property to five students from the start of the Autumn Term. It did mean that we would be committed to living on the 'married patch' for a few years, but it seemed a sensible decision in case Phil was posted back to Brize Norton.

In November 1991 Phil received confirmation notice of his next posting for Flying Instructor duty, and I began the usual removal preparations, including sending yet another change of address to friends and family with profound apologies for once again making a mess of section 'J' in their address books. Uncannily we moved from Cranwell Avenue at Brize to RAF Cranwell, and fortuitously we managed to arrange the removal for the week before Christmas.

We have very happy memories of that married quarter not only because we were extremely lucky to be allocated a quarter much larger than Phil's rank would normally have allowed but also as it had a lovely landscaped, mature garden backing on to the woods behind. Beyond the woods there were open fields and the North grass airfield, which was only used on the weekends by the gliding club, so we were situated in a very quiet location with the further benefit of being a good mile from the working runway on the base.

The detached house had been recently and carefully redecorated, completely re-carpeted throughout with brand new beige carpets, and the attractive, high quality curtains really complimented our furnishings perfectly. I have tried to push aside the only downside to the house which was the hopeless heating system; it stubbornly refused to work to order from day one. We had heating engineers aplenty trying to fix the problems for several days, including most of Christmas Eve, and in the end they left having provided ample portable heaters for us to enjoy Christmas. We purchased an enormous Christmas tree for the dining-room. We struggled to get all the roots into a huge pot, watered it lovingly and liberally for two whole weeks and then discovered to our absolute horror that the metal pot had rusted dreadfully, completely and utterly ruining the fine beige carpet underneath, which had now turned bright orange – a devilish turn of events to halt the prior weeks of serendipity.

We were very content at the idea of bringing up our young family at Cranwell. It was a great location, a pleasant country setting with lots of excellent facilities on base or a short drive away. I purposefully made a lot of friends 'outside the wire' in the local community, and we enjoyed a very comfortable lifestyle, wanting for nothing and feeling pretty satisfied with 'our lot'. Phil was very content instructing young pilots whilst adding yet another aircraft type to his bow, and we were optimistic that in three years' time, when Phil was due a posting, we would be able to move back south to Oxfordshire and Brize Norton. Meanwhile we decided we would take advantage of all Cranwell had to offer and commit ourselves to bringing up Rob and Amy in the best possible way.

For six months all went to plan until I rather worryingly began to feel unwell, became very fatigued and experienced some mysterious internal pains resulting in collapse, having to be admitted to hospital for several days. No explanation could be determined for my symptoms even though I had had to have several morphine injections to combat the severe pain. In the end we put it down to "just one of those things" and I tried to improve my fitness, but strangely a few weeks later similar symptoms developed, alongside which I had a horrible episode of pronounced shaking – a very disconcerting incident as I felt as if my body was completely out of my control. I was going to my doctor regularly and it was arranged for me to attend a military hospital as an in-patient for them to investigate my problems, but after various tests they were rather dismissive, and frankly I'm not surprised as otherwise I seemed really well other than having had a similar shaking episode. I am convinced that they thought I was imagining my symptoms for attention, but having experienced exactly the same frustration several years back with my tricky appendix I kept on beating the same drum of knowing there was something wrong. They must have been heartily sick of me down at the Medical Centre, and I tried to put on a brave face despite everything being such an effort.

I remember driving to Sleaford one day and suddenly I felt my eyelids being forced to close, which was a frightening experience. I stretched my eyes really wide, stopped safely in a roadside layby and peered at my eyes in the mirror, but nothing seemed awry. Two eyes... two pupils of the same dilation... nothing remotely obvious. However, the experience had been so worrying that I drove on straight to an optician and pressed him to do an immediate eye test, only for him to tell me not to worry as I had perfect eyesight.

I dread to think what was going through Phil's mind at the time as he worked hard on the Squadron and then often had to take over all the chores as soon as he got home. I was beginning to feel a bit of a hopeless wife and mother, and certainly not the efficient home manager / CEO I had been before. We tried very hard to make family life as normal as possible for our children, and fortunately they were distracted with school and nursery during the day.

One day, on hearing the doorbell chime, I opened the front door to have my second experience of an RAF chaplain standing on the doorstep! On this occasion the chaplain was not in the slightest bit serious-looking; instead he had a broad smile on his face and chuckled as he said, "Hello, Paulette!" I recognised him immediately as the padre I had known at RAF Coningsby when we had worked on the 'Listening Ear' project. I was delighted to invite him in, and we chatted about my health problems. He listened carefully to my problems and I was very pleased that he felt concerned enough to ask to visit us again.

The visits to the surgery didn't diminish, and I was very concerned that my body was beginning to cease to function. I was referred to the Royal Hallamshire hospital in Sheffield for neurological investigations, but a brain MRI revealed nothing untoward. I felt a complete fraud having wasted yet more NHS time and money, and quite at sea as to what to do next. I was even beginning to wonder whether I was indeed 'losing my marbles', yet really I knew deep down it wasn't in my nature to make things up or dally with ill-health as I loved living life to the full so much. I had got myself into a state where I seemed as if I was going round and round in decreasing circles. I really didn't know what was wrong except that there was something about me or my body which was in dire straits.

Three weeks later I was in a state of collapse again and was admitted to a general medical ward at St. George's, Lincoln where I spent over a fortnight undergoing various tests and being closely monitored. Another patient, Rosemary, a delightfully funny lady, was a great support at that time, and she and I were utterly convinced that we were the only sane patients on the whole ward. We became instant friends. We sought to find the funny side of our troubles, and Rosemary was very instrumental in helping me get through the day.[3]

I underwent yet another endoscopy, which revealed nothing out of the ordinary, but a member of the Endoscopy team had a hunch and decided to order an immediate chest x-ray, even though I had had one taken fairly recently. To her amazement she discovered the unmistakeable shadow of a tumour in my chest wall – that young registrar's action was my saving grace. A CT scan was carried out the next day and my consultant explained that there was a high probability that the tumour was cancerous but a biopsy would have to be carried out in another hospital to verify that fact. Meanwhile I was sent home to await a suitable appointment.

I was delighted to be home again, having missed seeing the children regularly so much, and the next evening the whole family went out to the Station Guy Fawkes Bonfire night at the top of our road. I remember feeling very weak after having spent a couple of weeks in hospital, physically and especially emotionally having received the recent shattering news, but delighted to be attending a normal event in the circumstances. Our good friends came to stand with us, and my friend Barbara had a bag of her homemade delicious

---

[3] Many years later I discovered that Rosemary was a Christian.

treacle toffee to share. I remember reaching inside the bag to pull out a gorgeously sticky piece, with the rockets exploding overhead in a myriad of stars, and thinking that I had to take everything in around me really in minute detail in case this turned out to be my last Bonfire Night.

That scene is still so very clear and vivid in my mind and it sends a shiver down my spine: the darkness, the cold, the throng of happy people, the colourful array of scarves, gloves and hats glimpsed for a few seconds by the powerful light from the fireworks, Phil holding my arm and our children's delight as we watched the lively scene as a family again. I don't know what was going through Phil's mind that evening, but he didn't seem to be at all negative, which helped me beyond any words he might have said. He seemed positive and strong and that gave me hope to be brave.

A couple of weeks later I had a biopsy in the City Hospital, Nottingham, which was extremely traumatic. The pain from the procedure was unbelievably terrible and the whole process felt like torture. It was very distressing and extremely difficult to endure. I remember thinking that death might actually be less painful and more preferable.

I was utterly exhausted afterwards and sat slumped in a wheelchair in the recovery room, completely shattered by the biopsy and the unbelievable pain I had experienced. The doctor who had carried out the procedure came into the room, bent down, took my hand and told me to have hope, as the pain I had experienced was indeed a very good sign that the tumour was not malignant, not cancerous. His kindness of bothering to encourage me was enough for me to summon up the strength to nod, give a weak smile and begin to live again. I can see his face as clearly as I write. I still feel enormously grateful to him for his kind and considerate manner as his compassion was so striking.

A week later his working knowledge proved correct and I had an appointment in the same hospital with a surgeon to discuss the removal of the tumour – not immediately, but probably in a couple of months. The tumour was a neurofibroma (as described in chapter one) and I felt a little concerned about the wait as I was keen to be rid of anything destructive from my body. The surgeon, known affectionately as the Knife, was an extremely pleasant and jovial gentleman who impressed us with his open and honest approach, which enabled me to totally trust his judgement for the right time to operate. He did make one request though: that if I experienced any difficulty in swallowing I should phone his secretary. I thought this rather odd at the time as I couldn't imagine what the significance of not being able to swallow meant. My throat seemed a long way from my lungs, and frankly I was already having difficulty in swallowing… the whole scary scenario![4]

In retrospect I needed those weeks to build up my inner resources in order to get in the right frame of mind for a major operation, and the extra time ensured another Christmas together as a family, which was something positive to focus on and really important for the children to enjoy some normality. We even decided to support our friendly chaplain and go to his Carol Service on base at St. Andrew's! It was a lovely, warm, cosy affair with the church full of flickering candles and beautiful singing.

At first I put some difficulty of swallowing down to being a bit of a Christmas fayre glutton, until the problem continued to reoccur at every meal and I called to mind the advice of my consultant. I bit the bullet and rang my surgeon's secretary in trepidation. A little later that day my consultant phoned me, and after a brief chat a date was arranged for an operation to take place in mid-January 1993.

Word soon got around the married patch, and many friends came to visit and wish me well. One day I opened my door to a lady, a passing acquaintance from the school run, who proceeded to explain to me that she and others had been praying for me for many months and that they would continue to support me in this way. I was quite taken aback and rather bemused at her words, thanked her politely, but then quickly closed the door. It was the first time someone had told me that they prayed, other than of course the kind padre whose job it was to pray anyway, and I was pretty astonished at this lady's boldness. I did think at the time that it was rather a liberty for someone to pray for me without asking whether I would like them to do so or not, but then the penny dropped and I remembered that she was American. She was probably just a member of a religious sect. *Phew,* I thought, *a close encounter and a very lucky escape!*

---

[4] I later learned that pressure from a tumour can make swallowing difficult.

CHAPTER SEVEN

Hold on to instruction, do not let it go;
guard it well, for it is your life.

Proverbs 4:13

In the third week of January 1993, seven days after my operation to remove the neurofibroma, I was discharged from the City Hospital, Nottingham. I was absolutely thrilled to be back at home, among familiar surroundings and the family, although a little nervous at first from being away from the constant nursing care. The sister on the ward had explained that I faced several months of slow recovery; however, I was optimistic that I could overcome any obstacles practically, sensibly and probably a lot quicker than most people, with dogged determination and positive thinking.

As the weeks passed my initial weakness and jarring chest pain began to diminish and I felt much, much stronger, began to put some weight back on and was determined to put the whole unpleasant ordeal of the past year firmly behind me. Yet one thing continued to disturb me: I kept reliving those moments of panic on the operating table, dreaming of being quite agitated as I struggled to think of somewhere 'peaceful, calm or tranquil'! Then I would wake in relief and realise that the operation was long and truly over. I strived so much to obliterate the nightmare from my mind, to distract myself from going back over recent events, and persevered to just concentrate on the present and the promise of the future. I knew that these thoughts were hindering my recovery psychologically, but I didn't know how to stop the nightmares. I could only give myself a good talking to and hope that eventually they would stop.

Contemplating the fragility of life after major trauma must be a common process and also for those close to the person experiencing the incident, accident or operation. The shock of Phil's accident in 1980, when he had ejected from his plane, had been a bombshell for me, although the shock and fear had naturally lessened as the relief of knowing he was fine became my greater emotion. At that time I remember thinking that if he had not survived how cruel and unfair life would have been for those of us left behind, especially me. I wrote at the time of feeling that the years would have been wasted if the outcome had been fatal, especially after I had expended all the time and energy in loving him. A rather heartless response, and it took my own close call with death to think more around the subject. I worried whether Phil might have had similar thoughts to me about wasted years if I had not survived the operation. He would at least have had the children, but then I feared that being so very young they might not have remembered I had been their mother!

Why, I asked myself, did I feel the need to be remembered, loved and yearned for in death? How very self-centred, and I felt a little ashamed at putting myself on a pinnacle in death when I had so little to show for in life. *For heaven's sake,* I told myself, as I felt a shiver go down my spine, *get a grip...* But what was there to hold on to? What could I grasp? Was there only self-reliance?

At the end of February we joined a Health Spa near Grantham to help my recovery. I drove there each weekday morning to use their pool – at first to walk widths, then to wade a couple lengths of the pool, and a few weeks later I was able to introduce a swimming stroke albeit with some difficulty. It felt as if I had to learn to swim all over again, which was a very strange feeling after thirty-five years of swimming confidently. Then, after many weeks of gradually increasing my ability, I swam a mile each weekday, which really encouraged my progress. I felt as if the finish line of the race to recovery was getting much closer.

Phil was busy getting on with his job of instructing student pilots, but unbeknown to me he was also very hard at work in putting together an aerobatic Tucano flying routine. He had decided to enter the RAF Cranwell Station aerobatic competition in March, having always been very keen on aerobatics. He eventually told me about the imminent competition and I didn't give it very much consideration, not realising the significance of the competition other than being really pleased that Phil was enjoying his job. We were both chuffed when he won the competition, especially after not having flown low-level aerobatics for fifteen years, since his Oxford University Air Squadron days, although his winning the competition was a two-edged sword and the competition's significance finally hit home for me. Phil was invited to become the Tucano Aerobatic Display Pilot for the forthcoming season, which meant that he would be away from home most weekends and additional weekdays, depending on the dates of the various air shows around the UK. Some might have thought that his choice to take on the role during my early stages of recovery was not the best timing, but I know that Phil needed a bit of a lift after all the worry he had suffered with my illness. He had stoically born all the consequences and I knew that he would absolutely revel in this new role, so I had absolutely no hesitation in agreeing to his choice when he asked me what I thought about him accepting the role.

Being a display pilot did involve a great deal of extra hours, especially in the planning stages, as Phil practiced his routine time and time again in order to safely reduce the height of the display from the initial five thousand feet to five hundred feet. He was given two days off during the week though to compensate for displays at weekends, which was a tremendous help during the week for me, especially with two boisterous children aged six and three.

Towards the end of his display season I signed up at Grantham College to do a 'Women Back to Science' course, which was a great way to coach my brain back to more intellectual thoughts. It also gave me a chance to consider whether I was actually fit enough or able to cope with the extra pressure of another activity in life as well as being a housewife and mother. Ultimately I wanted to go back to work. I realised that working as a social worker with its often unpredictable or unsocial hours was not going to be very practical for a military wife who couldn't rely on her husband being available at a drop of a hat to support her. I needed to consider something else in the meantime and, more importantly, something part-time. Therefore, after the first course I was easily persuaded by friends to do a second course, especially as they had all gone on to find employment. It was indeed an excellent course, extremely practical and consisted mostly of gaining a variety of computer and office skills. I quickly took to all aspects and I found all the work very easy to accomplish, which was a great encouragement. That same year Rob became a boarder at St. Hugh's School in Woodhall Spa and Amy began infants' school so it seemed the perfect time to look toward new horizons.

In the spring of 1995 we sold our property in Oxford, in preparation for Phil's expected and imminent posting in April away from RAF Cranwell, as we imagined back to Brize Norton. Our presumption was very misplaced as it eventually transpired that he was to be posted to fly the Nimrod MR2 at RAF Waddington, just south of Lincoln, a mere twenty minutes away!

I prepared myself for the usual scenario: change of aircraft type, change of pilot role, weeks of ground school, weeks of flying training, and 'short course' with no entitlement to a married quarter, although what I hadn't bargained on was the fact that the training course would be at RAF Kinloss on the Moray Firth in Scotland! However as the children and I were very settled in schools and college, it seemed reasonable to stay at Cranwell, particularly as the housing department agreed that we could remain living in our married quarter once Phil had begun his role at RAF Waddington.

Kinloss seemed a world away; a three and a half hour drive further north of our first home in Scotland near Leuchars, not to mention an eight-and-a-half hour drive from Cranwell – certainly not doable over a weekend. However, by unbelievable chance we were very lucky in the fact that the seven-week summer school holiday coincided with much of Phil's course and that he would also be given two weeks' block leave in August as part of a planned break in the course. With this fact in mind and another piece of good fortune – soon after Phil had arrived at Kinloss a colleague mentioned that he owned a holiday cottage a stone's throw away – Phil's grey cells jumped from aviation to other ideas. Phil chatted to his colleague again about renting his cottage for five weeks, and as it would be a guaranteed long let a very reasonable charge was proposed.

Even more good fortune came our way too in June, towards the end of my course, when I applied for the position of School Secretary at Kirkby-on-Bain Primary School, near Woodhall Spa. To my great surprise I was offered the job. I worked the last week of their summer term with the current secretary, by way of a short handover, in preparation for my official start in September, and the day after the end of term I drove our car, packed to gunnels, up to Scotland. We could enjoy our long school holiday in Scotland knowing we had much to celebrate – and what a marvellous summer it was!

We spent a lot of time on the beach at Hopeman, pottered with nets in the rock pools, and we were very elated when we found a Victorian necklace (authenticated by the local museum) in the same rock pool as a bright yellow rubber glove! Much to our astonishment and delight we even swam a couple of times in the normally cold Moray Firth.

Phil moved out of the Mess for those weeks, and as his course allowed he wallowed in our trips out to the beach and ordinary family life, if only to the supermarket. In fact after five weeks we felt so at home in Forres it almost felt as if we had moved there permanently, which just goes to show how very quickly military families are able to 'up sticks' and settle themselves quickly. We were certain that our good fortune in the holiday home and my forthcoming job had been meted out to us as recompense for my long illness, and we were very happy with the way the cards had been dealt.

Five months later, in February 1996, we had to truly 'up sticks' and resettle. The RAF asked us to quickly make the move from our Cranwell married quarter to one at RAF Waddington because a shortage of quarters had arisen. The 'married patch' at Waddington was a very different housing scenario. It was sandwiched between the village of Waddington and the high security fence of the main part of the RAF station – a very different setting from what we had been used to at Cranwell with the open fields and trees. By contrast it seemed very urban and the runway and taxiways far too close, with engine noise at extreme levels from the large aircraft (Nimrods and AWACS) operating out of the base, and many other jets from other RAF stations also flying practice circuits.

After a few months, living at RAF Waddington felt very superficial to us. Many of the quarters were unoccupied, we only had passing acquaintance with our neighbours, and the majority of Phil's colleagues lived off base. In addition Phil was often abroad, and I was busy either working at school or keeping up with friends further south in Lincolnshire. It really was the first place where we just didn't seem to be able to connect with our immediate community or surroundings and the house didn't feel anything like a home. I wasn't unhappy living there but it felt a strange period of insignificance and a vacuum of nothingness.

We both realised that we had reached the point when it was clearly time to buy another house. It made a great deal of sense to search nearer to Woodhall Spa, because my job was only two miles from Woodhall and both the children were now at school there, with Amy being a day pupil in the pre-prep at St. Hugh's.

House-hunting was far less an easy task than we had first imagined, because we seemed at a bit of a loss with what type of house we actually wanted. Unlike in the south of England where little was affordable, in Lincolnshire there seemed to be too much choice, and with Phil often away it was difficult anyway to get our act together to discuss the publicity received from the agents and to arrange house viewings. In the past we had quickly sought and bought a house, treating it just like a military operation, but this time we dithered about every single aspect. We pussyfooted around minutiae, and just when we had decided on a particular property we were overshadowed by huge doubt and couldn't commit to the idea of actually purchasing it. The whole episode was most peculiar. We knew we were both very keen to move off base and yet we just couldn't explain why we were acting so indecisively. Something was holding us back which we just couldn't grasp or articulate.

One Friday afternoon Amy bounced out of school very excited with her teacher in tow. Amy looked animated about something and her teacher (a wonderful, colourful character who with a certain look could bring children and parents alike to attention) called across to me.

"Mummy! Amy wants to tell you something."

I quickly moved to join them. "Yes, Amy, what would you like to tell me?"

She replied with great gusto, "I want to be part of God's family!"

I looked down at this little soul with her big eyes looking up at me and her teacher looking on with similar smugness. "Do you?" I replied inquisitively.

I took her warm hand in mine and we started to walk to the car. *My goodness,* I thought, *what am I going to do about this?* I knew I couldn't ignore her wish as a responsible parent, because I felt sure her teacher would question Amy on Monday, "And what did you do over the weekend?"

I looked down at Amy's bright, innocent face and with much astonishment I heard myself say, "Right then, we'd better go to church on Sunday!"

CHAPTER EIGHT

Know that the Lord is God.
It is he who made us, and we are his;
we are his people, the sheep of his pasture.

Psalm 100:3

The Station Church at RAF Waddington was a mere couple of hundred yards from our married quarter. From the outside it looked quite inviting: a single storey building, long windows either side of the double wooden entrance doors and a narrow concrete path flanked on either side with attractive flowering shrubs. Only the short cross on the apex of the building gave away the clue that the brick building was actually a place of worship.

Amy and I received a very cheery welcome from a smiling member of the congregation at the door, which certainly helped to ease my initial nervousness of not having attended a Sunday Anglican service for eighteen years! I felt very self-conscious once inside the church whilst Amy, in contrast, seemed very confident and enthusiastic. I chose for us to sit near the back, not far from the door, which seemed less threatening. I looked around at our surprisingly modern and pleasant surroundings: comfortable upright chairs placed at an angle on a rich blue carpet; attractively arranged flowers on a huge pedestal to brighten the magnolia walls; a simple unpretentious altar area; a soft play area for young children behind us, as well as a corner where interesting RAF memorabilia were displayed. This church was a complete contrast to my chapel days working in the private school; it was like coming out of the darkness into the light.

There were about thirty people in the congregation, many families and a few retired couples too. Various people turned to smile and nod at us, and as the organ struck up I began to relax. The chaplain entered stage right wearing a pristine cassock over his RAF uniform and we all turned to the first page of the service booklet.

The service brought back some memories of having worshipped as a teenager, especially when we sang a psalm antiphonally, which we had done regularly at Crowborough. I had forgotten a lot of the traditions, although I remembered with some trepidation that a sermon was soon due and wondered how long it might take and how boring Amy might find it. As it was I cannot remember anything at all about the sermon, although I do remember how fascinated I was to watch the congregation take communion afterwards. I couldn't help but stare at them as they followed through a ritual and wonder why they had such a look of emotion on their faces. What was going through their minds to have stirred up such serious contemplation?

Naturally Amy was also very inquisitive about the ramifications of communion; she wanted to know what they were eating and drinking, asking eagerly when we were we going to take our turn. I told her rather dismissively to "Shush!" as we were supposed to keep quiet and we couldn't take part in this part of the service.

After the service, friendly faces kindly invited us to stay for refreshments but I mumbled lame excuses. We prepared to dash off out of the church, but the chaplain blocked our escape, and after a few cheery words of welcome from him we took our leave... and urgh... promised to return! As we wandered back home I wondered what on earth had induced me to say that.

I am sure that Phil thought our "visit to a church for the sake of our daughter's curiosity" would be a flash in the pan, and he was surprised when we told him that we would be going back again the following week. It wasn't long before Amy joined the Sunday school and we both started to make new friends. In a few short weeks, going to church became a weekend habit, and a few weeks later even Phil joined us on the odd occasion, when he wasn't away with the Squadron or instructing as a volunteer at the Cranwell Flying Club – although I'm pretty sure that Phil only came with us because of not wanting to be left in the house alone on a Sunday morning.

It was quite a revelation to go to a church where the people understood about the military way of life, how it encroached hugely on our whole lifestyle and the many difficulties of coping with the children when Phil was away. I stayed for refreshments after each service and gradually got to know the congregation; I felt very accepted and comfortable. There was an instant rapport with other churchgoers because of our shared experiences, and conversations flowed easily. I was delighted to discover that a church family existed who wanted to reach out and support me, without offering advice or being critical but simply because I was their 'sister'. I moved to sitting nearer the altar, in the bosom of the church family with my new friends, and I began to soak up more of the service traditions, understood more about the different readings, sang the hymns with a much greater confidence, listened more carefully to the sermons, and concentrated hard to carefully say the words in the service booklet to understand more fully their meaning.

The biggest step happened when I decided to be brave and go up to the altar during Communion for a blessing. The chaplain prayed with his hand resting firmly on my head and I felt tremendous peace. I was conscious of something burgeoning inside me as I stood still. I imagined a door slightly ajar and on the other side it opened into a dingy, long, long corridor, but right at the end of the corridor I could just see a miniscule light shining incredibly brightly. I was intrigued and went and sat back on my chair with my head bowed. The miniscule light looked alluring and warm in spite of being so small and I very, very much wanted to go down that colourless corridor to investigate the light at the end, but I felt quite hesitant. How far was it to actually reach the light? Was it a true light or was it like in a nightmare where one is always attempting to get to a place but it always remains the same distance away in spite of the distance already travelled? How easy was it to make the journey? There had to be pitfalls on the way.

Such preamble was put on hold because all of a sudden our house-hunting seemed to fall into place. We viewed a house at Kirkby Green, a hamlet next to Scopwick, where the car had run out of petrol all those years before. I had actually passed and admired the house (an early Victorian property) many times before en route to Woodhall Spa from Cranwell to take Amy to St. Hugh's. It was currently being rented by a French family, and Madame showed us around trying to explain in her limited vocabulary the details about the property.

The house was spacious enough for our needs, although it needed much modernisation. Phil wasn't immediately struck with the back garden, which consisted of a poor lawn, a few diseased rose bushes, a large dilapidated wooden shed and a flimsy boundary line at the bottom. An uncared for garden wasn't on our wish list after our experiences of married quarters, but then, as we stared out across the garden, Madame asked whether we had "an orse". We looked at her rather bemused and she repeated slowly, "an orse, a small champ?"

Suddenly I was dragged back to O Level French and remembered 'champ' was the French word for 'field'. Surely... she didn't mean room for a horse... but yes that was exactly what she meant, and we trotted down to a fence at the bottom of the garden to investigate. Sure enough, extending behind two neighbouring properties, there was a large plot choked with broad-leaved weeds and thorny thistles almost taller than a pony! And on the other side of a short laurel hedge, at the far right end of the plot, was a small church with a very distinctive single bell tower standing tall above the main part of the building. We galloped enthusiastically back down to the house to have another serious look inside the property and agreed that every room needed a lot of improvement but – tally ho! – it seemed quite the right time in our lives to manage such a project!

All of a sudden our house-hunting doldrums were blown away by our enthusiasm, and without the slightest hesitation we put in an offer and felt certain that our offer would be accepted. It transpired that the house had been on the market for many months, even before we had moved from Cranwell to Waddington, although in all the journeys we had made past the property we had never seen a 'For sale' board outside. Whilst waiting for the sale to be completed, Amy was baptised into God's family during a Sunday service; it was a very special family occasion with her class teacher coming to support her as well as her godparents. We were very proud of Amy, almost as proud as she was of the lighted candle she had been given as a memento of her baptism. I felt particularly emotional and thankful because she had been totally instrumental in leading me back to church, to a new set of friends and a different attitude on life.

In September 1996 Amy became a boarder at St. Hugh's, having begged and begged us to start boarding so that she could be with her brother and other school friends. We gave in easily as we knew that sometime in the future Phil would be posted again and we would have to 'up sticks' and disrupt our family life. At least boarding school would provide both children with a continuity of education and peers.

Two weeks later we moved to Kirkby Green, and it was a fantastic feeling to be away from 'the married patch' and once again in our own proper home. We loved our new environment surrounded by countryside, crops to the rear and Limousin cattle across the road, with a ford around the corner for the children to splash in, as well as three quarters of an acre of garden to romp in – once we tamed those devilish weeds! For me, particularly, it was wonderful to know good health and to get stuck in with landscaping the garden and developing a large vegetable plot. The house seemed such a gift to us that it confirmed a growing realisation that we were in God's care.

Disappointingly, the Kirkby Green church only had a service once every six weeks, so without hesitation I continued to drive over to Waddington every Sunday, with Phil joining me more often than in previous months. I felt indebted to my church family there and didn't want to be separated from them, and I felt sure that they didn't want to lose us to another church either. We looked forward to Sunday worship, enjoyed the various church social activities and I decided to sign up for Confirmation classes as a means to explore the meaning of faith more fully. Being in a group, reading and studying Bible passages was very different from my experience as a teenager in the Bible study group, and it was great to be able to question and listen to the thoughts of the other Confirmation candidates. I liked the opportunity of being able to contemplate the current relevance of the passages from the Bible, and I analysed many of the circumstances of my past, which I had been certain before were chance happenings, mere coincidences, the lucky hand of fortune, my playing the dealt cards well – and doubts emerged about them all. It seemed that there was much more to life than these explanations.

I was conscious of something lurking at the back of my mind that was making me sift through my childhood and my early adult years, making me consider every episode and question whether in fact each occurrence was more to do with design and purpose; and then a surprising conversation was sufficient to force me to thrust chance and coincidence aside. Whilst chatting over coffee to our organist, he let slip that he had been a peripatetic music teacher in Hampshire (yes, I knew it)... in Liphook (gosh, really?) working for some of the time in the same school as me. I felt as if God was saying to me, "How many more times do I have to put people alongside you to make you realise what a great God I am?!"

I then recalled other occasions: a theatre nurse giving me a word of encouragement when I was about to have my appendix removed and recognising her as a friend from Girl Guide days and Hockey; a residential school social worker in Scotland whose manner and patience in explaining casework made me recall I had met him before in North Wales; a lady with agoraphobia who I had helped over many months and who, in changing beyond measure, was then able to childmind Amy for a couple of months in my own hour of need. So many other similar memories kept flooding back. I was clearly on a path with twists and turns and yet at each bump or change of course God had put someone in place to help me through. He had been my protector along the way as well as in all the times of serious illness.

Even more surprising was the awareness that many of these people couldn't possibly have all been Christian believers. God must have also used the capacity of non-believers to help me along my path in life, and it dawned on me how relevant each and every unique person is in this world; that everyone must be on a similarly individual path, with the freedom of choice to wander in any direction, yet along the way God places chosen people to iron out the kinks and help that path run smooth again.

I could have easily continued living my life as before, leaving God to 'rescue me' when necessary as it seemed he had done before, but I was disconcerted about the number of times he was prepared to help me and whether that limit had been reached. I felt uncomfortable that I had resolutely ignored God, and I hoped he would forgive me for having turned a blind eye to him. I had been quite remiss, and the past image of me ruthlessly nailing the coffin lid down on God made me squirm inwardly and left me feeling as ashamed, colourless and dingy as that long, long corridor.

Eventually it dawned on me that the light at the end of the corridor was most likely forgiveness and I needed to move fearlessly towards the light, trusting and completely hopeful of its promising warmth and insight. I read my Bible, underlined verses which were personally emotive, and hungered for a variety of Christian books. I wanted to hear as many testimonies from other Christians coming to faith, and I was constantly asking people to tell me their story. I began to grasp what it is like to have a true relationship with God, to perceive his grace, and take into my heart his mercy and moreover rest in the comfort of his unconditional love. The light at the end of the corridor was being transformed from something small and insignificant into a large beacon with marvellous flares of blazing light.

CHAPTER NINE

*I tell you the truth, no-one can see the kingdom of God
unless he is born again.*

John 3:3

The general public can be very scathing when they hear the phrase 'born again Christian', and comments are often made suggesting that such people are freaks, fanatics or just plain odd. Being 'born again' is exactly what happened to me when I got to the end of that dingy corridor and stepped into the Light. I had the wonderful sensation that I had stepped into a whole new world with a promising future. I asked God to forgive me for anything I had done to upset anyone else and felt the slate tangibly wiped clean. Anything which I was particularly sad about, regretted or ashamed of was far less of a burden, and I felt as if I had been given permission to put these things in my past firmly behind me.

Like a phoenix rising from the ashes, I was a brand-new human being with the promise of a fresh start. This might sound very fantastical and extraordinary, but just as a newborn baby is cleaned up after its birth I felt that I too was being cleaned up and made decent ready to be presented to the world... again. To feel so new gave me a newfound confidence to stand tall. I was determined to be a kinder person, a more caring wife, mother, daughter, sister, friend, colleague, neighbour, community member and Samaritan... Quite a commitment, but with God by my side it really felt possible.

A feeling of comfort and warmth surrounded me giving me much peace. I realised that I was out of the starting blocks on the track of a new beginning, with a new everlasting Father and a new unchangeable friend in Jesus, and the realisation was really exciting. I knew I had to trust God entirely; I had to turn to Jesus wholeheartedly and allow him to be my best friend and confidante.

As with any new birth I was also on an emotional high, and I was delighted to be confirmed by the Bishop of Grantham at RAF Waddington. It had been a culmination of a year's journey as I had met with other would-be confirmands in a class which met regularly to further our knowledge of the Christian faith.

With a new zeal and spring in my step, family and work life carried on as before but with a completely different slant on my capacity to cope with all the trappings of a military life. Even though we were settled in our own home, in an ordinary community, and tried to establish a normal civilian pattern for our family life, it was not possible to be divorced from the priority of duty to Queen and country. When Phil had reached the option to leave the RAF at thirty-eight, he had applied to stay in and was very pleased to be accepted as Specialist Aircrew, safeguarding his career until the age of fifty-five. He had been given a second tour of duty at RAF Waddington, and life had continued as before with the military way of life a dominating factor, not only due to the very nature of Phil's role as a Nimrod pilot, but also with all the extra accoutrements such as night flying, call outs, secondary duties, compulsory formal events and longer detachments. Not forgetting either an array of uniform, flying kit and long johns, which still had to be hung out on the washing line to publicise to all we were inherently military! Now though, with the support of my faith, extra pressures and tasks seemingly impossible to achieve or plain difficult became far easier, and when I was reticent to try something new I just had to remember that Jesus was beside me to help me. I surprised myself many a time as I stepped forward in faith and discovered that the more I achieved, the more I wanted to step further in faith to see what else I could accomplish. I was simply ecstatic to be reborn and immensely thankful – and who cared if someone thought I was a freak, fanatic or odd? Not me, as I knew otherwise what joy there was to be had in being reborn!

Phil and I were very happy working in our respective jobs, the children were doing well at school, and each of us was very settled in our own routine. Family life was marching along at a grand pace, mostly dictated by school term dates. Like very many families we very much looked forward to our holidays and the precious time to step off of the treadmill and relax together. Both children were particularly enjoying languages at school so we decided help their studies and renew our love of France. We headed for the Vendée department on the Atlantic coast – an area of France totally new to

Phil and me, as on previous holidays we had headed to the South of France or Brittany.

We went camping, for the first time as a family, to La Tranche-sur-Mer and stayed on a wonderful site, in spitting distance from a beautiful beach, and revelled in the French way of life and excellent weather for an outdoor life. The coastal scenery was very flat, but we were particularly taken with the whitewashed villas with their terracotta pantile roofs and attractive blue shutters, which were surrounded by a variety of pine trees and aromatic shrubs. Phil and I would often go for a walk and consider how very fortunate the local people were to live in such a pleasant place. We loved the shops with their array of different food items and the vibrant market with huge roasting trays of sizzling sausages, bowls of delectable olives, pungent goat's cheeses and delicious nectarines piled up high.

It was fun trying out our French on the stall holders and shopkeepers, although not all conversations went to plan. For example, there was one bewildering moment in the boucherie (butcher's shop) when I asked confidently for four nicely rolled up fillets of chicken in the display cabinet. The butcher waggled his finger at me and told me it wasn't chicken, it was dinde. Flummoxed because I didn't understand the word, I asked him with a bit of a grimace on my face whether he meant it was rabbit. "Non," he declared crossly, "c'est dinde." Panic set in and we excused ourselves from the long queue (with our bobtails between our legs) deciding that if it wasn't rabbit then 'dinde' had to be the word for 'hare'. A narrow escape as we couldn't have barbecued something so fluffy and cute as rabbit or hare. Out of curiosity we went straight into a bookshop a few doors away and had a squint in a French-English dictionary, which revealed that 'dinde' was nothing other than turkey! Oh dear, how foolish we felt! But now we were far too embarrassed to go back to the boucherie and begin the whole rigmarole again. Instead we walked off to the supermarket and happily gobble-gobbled sausages for supper and vowed to be more knowledgeable the next time.

Stumbling around the French language and laughing a lot at our mistakes and misunderstandings brought back so many recollections of previous holidays Phil and I had made to other parts of France, as well as our personal memories of school trips and family holidays. Amusing memories such as my paternal grandmother trying to defy a gendarme's persistent whistle in Le Touquet as she strutted in a determined "I'm British" manner across a forbidden park lawn; another occasion in Arras when my father attempted to drive the wrong way around a square and we all thought that the people waving at us on the pavement were ever so nice and friendly; of a primary school trip when I stayed in a Lycée (secondary school) and on the first night went to the refectory starving hungry to be thoroughly disappointed that the main course was detestable lamb's brains (I shudder at the memory as I write); and at fourteen on another school trip to Falaise in Normandy taking home a pleasing gift for my parents of a little brown jug of Calvados brandy! Easily purchased and without a hint of difficulty despite my young age.

Phil and I reminisced about the time we had made an achingly long motorbike trip down the eastern side of France. We had stopped near Grenoble for a night-stop and erected our two-man canvas ridge tent. We proudly covered it with a voluminous fly sheet his mother had carefully made from an old parachute Phil had purloined, only for heavy rain and wind to completely destroy it in a wink of an eye to shreds. Our tent and pitch were completely flooded out, although we probably had the best night's sleep of the whole holiday as the campsite owners came to our immediate rescue and kindly gave us a bed for the night in their own home on the site. We travelled on the next day and enjoyed a delightful holiday in the South of France, although on our return journey north we endured terribly heavy rain again and, being open to the full brunt of the elements on the motorbike, we became utterly drenched to the skin. We resolved that particular dilemma by purchasing a roll of large size bin liners, stripped off and converted them to wear as 'clothes' whilst we dried out our soaking garments at the campsite. The things we do when we are young!

With our love of France rekindled, we returned the following year to the same campsite at La Tranche. We had improved our French sufficiently enough to be competent in hiring a mobile home direct from the campsite owner, rather than buying an inclusive holiday from a UK-based company. This was a great achievement for us as well as enjoying the advantage of reducing the cost of the holiday by over a third. We had a wonderful time, basked in extremely hot weather and lapped up even more of the local culture; we even shopped for turkey steaks for the barbecue at the same boucherie.

The next year, in 1999, now bitten by the Francophile bug we headed for the Loire valley and for the first time rented a gîte, at

Cherverny, which was nestled amidst the neat rows of a white wine vineyard. It was run by a lovely young couple, and the husband was a larger than life character who had trained as a chef in Liverpool and delighted each morning in greeting us, not with "Bonjour!" but a flourish of a bow bellowing, "God Save the Queen!" He was an excellent chef and we enjoyed several meals with him, his family and several more of their guests from other European nations. We all sat convivially around a long table in their courtyard, and it was a real joy to try different culinary delights, converse with everyone, share life experiences and discover how each nation ticked. We began to feel much more European than British.

By the time we had returned from holiday, the United Kingdom was emphatically on the bandwagon of promoting the forthcoming Millennium, and everywhere there was a plethora of Millennium publicity, which soon escalated beyond imagination. A crescendo of craziness evolved, and many wondered whether the world, so dependent on Information Technology, would come to a standstill, whilst others predicted doom and gloom. Still others saw it as a time for reflection, a time for change and a time to herald in a new beginning. Many thought about the future, their hopes and expectations, as we did too, and by December the Millennium hype was at fever pitch and threatened to swamp everyone in its wake by Christmas, let alone survive until New Year!

On New Year's Eve we went to a party with church friends, to make merry, and later that evening enjoyed a very special service of reflection in the church at RAF Waddington, as we celebrated the greatness of God and his many blessings on each of our lives. We prayed for Jesus to direct us in the next Millennium. As the service came to an end an enormous explosion from the first firework filled the air and we all went and stood outside the church, revelling in the array of firework displays to add to the glittering starry, starry night. It was an astonishing spectacle, and as we all stood together looking up at God's awesome celestial creation, alongside the outstanding man-made pyrotechnics, I felt sure that I wasn't alone in feeling tremendous joy, curiosity and anticipation at what the year 2000 had in store for us all.

CHAPTER TEN

Dear friends, do not be surprised
at the painful trial you are suffering
as if something strange were happening to you.

1 Peter 4:12

Millennium or no Millennium, the year 2000 began in the same familiar way as the start of any new year. The same scenario was played out by friends and colleagues: discussing their New Year resolutions – whether to get fit, lose weight, kick a bad habit, make contact with someone, join a new club, make some sort of change – with every good intention over the first couple of weeks, and then generally becoming fed up when they failed the first hurdle of the new challenge. I have read that only 8% of people succeed in carrying through their resolution!

In the past I had been no better than the rest, but this year being a Millennium and a little bit special I was determined to overcome such a downfall if I could only choose a sensible challenge to embrace. I wanted to establish an abiding commitment and sought a resolution which would not only challenge me daily but would bring about real change in all areas of my life. With that in mind I took out an annual subscription to receive booklets of daily Bible readings on a quarterly basis. I also invested in a study Bible full of explanatory notes, maps, good clarity of teaching and thought-provoking comment extremely pertinent to modern day living. After the first week I was hooked on my habit of doing the suggested Bible reading for the day first, reading the explanatory notes, and then taking time in pondering over the thought-provoking verses. I was quite surprised how coming into God's presence each morning gave me the encouragement to lead my life in a different way. It even gave me the answers on how to persevere and strengthen my will-power to get fit, lose weight, kick a bad habit and begin another new venture!

As a family our New Year resolution was to create a small Millennium garden within our garden to hide a shabby area in which lurked all sorts of paraphernalia, compost bins and an incinerator. As ever, Rob and Amy were very keen to get involved with the idea, and from their design we erected panels of screening, planted up fragrant climbing plants, planted a mini knot garden with lavender and box hedging, put gravel down underfoot and then surrounded the whole area with fast growing mixed foliage shrubs to develop a very attractive private space. We installed a bench seat in front of the screening, and underneath it, in the spirit of the Millennium, we buried a time capsule with a cache of interesting things relating to our home. We then puzzled as to the most appropriate location in which to place a plaque pointing to the capsule's existence, because we didn't want a future proprietor not to know of its existence after all our thoughtful efforts, yet we didn't want anyone to dig the capsule up too early either. Rob resolved the dilemma by suggesting that the script should be in Latin in order to put any would-be burglars off the trail! Amy duly involved her Latin teacher with the translation (much to his amusement or bemusement) and the plaque was quickly produced and proudly erected.

Like many families that year we had many aspirations for our future, as well as good intentions to visit family and friends we had lost touch with over the years and our general desire to explore new horizons. Unfortunately something rather strange began to happen to me, which threatened to interrupt all our hopes and dreams.

The previous October I had begun to suffer a niggling pain in my side which I had ignored for a long time, putting it down to probably having sprained a muscle whilst digging out the Millennium garden. After the New Year I couldn't ignore the pain anymore and eventually was referred to the local hospital for a CT scan. Thankfully it revealed nothing untoward and certainly no evidence of a recurrent tumour, which was a great relief. I prayed to God, asking him to keep me fit and well, not only for the sake of my family but also for myself so that I could keep working at the primary school – a job I absolutely loved. It was such a joy to get up and go to work.

However, as the year progressed, having tried so hard to pay no attention to the wretched niggling pain, I felt that my health generally was beginning to spiral downhill. I didn't want to believe the pain existed but it refused to subside. Instead it was frustratingly persistent and, as if to flaunt my intention to stem it, kept intensifying. I was referred to a Chronic Pain Clinic where a Pain Management Consultant attempted various excruciating interventions to block the pain and prescribed a range of medication for neuropathic pain (some of which produced the most horrible side effects). I really didn't want anything to do with this pain or its treatment, but I was clearly stuck with it and I tried to manage as best I could. Surprisingly, a great help was the morning ritual of reading the Bible and devotional notes. It helped me to put things in perspective and inspired me to get on with life when I felt a bit low.

Our summer holiday approached. We decided to travel to Northern France and caught the car ferry from Portsmouth in order to cut down on the number of driving hours for Phil. He had to be the sole driver as my ability to drive had reduced so drastically over the months to a mere twenty minutes. I was finding it more and more uncomfortable to be able to sit in a car for any length of time, even as a passenger, because when the car braked or went over the slightest bump or pothole it would set off the jarring, stabbing pain. I seemed to spend the whole journey hanging on to the inside support of the door or with my arms stretched out against the dashboard bracing myself to try to minimise the pain; not very encouraging for Phil or any driver!

We spent the first week at a campsite near Granville in Normandy and then moved on to a site in Brittany near Quimper, famed for its Festival de Cornouaille (an enormous street parade of Breton folk in traditional costume alongside a riot of Celtic music and dance). Our campsite was beautifully sited alongside a beach, although we mostly stayed around the campsite to use the very large and well-equipped swimming pool, where we could relax on loungers whilst the children continually delighted in the impressive water slides.

I really didn't feel like doing a great deal, but one morning we decided to stroll into the village as a traditional fête / folk day had been organised. This day became the most memorable day of our whole holiday as we experienced the French enjoying themselves as they do best with family and friends in their quintessential 'joie de vivre' spirit.

As well as a traditional market there were artisans demonstrating their crafts and celtic music bands with their traditional pipes, flutes, violins and accordions. Female dancers of all ages, attired in long black costumes adorned in pearls with plain coloured aprons and intricately crafted, stiff, white lace hats and collars, danced beautifully on the makeshift stage. It was such a striking sight and a day which really lifted our spirits. We paid to join in with a community meal, and for eight euros each we sat under huge awnings at long trestle tables and savoured an excellent three-course lunch of traditional fayre, all catered for by the local people, and all washed down with Breton cider.

We popped back to the campsite for a very necessary siesta and then in the early evening returned again to the festival site and watched a theatre production about Breton customs, from the countryside to the sea, the conclusion to the marvellous day being a superb firework display. Our love for France was well and truly cemented that day.

I had hoped that the holiday would have restored me physically, but I struggled through the rest of the summer holidays needing more and more help, and when I went back to work at the start of the Autumn Term it was difficult to cope with a busy school day. I really began to wonder where all this ill-health was leading me and got a little desperate about what I could do to stop the rot. I received lots of advice from family and friends but my confidence was really knocked sideways when a friend suggested that the reason for my pain and suffering was because I needed to ask God to forgive me my sins. I felt very confused and bewildered about this comment, particularly as I asked God daily to forgive me my trespasses.

One Sunday at church our chaplain organised a part of the Communion service to include prayer for healing, inviting anyone who would like healing to move across to the Side Chapel. I certainly wasn't going to pass up such an offer and almost rushed across to be the first person to be anointed with oil on my forehead. I walked back to my seat afterwards, bowed my head and waited patiently for some sort of sign. I hadn't expected to receive instantaneous healing but I had expected to feel some sort of rush of emotion and restoration from the actual act of being anointed with holy oil. Yet not a single tingle of emotion was felt.

Later that day I thought back to the moment of the anointing and rationalised that perhaps instant healing hadn't occurred because God felt that I was too greedy in wanting a quick result. Perhaps, too, there was a lesson to be learnt about not being too impatient for him to act. Therefore I vowed I would try to be more patient and settle instead for a slower reaction of significant improvement. Perhaps if I played my part, God would act and heal me?

But – oh – what disappointment I felt when the only significant thing which happened over the next couple of weeks was my having to take yet more time off work. I had become utterly exhausted in trying to cope with the pain, which had left me very debilitated. The only way to cope was to spend time in bed when not at work, which was very disheartening especially as the jobs around me mounted up. I couldn't understand why I struggled to do even the simplest chore, and I was losing my strength to lift anything of even light weight. I broke so much crockery as a result. In a space of a few months I managed to smash to smithereens the remainder of our wedding gift dinner service, as well as a fine decanter my brother had given us and countless other treasured ornaments! I was beginning to get a reputation as being totally clumsy as well as in danger of upsetting my family.

Getting up in the morning had become a real trial and an even greater one was literally crawling up our steep cottage stairs to bed each evening. After a long time off-sick I returned to work only for the same problem of fatigue and inadequacy to rear its ugly head again a few weeks later. I became very frustrated and my faith certainly took a wobble. I seemed to be going from bad to worse, and nothing seemed to be stopping the downslide, not even God. I absolutely couldn't fathom why not.

My hospital consultant decided to lend me a TENS machine (transcutaneous electrical nerve stimulation) which releases an electrical pulse in an attempt to confuse the brain and block chronic pain for a short while. As a result I discovered that I clearly do not have the type of brain which likes to be manipulated by scientific intervention because when I used the machine it produced unbearable pain even greater than before. A week later, with my pain totally out of control, I was taken into hospital overnight. I felt so sapped of life my doctor didn't have any other option but to put me off work again, this time for a fortnight. In the meantime my Pain Management Consultant tried some further steroid injections, in the upper part of my back, along the line of my operation scar, in the hope that the result would be to suppress the pain – but the process was excruciating. The third attempt with the injection had me yelling so much that the sister said she was convinced that the team would be having a very short day at work because I must have cleared their waiting room!

I started back to work two days later but it was a complete mistake. I was completely wrapped up in pain. I knew what a terrible liability I had become to the school, physically and financially, therefore I decided that the only course of honourable action was to stop being a burden on them. The next day I handed in my resignation letter giving the minimum of four weeks' notice, although not actually knowing how many of those days I would actually be able to come to work. I felt completely wretched about letting people down. For the first time in my life I felt very prone to depression, but then that same afternoon I received a surprising and beautiful bouquet of flowers from friends, which lifted my spirits enormously and put a smile back on my face. Sadly I only managed to work a further three days and received the final kick in the teeth when I was put off-sick until the end of my notice. Just to rub extra salt in the wound that day my husband, best friend and right-hand-man left with the Squadron on detachment to Italy and our troublesome heating boiler broke down completely. It never rains but it pours!

Officially my last day at work was 2nd March, 2001, and as it dawned it felt the oddest of days. For most of the day I wondered if I would ever work again. I dared to hope that it would be sooner rather than later, yet in my heart of hearts with such a catalogue of pain and illness I felt more certain that it might be 'never work again' rather than 'ever work again'. I had clearly reached a life-changing moment and had to mark the day in some way. With a flourish I took off my only wristwatch, having thought desperately at first of taking a hammer to it, then went to the cupboard and stuffed it deep into the charity shop bag, which was to be collected later in the week. I thought someone else could benefit from my misfortune in not being able to work, and in truth I couldn't bear to look at it. I wonder to this day who might be wearing it!

CHAPTER ELEVEN

Your hands shaped and made me.
Will you now turn and destroy me?

Job 10:8

Imagine peeling an orange by means of taking a small, sharp knife, forcing it through the peel at the top and then drawing the knife around the orange to the bottom several times, forming curved sections all around the orange. Then waggle the point of the knife into the top of the orange to lift the start point of one section and peel each section away. By adding a bit of force to the blade of the knife the peel will generally come away without too much difficulty, tearing off most of the unpalatable pith... but never all. What remains is an orange that has been methodically stripped bare of peel; left disrobed, without protection, naked, defenceless and vulnerable to the touch. I was like the orange with all my parts stripped back. My rich, shiny hue of bright-coloured peel had been discarded and a normal, healthy lifestyle had been torn from me. I was disrobed of an opportunity to work and fully exposed as a non-functioning person. I felt miserably laid bare, with the remains of bitter pith stuck fast. Pith normally stores and carries nutrients to the plant to make it healthy, but when cells are destroyed and torn then the system breaks down and cannot function. I knew I was in the process of breaking down too and in my frustration was disagreeable with others, in my bitterness acerbic with them and generally lacking in grace. But how to stop the downslide?

Around me the world carried on as before and the family carried on regardless and expanded its own experiences whilst my world contracted and became emptier. My brain was so befuddled with medication and I feared that I would soon lose the ability to process complicated thoughts and techniques. I worried that I would be reduced to being a complete burden on my family as had happened with my job, and Phil would become fed up with me to the point that I would lose his love. I wondered whether my infirmity from chronic pain was similar to being put in solitary confinement, as the invisible walls built up around me, especially as I was ousted out of family activities because I simply could not manage to join in. Living in a small hamlet in itself was socially isolating and when initial visits from friends grew few and far between I felt very lonely.

The narrowness of my daily existence threatened to seriously get me down, but what depressed me more was simply not being able to fathom why I was suffering so very much. What had I done to merit such a protracted illness? Was it a wake-up call to enable a change in our lifestyle? Had I simply been in the wrong job? I dared to imagine that in fact this experience, dreadful as it was, was part of God's purpose for our future. Perhaps my experience of suffering and illness was mandatory so that I could be better equipped to help others in a similar position? I also constantly wondered and questioned if indeed I was being punished by God because I needed to be taught a lesson? Was I really a bad person? I was unable to see my wrongdoing and prayed that I could be forgiven for whatever needed pardoning. I thought back constantly to the healing service where I had felt devoid of emotion and that left me feeling even more confused.

Then in desperation I began clutching at straws in the hope of a cure. On a recommendation from a friend I booked a session of reflexology; I had an appointment with a homeopath and came away hopeful and clutching a bagful of pills and potions for nerve endings and cell repair. I rubbed 'miracle' oil into my long scar in the hope of amazing results. I even arranged a private blood test and from the results changed my diet, eliminating a variety of food products which I was supposedly intolerant to. I optimised my intake of all the right nutrients and vitamins, wore various recommended bracelets to thwart pain, tried a number of heat pads on the trigger points of pain and when those produced no results changed tack to cold compresses using packs of frozen peas. Many friends and family were certainly not slow either in adding their twopenny worth of advice, which often proved conflicting, and I listened to a host of old wives' tales and even followed some! I was referred to an Extended Scope Physiotherapist, who recommended certain exercises and getting an exercise bike. Naturally, we dutifully purchased the right model, and I attempted to ride it for a certain amount of time each day until the pain was too great in trying to lean forward to reach the handlebars.

My GP arranged an appointment with a neurologist, and I went to the appointment hoping for a breakthrough only for the consultation to end by telling me in no uncertain terms to "go and get a life". I was devastated and felt extremely misunderstood. I hoped that our paths would never cross again, but no such luck there as a year later, much to my surprise, I received an appointment to return to his clinic for a review. I was very reluctant to go, and as I sat in the waiting-room I felt very nervous. Finally it was my turn and the sister in charge led me down the corridor to the consulting room. As we reached the door she told me the neurologist was feeling rather sorry for himself. Slightly puzzled I looked at her askance and she smiled rather wryly at me. I gingerly opened the door to see him hunched over his desk, looking very uncomfortable with his arm in a sling and clearly suffering. Suddenly all my fears evaporated and I resisted in telling him to pull himself together... only by the shortest whisker!

I started writing a journal that year, and the act of putting my feelings down on paper was a surprising release. It was far better to commit my frustrations to a diary rather than bend someone else's ear. I recorded family events, daily successes, weather (oh so British!) and world events. I hoped too that a pattern might emerge to help me ascertain if there was something blatantly obvious I had missed hindering my getting better. Some days were better than others, but I was flummoxed as to why this should be. Sometimes I was fearful as the pain spiralled out of control and I was reduced to bed rest whilst on other days my chest felt so incredibly heavy. It really did feel as if my upper body was made of concrete. On other days I catalogued the disappointment of having to cry off an event and apologise to the children that parents' night would again be missed, and I wrote about my general lack of ability to be a wife and mother. I noted that there were many days when I just wasn't able to get to church because of being unable to get up in time, or if I could manage to be on time then not actually feeling able to drive. As Phil was busy instructing at the Flying Club he wasn't always free to give me a lift to church either, which was disappointing. I revelled in the fellowship of Lunch+, the ladies' Bible study group, but for the same reason often missed out on that too.

In September the dreadful, traumatic events of 9/11 occurred and the horrific collapse of the World Trade Centre twin towers unfolded in our cosy sitting room. That painful experience alone should have been enough to take away my pain. I repeatedly asked myself where

God was in all the suffering which ensued. Had he caused the suffering? No, I was sure that the root cause was inherent in the evil of mankind. God gave man free will to either be kind and loving to fellow man or to sin and create evil actions. In these events man had chosen to maim and kill for man's own glory. God must have been on the sidelines watching and weeping.

But why did God allow suffering to that unbelievable unfathomable extent? Perhaps to show a shocked world the reality of all man's grave actions so that we might finally grasp the notion that enough is enough and seek another way – his way – and rally around and assist one another. Perhaps it was intended for us to finally grasp God's purpose for his created world and to strive for unity and peace. Common to any tragedy, God was most evident in the subsequent amazing stories and miracles which were witnessed by the victims and rescuers involved in this terrible disaster.

In our generation it is easy to imagine the various corners of the world as names of places or countries are flashed across our screens every day. We have the benefit of brilliantly produced geographical programmes unfolding on our television screens each week, and we can search the internet in seconds for impressive and sharply produced images to fill in our lack of knowledge of places and events. So many diverse habitats to wonder at; therefore it is only natural to ask why God allows natural disasters to threaten the beauty of our world. Why would he want to destroy something that he has created from the beginning? Perhaps he even wanted to destroy me...

Research has proved time and again that a natural cause for tragedy, such as an earthquake or flood, is so often exacerbated by humans in their quest for resources, in search of a vital mineral or substance in their quest to be rich or powerful. With our God-given talents to care for his world we seem hell-bent on destroying his creation, at whatever price, and what we do in one part of the world can have a ripple effect of repercussion around the globe. How God must cry out for our inadequacies in caring for his phenomenal creation!

Often as outsiders to a particular tragedy we naturally criticise the faults and deficiencies of other countries, coining the phrase, "It was a disaster waiting to happen." Some observers are more realistic and recognise that the same problems exist within their own country, yet they carry on with their lives not giving it another thought, commenting, "There but for the grace of God go I." Others will openly admit that problems in other countries and places are the same in their own community, threatening their own family and friends; and a tiny minority actually will admit that they made a gross error and are themselves culpable.

My suffering seemed a mere drop in the ocean compared to world suffering – but I was suffering. I also wondered whether God allowed tragedy to occur in his desperation that we might fathom our mistakes and lead one another to obedience. I couldn't fathom my mistake but I could try to become more obedient. Like the rest of the world, perhaps I needed to walk closer to God.

In October 2001, in response to the attacks on 9/11, 'Operation Enduring Freedom – Afghanistan' was launched in an attempt to fight terrorism; a joint U.S., U.K. and Afghan operation which involved Phil's Nimrod Squadron deploying to Oman for operational duties. Fortunately part of Phil's time away coincided with the children's half-term, and with the help and the support of my parents we managed to get through his four week detachment.

Phil arrived home on 2nd November, and three days later, after more than six years flying the Nimrod, he was posted to RAF Cranwell to join 55 Sqn, his role being to pilot the Dominie aircraft in support of the training of navigators for the Flying Training School. I was very thankful for this posting because very little needed to be changed in our home situation, and Phil was equally delighted, not only because had he been granted a choice of posting for which he had asked and hoped for but also he would rarely be detached away. We had the additional bonus of his flying training course for his new role being conducted at Cranwell. For once, in my time of need, he would not be leaving me bereft for several weeks (or months!) nor would he have to bean-steal in the Mess, which Phil loathed. We had been truly blessed and were full of gratitude. Instead of driving to work north-east from our home at Kirkby Green he simply had to make the comparative fifteen minute drive in a south-westerly direction. I do have the sneakiest feeling that Phil also considered the most beneficial plus of his posting was the prospect of being able to chalk up yet another aircraft type in his flying log book!

It actually felt quite strange to make it full circle back to Cranwell. It had been ten years, minus just one month, since we had moved into a married quarter with our young family and all our hopes and dreams for them. We had accomplished a decade of family life, the children had grown to be teenagers, and we had endured a hugely challenging time with the blight of my poor health affecting us all in different ways. I certainly didn't want to turn the clock back and think about what might have been, because it was encouraging to see that in the midst of all the unpleasant and fearful times there were many times of real joy. The most treasured thing I held on to was the comfort of knowing that I could cope with every dark and miserable moment only because of a special friend, who walked alongside me and encouraged me to persevere.

CHAPTER TWELVE

Be ever hearing, but never understanding,
be ever seeing, but never perceiving.

Isaiah 9:9b

Just north of St. Andrew's lies Tentsmuir Forest, a vast pine forest, a mere stone's throw from RAF Leuchars in Scotland. It is bordered impressively on one side by dune-clad beaches and the North Sea. Whilst we had lived at Leuchars back in 1983 it had been a great place to walk, to follow a trail through the forest to the sands and then trek up the long beach to Tentsmuir Point in the hope of seeing seals. I remember one bitterly cold afternoon in February when we had started a bracing walk up towards the Point, but the fierce northerly wind had quickly forced us to opt for a hasty retreat back to the car park. We left the beach and walked through the imposing pines to a clearing, which opened up to reveal not only the car park but a very large, wooden see-saw. We were really surprised to see two diminutive, elderly ladies with matching bobble hats having an absolute 'whale of a time' on the see-saw as they took it in turns to propel each other high into the air. Once Phil and I got over the amazement of watching elderly people actually daring to act like youngsters, we couldn't wait to have a go ourselves, although we had to wait a good while for the other 'children' to finish their turn first!

See-saws are exhilarating, even at a balanced height oscillating gently from one position to another, with little change between being up and down, allowing your feet to lightly touch base. It is fun and enjoyable using just minimum force, but as a result of great force, you can have your heart in your mouth as you pivot high in the air, grasping the rail to cope with the jerk off the seat at height. At the highest point of travel there exists the slightest fear that the other person, far below, will unwittingly leap off of the see-saw at that point. On one occasion that happened to me, and with no hope of bracing myself I came crashing down onto the hard tarmac, experiencing the full realm of gravity, fear and an extremely sore bottom.

Suffering chronic pain is remarkably like being on a see-saw. You know from experience that it is not possible to stay up without pain forever, even though you hope upon hope that being 'up' will last as long a time as possible. You try very hard to make the descent slow and measured, but mostly you come crashing 'down' without any premonition: undignified, frustrated, fearful, bruised, hurt, in pain, disillusioned yet with very little choice but to get back on the see-saw and have another go.

By the middle of 2002 I plunged downwards, experiencing a different type of pain to add to all my physical pain, the pain of social stigma associated with not coping. I had put in a claim to social services for assistance and was awarded Incapacity Benefit, with the addition of also being awarded a Disability Living Allowance, begrudgingly having to rely on a disabled parking permit to help my independence of being able to drive, and using my benefit money to pay for home-help three times a week to try to keep home life as normal as possible. The general public can sometimes be very scathing of those on benefits, and I seemed to spend a great deal of my time apologising to friends that I had to make a claim. I don't think many even contemplated the negative effects I might have felt on being reduced to such a status; however it certainly opened my eyes to all aspects of the stigma.

In an attempt to alleviate some of my pain, my consultant decided to freeze the trigger points of my nerve pain using a cryoprobe (an instrument of microtechnology) being hopeful that the treatment would last six weeks to allow the nerves in that area chance to heal. I wasn't exactly thrilled with this proposal after my last experiences of injections in Day Surgery, when my screams had frightened the other patients, but if my consultant thought it might help then I was prepared to be subjected to the treatment. I was given the first appointment in the afternoon for very obvious reasons! Soon afterwards I felt stiff as a board, whether from the result of the actual 'freezing' treatment or the local administered anaesthetic, and the following day I had dreadful nausea, then a further ten days of lethargy, drowsiness and immobility. I fought to stay awake for any decent length of time, and for two of those days Phil came home from work and woke me at 5.30pm! It felt as if I had slept the whole day.

I spent more and more days in my pyjamas and dressing gown, barely able to find the energy to wash, shower or prepare a snack, let alone cope with doing anything in the house – how very demoralising that must have been for Phil when he came home each evening. We both were in need of a dramatic change, something to look forward to, a glimmer of something more normal, something which would lift our spirits. It had not been possible to take a summer holiday in 2001 but this year we had to be more determined and we decided to plan a return trip to Brittany and the Loire valley and invited my parents to join us. It was good to have a goal on the horizon.

I was really low and downhearted a few days before we travelled, having struggled to pack. On the long journey south from Lincolnshire to Newhaven, the ferry port in East Sussex, I suffered a great deal of pain and discomfort. When we finally embarked on the ferry for the longer crossing to Dieppe, I found the passage purgatory. I couldn't bear the jolting or vibrations of the ship, and I had to lie down for much of the journey to try to get even remotely comfortable. As I lay down I worried we had bitten off more than we could chew.

Our first night we stayed in a Chambre d'hôtes (B&B) in Normandy, and I was beside myself trying to get in a position in bed to escape the searing pain. I had a truly horrible and anxious night, and I was little better the following morning when we met for breakfast. Later that day, whilst the rest of the family explored Bayeux, I spent the morning resting in the car, not wanting to move, and I seriously wondered whether it had been a really grave mistake to come away on holiday. We had genuinely needed a relaxing break and were very keen to show my parents why we adored France, but what seemed to be unfolding was the realisation of having made a massive error in deciding to come away and the mistake in being so far from familiar medical assistance.

Fortunately I improved a little as the holiday progressed, but mostly I had a lot of debilitating pain, felt exhausted and generally very out of sorts. Yet amazingly we had many blessings too. Not only was the weather kind to us but it was super for the children to have their grandparents around them for a much longer period of time than usual. Also, at the campsite in Brittany, Rob unexpectedly met up with school friends (where else but at the top of the waterslide!) and one evening after supper as we ambled around the site we rounded a track to see RAF friends playing a game of badminton! We hadn't had the slightest idea that they were in France and it was wonderful to catch up with them. Even in my lowest moments these blessings helped to distract my thoughts and worries of being so far from home.

During the holiday I developed a much greater difficulty in walking up steps and inclines, and it became more and more apparent that walking was becoming very demanding. On our return to the UK I purchased a folding walking stick to help my balance, and my GP decided to contact the Pain Management Consultant again to explore the possibility of introducing yet stronger pain killers. Thankfully the cryoprobe treatment was off limits, after the poor results; however, I was wary and fearful of the possible side effects of yet another drug. I began to consider whether it was time to actually reject any further treatment, and I prayed to God and asked Him to show me the missing link in my life. What was I failing to grasp about this whole situation of chronic pain? Were the medics continually making bad choices about my treatment or was something causing me to be unresponsive? Where was I at fault?

Before I resolved that dilemma another drug was introduced, whose properties masked the brain in the attempt to stop communication between the brain and the nerve endings. The drug promised the usual lengthy list of side effects and hence required a very slow programme of introduction. After only a couple of days the outcome was a burning rash, difficulty in focusing, and being even more unbalanced and disorientated, but I persevered over the weeks and months even though the drug left me very woolly headed – if it was possible to be more woolly headed than before! As a consequence I managed to make a huge mistake whilst shopping online. Whilst organising a supermarket order before Christmas I gaily added twelve lemons to the order, but the next day when the delivery man unloaded the shopping from the van, his pièce de la résistance was a large fruit box of 144 lemons! I scanned the printout, but the fault was all mine as I had failed to notice the item on the website was for a pack of twelve lemons and not a single lemon. In the New Year many a friend appreciated the story and a jar of marmalade!

By Christmas we had finally swapped our allegiance from the church at RAF Waddington to St. Andrew's Church of Scotland at RAF Cranwell. It made sense to be worshipping at Phil's place of work, and it was nice to become involved with a different congregation and get to extend our Christian family. Interestingly it was the very same church where we had previously attended our first Carol Service as a family in 1992, the very same building in which Amy had been to nursery school, and alongside the church car park there was a gate guardian in the shape of a Jet Provost aircraft, which was the same mark from which Phil had ejected all those years ago. Every time I went to church that Jet Provost aircraft served as a reminder of what might have been and how very thankful I ought to be for our present life, regardless of my suffering and difficulties.

Worship in the Church of Scotland was much freer than in the Anglican Church and we liked the change of style and form. It refreshed me spiritually and mentally, and I felt really moved by the presence of the Holy Spirit in that building. It was heart-warming to make new friends, gain extra support and, with their encouragement, be more determined to get through the low points.

One day I managed to attend a Ladies' Lunch in the Officers' Mess at Cranwell. I only knew a handful of people as it was a rare occasion for me to make a social appearance, and I felt a bit of a wallflower as I stood on the fringe of the gathering in the dining room. To make matters worse there was no seating plan, and I dithered in making a choice where to sit, eventually choosing to sit next to another lady who seemed equally alone. I quickly made an astonishing discovery: my lunch companion had been a chronic pain sufferer for twelve years! We spent the whole lunch animated in conversation, pretty much in seclusion from the others around us, as we compared our debilitating similarities and discussed the see-saw effect. We laughed so much about our troubles and misfortunes and the ridiculousness of our situations... yes, actually laughed from the delirium of discovering we were not alone in fighting chronic pain. I wondered if there might be a support group locally which I could join, but there was nothing within my ideal driving distance of twenty minutes.

However, once I started to think about support groups I turned over various ideas in my head and eventually realised that what I really needed to do was to get a Lunch+ group off the ground at Cranwell, in a similar format to the group I had attended at Waddington. A support group with a difference: a fellowship and Bible study group, where a snack lunch could be shared, somewhere to lay our burdens before each other and God, with time for prayer and for one another. Quite the best type of support group, and we would have the ideal president, Jesus, who had endured the pain of all pains in being nailed to the cross. I knew he would be our perfect president, showing up at the meeting before anyone else got there, knowing everyone personally, understanding the dynamics of our group, feeling that everyone was worthy and important regardless of social status, and most importantly hearing their questions and responding to them appropriately and individually. I put in a request to the chaplain's office for permission to run and advertise such a group, and a month later we held our first meeting. What joy!

It was a huge struggle for me to get there each week but it gave me purpose to lead and prepare the studies, and to have yet another reason to delve into the Bible made me focus on all things spiritual rather than physical. I began to conclude that although pain relief drugs were sometimes capable of making slight differences in reducing pain they were unreliable as a constant, sure relief. I was beginning to perceive that my reliance on a pain relief regime might have been my greatest misunderstanding. My constant, sure, reliable comfort and relief from pain was Jesus, and I needed to increase my dose.

CHAPTER THIRTEEN

Do not conform any longer to the pattern
of this world, but be transformed
by the renewing of your mind.

Romans 12:2a

Looking back at my journal entries over the previous two years it was concerning to read how chronic pain had become such an overwhelming component of my days, weeks and months. My entries read more like a medical file: recording problems, investigations, findings, advice given, treatment, drugs prescribed... *Heavens,* I thought, *how very dull I have become!* Not at all what I had actually hoped to achieve when first setting out to write my journal; at the time I had dreamed of a descendant of mine uncovering my dusty journal whilst clearing out a cupboard, reading a snippet, not being able to put it down in astonishment and then searching out the next thrilling instalment to satisfy their curiosity! If that were to be the case I would clearly have to improve my outlook on life and in doing so improve their appeal, by writing in a much more positive and interesting way.

With this change of focus my 2003 journal included not only accounts of our children's achievements but also all our family news, concerns, our blessings, book reviews, social changes, photographs and world events; the feelings of fear when the Iraq war threatened, the unbelief of US air strikes on Baghdad, the awfulness of a terrible earthquake in Iran, the India/Pakistan conflict, as well as my prayers for everlasting peace in our very troubled world. The change of focus had the positive effect of making me concentrate on the other areas of my life and trying to redress the balance by keeping medical issues to a minority.

By the end of 2003 I had actually reduced some of my medication as I focussed on other ways to combat pain. I had read on the

74

Internet various articles suggesting that distraction techniques were beneficial in reducing pain as well as trying to introduce gentle exercise into my week. Another useful distraction was a holding cross – a gift from a dear, caring friend – a hand-held wooden cross, carefully carved from an olive tree in the Holy Land. It was strangely tactile and I could keep it under my pillow at night or in my handbag during the day. It enabled me to centre my mind on Jesus as I held it tight and battled through the pain; a reminder that my suffering could never be as severe as that which my Saviour had endured on his cross. I was determined to remain strong and keep my roots firmly planted in the confidence that God would eventually show me mercy.

I went to the hospital in January 2004 for a Review, and after discussion about having reduced some of my medication, I agreed with my Pain Management Consultant to be discharged from his care back to my GP. At the same time I took up his offer of a series of acupuncture treatments to be carried out at the hospital, and as the clinician later explained in my first acupuncture session, "We cannot cure your pain, but we can arrest the decline." If a cure wasn't possible then putting a stop to my decline was paramount and I was happy to subject myself as a human pin cushion, especially if it kept me from the prospect of having to look to a future of using a wheelchair. Several friends, Christian and non-Christian, were negative about the value of acupuncture, as if I was signing up to become a human voodoo doll! I just dismissed their comments and was thankful that at least some form of treatment had been offered to me.

I was beginning to be much more accepting of a lifestyle with chronic pain, knowing that acceptance was far less stressful than denial, although what I did find difficult was accepting my inability to plan a day out, attend events and functions, and go to church regularly, because I simply did not have a clue what my pain tolerance would be like on the day. However, I tried very hard to not wallow in misery when an event was cancelled but to use the time more imaginatively, by thinking of the time as a blessing to get something else achieved and focus on that activity instead. For example, I furthered my Bowey family history research and tackled the most intricate cross-stitch kits. Both involved a lot of concentration and served as a positive distraction as I produced results from a 'failed day'.

In the middle of May, Phil and I crossed the Channel to visit the First World War battlefields in Northern France. Both Rob and Amy were away at school and it provided a perfect opportunity for us to have a low-key, five-day break, with a shorter journey for me to have to cope with rather than travelling further south or west. From bitter experience of having to cancel previous planned trips we purposefully didn't book much in advance, except for two nights' accommodation in a charming Chambres d'hôte six kilometres from Douai. The young and enthusiastic owners had recently purchased a large, grand house complete with a quadrangle of rambling farm buildings and barns, which they were in the process of renovating to use as a function venue. We admired their foresight in having seen the potential in their property and also their enormous enthusiasm and warm welcome.

The following morning we headed for Albert, a key location in the Somme, and after making an enquiry in the local Office de Tourisme to arrange a Battlefield Tour we booked places on a minibus tour, with a personal guide for the day, to visit the major sites. We were delighted to discover that we were the only tourists on board that day and thus we could travel at our own pace which was a tremendous blessing.

We began at the Newfoundland Park, near Beaumont Hamel, where on 1st July, 1916 the Battle of the Somme began, with staggeringly heavy losses of thousands of lives. We were immediately moved and saddened by the enormous scale of the Great War, which without too much imagination engulfed our senses as we walked upon the very ground on which the battle had been fought.

We moved on to view the gigantic, forty-five metre high Thiepval Memorial with over seventy-three thousand names of British and Commonwealth officers and men with no known grave, and the terrible events of the past became more real and indeed personal as we were able to locate the name of my ancestor on the stone of the monument. In one day our hearts had been moved beyond our imagination, yet we had only experienced such a small section of the Battle of the Somme.

For the rest of the day we were taken to other battle sites, memorials, cemeteries and the astonishing site of the enormously deep Lochnagar Crater, which was blown on the morning of 1st July as a two-minute precursor to the start of the Somme offensive. We walked carefully around the lip of the crater, which is ninety metres in diameter and twenty-one metres deep (sadly reputed to be the largest crater made by man in anger) and we were surprised to regard a plaque commemorated to a battalion of the Lincolnshire Regiment. Coming from Lincolnshire brought the terrible consequences of war marring landscape as well as lives even closer. Later that afternoon we returned to Albert, deeply moved emotionally by what we had experienced and saddened by the parallels with this Great War and the current fighting and conflicts across our world. Why did man not learn his lesson?

We concluded the day at the Somme 1916 Museum, which occupies the crypt beneath the basilica in Albert. The various dark, sombre narrow tunnels and musty passages were used as shelters in the Second World War but have been utilised to show scenes and exhibits of trench life, including a host of artefacts found on the battlefields. Halfway around the museum I suddenly felt a dreadful foreboding of death and destruction, and I totally panicked about being underground. We had to rush through the corridors, up and out of an escape exit. I was desperate to get into the open air, but once sitting on a bench in the sunshine I felt utterly ridiculous at being so scared.

The day's events haunted my dreams that night, and I felt very aware of the appalling and disturbing fear the soldiers must have endured as they fought to stay alive in the trenches and survive the choking gas attacks. My panic attack was something they had had to endure every day of their trench life, and there had been no exits for them to rush up and out into the beautiful calm of an ordinary summer's day. I could also empathise with a part of their monstrous fear, of being petrified of the unknown and wondering if one was losing one's mind. Yet what I couldn't envisage was the danger, the dire, the hideous, the odious and repulsive facets of their war, and I felt ashamed to even use the word 'suffering' for myself.

We returned to our accommodation that evening exhausted and ravenous, looking forward to dinner with our hosts and further relaxation; however as we drove under the entrance arch into the courtyard we found our hosts grappling alone with trying to erect a small marquee on the gravel. We got out of the car, and even with our limited French we quickly tuned into the urgency of the situation. We immediately dashed around to hold poles, grab tent pegs and mallets, and heard in disbelief that tomorrow was to be their first big function... and a wedding to boot! At that point I think we both felt numb as if it was our responsibility too!

Whilst coping with their exuberant setter, bounding around our feet and generally being an utter nuisance, we tried hard to grasp their quick fire instructions and carry out the tasks quickly and effortlessly, not only to do all we could but also because we were extremely hungry. It soon became clear that our pre-booked supper was rather low priority and learnt that there was a large gazebo to erect next plus several other jobs to do in preparing their very dusty and cavernous barn for the chic wedding breakfast. By that stage the jury was definitely out on which couple was panicking the most under stress, and by the time we sat down to our meal at 11pm we were all a little delirious from the effects of hunger and thirst.

The next day we left for Belgium, wishing our hosts the very best of luck in their venture and praying that the wedding function would go off without a hitch. Amazingly the whole experience didn't put us off staying in Chambres d'hôte accommodation at all; in fact it made us all the more eager to always choose such accommodation and to look forward to coping with the unknown factor of the night's stay.

On crossing the Belgian border we headed for Ieper (Ypres) in the Flemish province of West Flanders – a town completely rebuilt out of the ruins of war as closely as possible to its original medieval design. We marvelled at the reconstructed medieval architecture in the impressive market square and visited the Cloth Hall, which was one of the largest commercial buildings in medieval times and took thirty plus years to restore after the ravages of war. It houses the Flanders Fields Museum and we spent a couple of hours looking at many haunting photographs of Ypres devastated by artillery fire, bedraggled soldiers limping along 'roads', men slumped head in hands in the trenches, the young with 'old' faces, looking drawn and hopeless, and photographs of many civilian casualties too. We read letter upon letter put up on display, were fascinated by them having survived the ravages of war and by their astonishing content, and we were saddened by the evident mental trauma expressed between the written lines and further shocked by the dreadful consequences of war.

A short distance from the market square is the imposing Menin Gate Memorial with its arched Hall of Memory, over thirty-six metres long and twenty metres wide with its arches spanning the main road – a vast memorial with a terrible count of 54,389 names engraved on the stone of those missing on the battlefield of the Ypres Salient, who fell before 16th August, 1917.[5] At the Menin gate a short ceremony is held every evening at 8pm, which has been the custom since 1927, and has continued every day since except for the period of the Second World War when Germany occupied Ypres. We gathered early with thousands of other people and stood reverently as the Last Post was played by buglers from the voluntary fire brigade in their dress uniforms, and watched in silence as several wreaths were laid in memory of individual people being honoured that day or certain military units depending on who was there to represent them. It was a very humbling moment, tear-jerking and a culmination of our emotionally charged short break. As we made our way back to our accommodation we were markedly touched and changed by our experiences over the past few days. We couldn't help feeling that if everyone did a Battlefields Tour then the world would become a better place as people would be inspired to promote peace at all costs.

Our few days' holiday had gone surprisingly well, with my pain manageable, and it had been a very special, thought-provoking time. The following morning we crossed back into France and reluctantly headed north. Both of us were subdued in the car, not saying a great deal and seemingly not keen to make the ferry port in haste. As we neared Calais my heart was in my mouth as I blurted out to Phil that I felt that God wanted us to be in France. It was an extraordinary statement, and to this day I can recall vividly that exact moment in the car, feel again the hairs standing up on my skin and hear Phil's quiet voice say in affirmation, "I do too." The conversation then flowed thick and fast as we talked about how it might be possible to spend longer periods in France. We toyed with an idea for the future when Phil would retire from the RAF in May 2012 of buying a motor home and travelling around the country. By then our children would be independent and anything might be possible, even perhaps running a Chambres d'hôte business, although certainly not as a wedding venue! We were cheered up by hopeful expectation, and in a much more buoyant mood we stood on deck to scan the horizon for Blighty, whilst the French coastline faded slowly into the distance behind us.

---

[5] This memorial is only one of many across First World War battlefields with thousands upon thousands whose memory is upheld in absence of no known grave.

Once home that buoyant mood was soon deflated as the onset of debilitating pain returned with vengeance. In desperation, following up a suggestion from a friend, I had a private appointment with a physiotherapist to see if her expertise with lung and chest patients could help me in any way. As the sessions unfolded I felt very encouraged and religiously did all the exercises I was given at home. A slightly odd sensation developed in these sessions as in my mind's eye I could see how my body was behaving inside me, a vision not too dissimilar from looking at a scan in black and white – no technicolour drama! At this point you can be forgiven for thinking that I had finally become deranged, but truly that really was not the case. I was perfectly sane, only rather unnerved by this realisation of being able to watch my muscles flipping and flopping, cartilage twisting within my rib cage and bones rubbing. Unbelievable, I know, but a couple of health practitioners confirmed that what I described was in fact what was happening, although their descriptions used clinical terms. In knowledge of this truth I further worried if something was taking control of my mind, giving me this knowledge, and sought ways to obliterate the insight, but it remained a constant nuisance and a dreadful hindrance. As I tried to distract myself from pain the vivid body scenes would force me to concentrate even more on the pain itself, and it was almost impossible to distract myself from it.

I should have asked for help to combat this curse but I was too embarrassed and worried in admitting something which might thrust me into the clutches of mental health professionals. More importantly, I really should have asked for prayer from all my Christian friends, but even with them I was reticent since they must have been getting heartily sick of my constant prayer requests without asking them to add a 'weird dimension'.

Clearly more distraction was needed; I threw myself into re-learning the French grammar from my schooldays and watched an Early Learning French DVD I had bought the children, in my effort to learn the language. In a nearby village shop I occasionally found a Le Monde newspaper lurking between the British papers. Seemingly the shop only stocked one copy, and I often wondered who I deprived of reading the widely respected news coverage whilst I attempted to read only the shorter articles, adverts or picture captions. I spent a fortune on an enormous French/English dictionary, which turned out to be extremely cumbersome and heavy for me to use, although jolly useful for standing on to reach something from a top shelf! I justified its expense with the knowledge that we would sometime in the future need it, although I was soon sellotaping the spine from constantly mishandling it and dropping it on the floor.

In February 2005 I was able to put my study into practice as we flew into Tours, which is situated on the lower reaches of the Loire, for four nights. Phil had previously visited the city on an RAF training flight and had been impressed enough to arrange a short break. I was very impressed with the city too, with its bustling medieval quarter and half-timbered buildings and their quaint exterior staircase towers. We pottered around the old quarter and the modern parts despite the bitter, close-to-zero temperatures. On the Saturday we had a fantastic lunchtime meal in a tiny bistro. It was a tiny restaurant but with huge atmosphere and cheerily decorated in bright red gingham. The windows were completely steamed up from the body heat of the diners squashed up close together and by two waiters rushing around to fulfil the orders with lightning speed.

We chose a formule (set menu) and the food was utterly delicious. The restaurant might have been small but the cheeseboard was far from petite. We were goggle-eyed when the proprietor proudly placed a selection of forty goat cheeses down on the corner of our table and whilst he balanced them proceeded to rattle off the characteristics of each one. Some cheeses looked as if they might have actually been produced in medieval times being dubiously very black, or knobbly, wrinkled and misshapen, whilst others were perfectly produced pats of all shapes, sizes, various strengths of flavour, pasteurised, unpasteurised – and one log-shaped cheese curiously had a length of straw running through it! A piece of that had to be part of our choice... bien-sûr! We were hugely impressed by the quality of the food, especially as the whole four-course formule had only cost seventeen euros each.

We wrapped up well and went back out into the bitter cold air, intending to go back to our hotel for a much needed siesta, but noticed that the streets were remarkably quiet and surprisingly many shops remained closed. A couple of young men walked briskly past with flags rolled up under their arms and we assumed they were going to a football match, but... as we turned into the Rue Nationale and looked down towards the Boulevard Béranger we were met with a scene which made us suddenly quite unsure whether to proceed further. Hundreds of people were milling about waving large flags;

there was a great deal of commotion and a cacophony of sound with the most deafening element being a banging of many drums. High pitched whistles were being blown at full pelt and horns blared, as well as a host of gendarmes and Police Nationale taking up positions all along the boulevard. We certainly didn't fancy getting caught up in the type of nasty Paris suburb riot which we had seen on UK television but on more careful observation thought the hundreds of people stretching down along the boulevard could not be rioters as there was far too much of a party atmosphere. In fact there were whole families out together, grannies waving flags, mothers pushing strollers, men smiling and shaking hands with one another, and union officials calmly handing out information about the cause. We experienced our first demonstration of the French protesting in a way that was serious but unthreatening.

The march that day coincided with many a protest across France against extending working hours beyond the thirty-five-hour week, which would have undermined benefits, pension rights and health care. Instead of a siesta we actually sat at a café outside on the pavement, in the bitter cold, with a large hot chocolate and lapped up the atmosphere! No wonder the city centre had been like the deathly hallows, because this was the scene of the action, the place to be and to be seen, and a wonderful piece of street theatre for us to experience.

That same evening we enjoyed another form of entertainment, a concert by the Tours Symphonic Orchestra in the opulent Italian style Grand Théâtre – a completely different, sophisticated experience of French life. The theatre, a very impressive building from its original façade outside to its restored interior, has an auditorium providing comfortable and luxurious seating for a thousand. The comparison with a British theatre fell short as we were shocked to discover that for our desired delectation there was no bar, sweets or even ice creams for sale during the interval! In fact, virtually the whole theatre emptied during the interval to frequent the local bars or to loiter in the cold night air, with a cigarette for warmth, whilst we aimlessly climbed every staircase in search of refreshment. What a missed opportunity on the part of the theatre management team, we thought, as we couldn't but salivate because of our conditioned response to British theatre-going. Heavens, there was much more to perceive about France than we had first imagined, and we clearly had a lot to learn about the many cultural differences between the French and the British.

CHAPTER FOURTEEN

Whether you turn to the right or to the left,
your ears will hear a voice behind you,
saying, 'This is the way; walk in it.'

Isaiah 30:21

When I was a child I loved playing the childhood game 'Hunt the Thimble'. Whether we actually used a thimble I cannot recall, but regardless the 'thimble' was always carefully hidden to try to prevent the seeker from finding it too easily. At first it took me a while to catch on to the point of listening to the clues being given as to its whereabouts, because my first impulse was to rush blindly around the room and turn everything upside down at random in the hope of finding the thimble. Later I learnt to move purposefully and methodically around the room, carefully watching people to see if they would give away a clue unwittingly, heedfully listening to their instructions of "fr-r-ree-eezing"or "b-b-b-boiling hot" and making sure to ignore the false clues given to try to slow my progress in seeking the thimble.

Listening to God's direction is actually similar. It is human nature to ignore him and instead rush around in all directions trying to accomplish the various goals we set ourselves solely by our own efforts. We tend to believe, often stubbornly, that we are going about things in the correct, methodical way yet we often get drawn down the wrong route because of listening to or being influenced by someone else, only to have to retrace our steps. Sometimes we might actually be at a standstill, without any clear idea in which direction to turn, and in our quandary we can waste time, energy, material resources, finance and become quite disillusioned with everything and everyone around us to the point that we even forget what our actual goal was in the beginning! God's voice is there to guide us if we are prepared to tune in to him and rest in his presence... listening. This requires effort, practice and perseverance, and it was not easy for me to put into practice either because of my persistent attitude to be self-reliant and not God-reliant.

By the middle of 2005 my chronic pain problems had not dramatically altered, and I had notched up over four years of being unable to return to employment. The 'thimble' I had been seeking was to banish chronic pain, but in four interminable years I remained lukewarm. Looking back I reflected whether I was guilty of having flitted to and fro – passionate in faith then failed to listen to God's guiding voice. In truth I wanted to be 'boiling hot' and desperately wanted to hear God's voice in my every step and action. The only way forward was to read my Bible more often each day, not just the verses for the daily devotional or chapter for a Bible study, but deliberate, in depth reading.

I began with the psalms and they had an immediate impact as I was amazed to connect with the psalmist's affliction. I filled the inside covers of my journal with the verses I could easily relate to, and looking at the inside cover of my journal now the page could be entitled 'Woe is me'! Fortunately as I read the commentaries and the God-given direction to combat affliction, pain and suffering, I noticed the verses I was now recording were enlightening, positive and useful. Most required me to put effort in to change in some way: whether a thought process, an action, to admit I had sinned or fallen short, to forgive even when forgiveness seemed unwarranted, or to love unconditionally.

From time to time the small light I had sought at the end of the corridor would pop into my mind as a constant reminder that Jesus was the Light of the World in the Old Testament as well as in the New Testament. Often I opened the Bible at random and was thrilled to discover a relevant passage leaping out from the page pertinent to my situation. It almost became a game to see how many times that worked.

Another change I made was to accept that our house and garden were too large for me to manage, even with help, and there was no denying the fact that we were too far from shops and facilities for my independence. If I couldn't rely on being able to drive then I needed to be able to walk to shops. I prayed to God for his guidance, feeling a little nervous, but we soon felt at peace with the idea of moving. We put the house on the market, and after a couple of hopeful viewings explored the larger villages with full facilities and market towns close to RAF Cranwell. It was difficult to decide where to move to, and we ended up deciding to restrict our search to Woodhall Spa, ten minutes' drive away. My parents lived there. We had confidence in my GP and knew that if Phil was posted away from the area we could let a property easily. We found a suitable family home and remained convinced a quick move was on the cards, until we fell at the first hurdle: little interest in our own house. History had actually been repeated, as nine years previously we had tried on two occasions to purchase properties in Woodhall and both had dramatically come to nothing. In the light of this third experience we felt rather uneasy about looking for another house in Woodhall.

I prayed to God and asked him how and where I could be a better witness to him, using the gifts I had (limited as they were), rationalising that with this knowledge we could decide on the ideal location. Phil and I prayed together and felt closer in our Christian walk with God, yet as the months passed it became obvious we were not getting clear direction as to what and where we should move. We wondered what the block could be; either we were looking in the wrong direction, the timing wasn't right, we possibly received bad advice regarding our house sale, or we were failing to grasp something more vital. We needed skins as thick as rhinoceros' to ride out our disappointment, and clearly had to exercise calm restraint and patience. Easier said than done, but we continued to pray together and trust God that he had our interests in hand.

One afternoon I popped into Sleaford to see a friend, hoping to lift her spirits. She was very unwell, and her brother, who had flown over from Mexico, answered the doorbell. After the initial introductions I learnt he was a clinician and his sister had told him all about my problems. I felt very embarrassed because I had come to boost her morale not focus on myself, and my heart sank further as he explained he knew about thoracotomy operations. *Oh, dear,* I thought, *please God, not another one, please don't inflict this upon me.* You see, at the beginning of the year I had met a surgeon from Lesotho when I presented for a pre-appointment for carpel tunnel release surgery. The surgeon was incredibly friendly and enthused about how wonderful it was to meet me! As a result of my previous experiences of some consultants his enthusiasm seemed worryingly misplaced! However he explained that his interest was in my having had a thoracotomy and my current good health, as he had carried out several but few had survived his operations! *Great,* I thought! How much more I now looked forward to him slashing my wrist! Fortunately he quickly explained his poor record was only in the case of thoracotomy operations and that the failure rate was because all his patients had had the complications from having been shot!

In Mexico, they clearly had had more luck with their patients presenting for a thoracotomy and knew a great deal about their aftercare. Now my friend's brother told me simply and plainly that my symptoms were those of post-thoracotomy syndrome. You could have knocked me down with a feather! After all the years of searching for a reason for chronic pain it seemed I might actually have a name for my condition, and what a blessing this encounter had been. God's intervention left me feeling very humble.

We re-advertised the house with another agent in January 2006, and on the advice of a lovely Christian friend explored the market town of Bourne in South Lincolnshire. Bourne is about thirty-five minutes south of Cranwell, nestled between the low-lying fens to the east and a ridge to the west of the town, having a population of fifteen thousand. It provided all the facilities we wished for, plus a great bus service around the town and further afield to Stamford, Peterborough and Spalding. It seemed to tick all our boxes. Previously we had tried to keep within the catchment of my medical treatment, but this same friend had prayed a great deal for me and felt that a change of medical advice might prove to be a good thing. Encouraged, we began to look at properties, get to know the town better, and we were surprised that viewings for our property increased by early April, with suddenly much interest being shown.

One afternoon I was tidying up the front flower bed and a couple stopped their car to look at the outside of the house, having spotted the 'For Sale' board as they were driving by. I could hear them talking so I popped my head up over the wall to say hello. After a short conversation they seemed genuinely interested and I invited them to view the property. On seeing our RAF memorabilia the gentleman admitted to being an ex-RAF pilot. Small world.

Within a fortnight we had more viewings, and the couple mentioned above and another couple both put in an offer on the same day! What is it they say about buses?! A sale was agreed with the first couple, and we dashed down to Bourne to view a new build townhouse on an estate, which had very much appealed to Phil. I was really unsure about the convenience of such a property as I already struggled with one set of stairs let alone coping with two flights in a townhouse! However, a plus point was the miniscule garden – small as a postage stamp! – and I could see the appeal of a brand new house promising ease of maintenance; it also had a sitting room on the second floor with super views across a nature reserve, to bluebell woods and hills beyond. We toyed with the idea that once Phil had retired from the RAF the house would be ideal to leave for a couple of months whilst we travelled around France. I quickly became as smitten with the house as Phil was.

There was a long chain involved with our house sale, but we weren't disheartened because everything had come together at once and we felt very much that God's hand was firm and sure on our move to Bourne. So sure in fact that we took a week's holiday in June to visit the area around Montpellier, on the Mediterranean coast.

We touched down on the tarmac, absolutely thrilled to be back on French soil. Taxi-ing toward the terminal building, I looked out of the aeroplane window with enormous pleasure at the scene which unfolded. A brilliant blue sky without a cloud in evidence, a shimmering heat haze across the flat, parched marsh land adjoining the airfield where flocks of brilliant pink flamingos were feeding. What a breathtaking start to what proved to be a scorching, wonderful week! I had few problems and such good health that I only had to miss out on one day's planned activity, to a water park. I was even able to swim a little too in the lovely heated pool. It was the nicest and most blessed of our holidays in a long time, not only because my pain remained at a low threshold, but also because of such an immense feeling of being at peace. This peace was derived from having persevered in fathoming God's direction for our lives, from having tested a closer walk in obedience to his Word and having received blessing upon blessing individually, as a couple and as a family. Who would not want to seek such peace?

CHAPTER FIFTEEN

You, O Lord, keep my lamp burning.
My God turns my darkness into light.
With your help I can advance against a troop,
with my God I can scale a wall.

Psalm 18: 28-29

September 6th, 2006 was a glorious hot day and quite perfect for our removal from Kirkby Green to Bourne. What a scorcher of a month too, with 30.5°c being recorded one day at Kew Gardens, and the heady days of an 'Indian summer' added to our overwhelming happiness of being in our brand new home in a new and different environment. In between the unpacking we used the opportunity to investigate various footpaths into the centre of town, walk in the lovely, leafy park and indulge ourselves royally in many of Bourne's teashops. The treasure trove of individual shops and supermarkets far exceeded my expectation, and the yearning for independence and company around me had been fulfilled.

I purchased the local paper to get more of a feel for our surroundings. The articles mentioned a whole host of unrecognisable place names to seek out on the road map. One article caught my eye particularly, and astonished I read that the average price of a house for a first time buyer (across the UK) had reached the staggering sum of £196,000. Phew! In comparison with the cost of our first property purchase of a two bedroom bungalow in 1983 this seemed absurd. I carried on flicking through the paper, then did a theatrical double take of moving back from holding the paper arms outstretched to peering closely again at a bold typed advertisement. I sat still for a moment, astonished that I had even spotted the advert for a French Improvers language class, doubly amazed that the lessons would start the following week, and even more astounded that they would be held in Bourne! I couldn't have received a clearer sign of direction and lost no time in picking up the phone to register. I needed no second bidding in trusting that this was a divine opportunity. You might be tempted to think that I responded to the advert simply to fulfil my own inclination. After all, we had spent many holidays in France and planned many more in the future, hoping to return for really long periods, thus a practical solution to improving my French. Certainly a great many decisions one undertakes do make good sense and are rooted in practicality. Someone might suggest that it was a coincidence to decide to buy a paper that day, another that it was actually a coincidence to purchase the correct paper publishing the advert, or another that it was a coincidence to open a certain page or a coincidence to read that particular advert among several, or perhaps even a coincidence to take in the detail of the advert when I should have been concentrating my efforts on unpacking! How many coincidences does one need in order to stop for a moment and consider their meaning? Surely even a person with the merest grain of faith must puzzle over such providence!

Quite unwittingly, people of little or no faith use words of faith to explain such a phenomena by saying, "What a godsend that was", "What a blessing", even "It was a miracle waiting to happen"! Christians recognise God's hand in these instances, and we give thanks and praise for the unexpected, knowing that these are not coincidences as God is working his purpose out by giving us a little nudge along the way to direct us down an amazing path.

Four days later, I needed all the courage I could muster for the first lesson, especially as it had been thirty-two years since I had last participated in any French language class. I thought I had learnt quite a lot of vocabulary on our various holidays and having worked occasionally on grammar exercises at home, but there was no denying the fact that I was much unprepared for the intensive two-hour class. My brain felt like mush and the words absolutely failed me!

Our teacher was a lovely, encouraging young woman, a native French speaker from Paris and clearly a superb teacher regardless of any subject needing to be taught. She tried to limit herself in speaking English and cleverly mimed many words and phrases, alongside speaking French, a superb method which kept our attention and made the class entertaining. My classmates were a friendly bunch, obviously Francophiles, with some having a home in France and/or planning to emigrate at some time in the future. As the weeks passed, the class indeed was a godsend. It ran at a fast pace but was extremely interesting as it was tuned to teaching about everyday life in France – health, education, politics, current affairs, French literature and music, to name but a few topics covered. It gave me a real purpose to fill some of my days with learning, as another form of distraction from being languid when pain hit with a vengeance.

We joined a medical practice and my GP referred me to the Pain Management team in Stamford. I went along to the consultation expecting little intervention but was pleasantly surprised as the consultant showed much interest and understanding in my tale of woe in coping with chronic pain. She recognised post-thoracotomy syndrome, put in place a change of medication, offered six weeks of acupuncture sessions as soon as the waiting list allowed and also talked about recommending me to attend a Pain Management course at Edith Cavell Hospital in Peterborough. Meanwhile an appointment was arranged to see a physiotherapist from the Pain Management course team who would help me to arrest any further decline in my health until a place on the course became available. I was really thankful, and all praise goes to my 'praying friend' who had been right in her deduction that moving house to another area might be beneficial. Coincidence? I don't think so!

The conundrum of choosing a new church in a new locality was easily solved by going to the Sunday service at St. Firmin's in the nearby village of Thurlby – a beautiful church dating back to 925AD, yet with the modern touch of having had the pews removed. It was a convenient couple of minutes' drive from home, a short cycle or a pleasant walk along a disused railway line and through the village. On the first Sunday we received a wonderfully warm welcome from Audrey, a door steward, who made us feel very special, and after an enjoyable service we didn't see a need to try elsewhere. A few weeks later we went along to the Church Hall to support a fund-raising event and promptly won the star prize of a large Christmas hamper! We both felt undeserving of such a magnificent prize and hoped everyone in the room wouldn't begrudge us a win as new kids on the block! Fortunately we were among Christians, unlike a similar situation in another small village in Devon, twenty-five years previously, when our local shop had set a competition "to find as many words as possible from MERRY CHRISTMAS". We had recently moved to the village and, with plenty of time on my hands as jobless, the competition had really appealed to me. I had gone through the dictionary meticulously, page by page, line by line, as if my life had depended on it, and recorded a grand list of four hundred and twenty words. I romped home in first place beating the previous entrant by more than three hundred words! I was pretty pleased with the result of actually coming first in a competition but then had misgivings in my being new to the village. My concern was completely justified as when I went to collect my prize there was a tangible reticence in handing over the large hamper of food! I always felt slightly apprehensive each time I shopped there afterwards.

On January 17th, 2007 a severe weather warning was forecast with winds of eighty to one hundred miles per hour predicted to batter the country, which coincided with a rail journey to London for 'The France Show' (the largest French exhibition in Britain). The trains travelled a little slower than usual because of the blustery conditions but we got to London safe and sound. Later that evening we read that part of the canopy across the front of the station had collapsed due to the ferocity of the wind.

Stepping inside the Exhibition Hall was intoxicating as we left behind the menacing gales and entered an atmosphere of buzz and passion for all things French. We loved and appreciated the whole event as we listened to the many babbling French voices and re-immersed ourselves in the culture of La Belle France. There was a huge variety of commercial stalls, wine tasting stands, inspiring cookery demonstrations with top French chefs, a plethora of companies advertising properties, food outlets, as well as interesting seminars to sign up for in order to further our knowledge on specific financial topics, and various stands representing regions or holiday pursuits.

At one stage we were taking a breather, standing by the Niort[6] tourist office stand pondering in which direction to go next, when a representative accosted us, having taken advantage of our dithering. She offered their brochure and we listened politely to her whole spiel and were happy to chat amiably; we learnt that although originally from the UK, she had lived in France for over thirty years. Well, talk about a 'red rag to a bull'! Now *we* were the ones doing all the running as we asked lots of questions about her region, saying rather timidly that one of the most important things for us, if we were to settle in France, was to live near to an English-speaking church. She responded immediately, "I'm a Christian and there is a church at

---

[6] Niort is situated in the Poitou-Charente region in south-west France.

Parthenay, close to Niort. You must make a visit. You really would be surprised at the number of places to worship." We were impressed and needed no second bidding in taking her leaflets.

In late April, much enthused by her information, we landed at Poitiers International Airport (the international part being of great importance to this small provincial airport).

Parthenay is a fortified town, fifty kilometres west of Poitiers in the department of Deux-Sèvres, with a citadel perched high above the meandering river Thouet which loops around one side of the town. There is an historic part, and the day we visited the medieval quarter, with its half-timbered buildings, it resembled a deserted film set. There was not a soul in sight (no actor, no one). Later we realised that the reason for so little activity was because it was a Monday, when most shops are closed for a half or full day; however, we experienced an eerie stillness hanging in the air, and we felt a chill even though it was a pleasantly warm day. It was the oddest sensation, and perplexed we trudged back up the hill to the citadel and drove away from Parthenay as quickly as possible.

We felt confused and disappointed having pinned such hope on the town. We had thought coming to Parthenay was God's direction, yet from our experience it seemed far from the case. Had God turned us away? Or had the Devil tried to thwart us?[7]

We drove east across the countryside, which reminded of East Sussex with its hedged fields and woodland, to stay in a gîte barn conversion of which the proprietors turned out to be British. Previously in booking accommodation we had always made a point of choosing French proprietors so that we could practice our French and somehow must have overlooked the fact when booking. They were a very pleasant couple and in discussion about places to visit in their area suggested the town of Montmorillon in the neighbouring department of Vienne. On the map it seemed a reasonably sized town, within easy distance of the gîte, and so we made it our first point of call.

We parked on the edge of town and immediately in getting out of the car felt our spirits lifted. It was quite an extraordinary feeling, because we had parked in a very ordinary car park, but we both remarked on the feeling. We strolled down to the charming town

---

[7] For all those in praise of Parthenay you will be encouraged to learn that we have since discovered it is a very nice town.

centre, wandered around a bustling market in the square and then crossed the river and discovered a beautifully kept medieval quarter with narrow streets winding up and around. There were many quaint shops with various craftsmen plying their trade mostly in relation to books and bookmaking. We learned that Montmorillon is also called 'La Cité de l'écrit et des Métiers du livre' (city of writing and bookmaking) and we couldn't help but be fascinated by such a picturesque spot.

We ate a picnic, a stone's throw from the tumbling waters of the river Gartempe which was well stocked with large trout, and then investigated the back streets of Montmorillon before heading back towards the main square where most of the action seemed to be. As we turned the corner of an unassuming building we were taken aback to see an advertisement in the window, in English, promoting a forthcoming Alpha[8] course. Curious, we read all the notices in the window, and it appeared that the building was being used for worship by the Protestant Eglise Evangélique. The fact that they were running an Alpha course looked very promising, and we made the decision to attend their Sunday worship service.

We returned to our gîte full of the joys of spring, having enjoyed a super day because of our host's recommendation and later in chatting with them discovered that they too worshipped at the same Eglise!

We were up bright and early on the Sunday, expectant of a new experience and keen to drive across for the service. The French/English congregation welcomed us royally. The sermon was translated, the music and worship gratifying, and we quickly felt very at ease, especially when introduced to a couple hailing from Lincolnshire with whom we had a mutual friend! In chatting to other ex-pats in the congregation it was clear that they had few regrets in moving to France, and their wholehearted enthusiasm raised our ardour about considering a permanent move to France.

As usual, on the morning of our departure we were very melancholy as we went through the process of leaving the country and all things French started to slip through our fingers. We handed back the keys to the gîte, dropped the hire car back to the airport, had our passports checked, and were given the OK to leave the

---

[8] Alpha is a way to explore what it means to be a Christian in a very unthreatening way. It is great for people who are curious about having a faith but want to explore the issues without feeling pressurised.

country – hoping they would find some reason why we couldn't leave! Finally, after a last fleeting walk on French soil, we reached the point of no return. The cabin staff checked the doors of the aircraft cabin were locked and crosschecked just in case anyone wanted to escape!

With nothing much to do during the hour's flight other than flip through an airline brochure about dining in some far flung place such as Bulgaria or Latvia, my thoughts turned to the abundant blessings we had enjoyed during this last week and how very blessed our lives had become on moving to Bourne.

I personally didn't have any reasonable excuse to feel gloomy and dispirited. How very selfish of me in wanting more of France when just the week before I had written in my journal of my grateful thanks of what I had gained since September in Bourne! After only seven months a huge burden overshadowing my life had been lifted, my independence had made gigantic strides, and we enjoyed church life with the spin-off of great fellowship. We had a host of new friends and in any case were surrounded by all things French: through my language lessons, French productions at the local Arts Centre, the occasional French market in town, and in being able to have regular holidays in France. What ungratefulness on my part! What lack of grace! In being given an inch, I had wanted a mile, and how ashamed I felt of my greed!

We celebrated Phil's fiftieth birthday at the end of May 2007 with a special meal at home and an 'Amy's special' chocolate cake. On reflection it wasn't much of a celebration for a 'special birthday'. The weather was nondescript, I was suffering from a bout of pain and not able to go out, and Rob was at University three hours' drive away in Newcastle. Nevertheless, a couple of months after the occasion Phil realised that his fiftieth had been very special and significant as, if desired, he could actually put in a request for Premature Voluntary Retirement from the RAF after turning fifty, which might result in him being released from a military career in a matter of months. Some of his pilot compatriots had recently joined an aviation company called NetJets which had pioneered the idea of fractional aircraft ownership, giving individuals and businesses control of owning a jet without the management responsibilities or costs of full aircraft ownership. Phil had the requisite qualifications and experience; therefore he decided to test the water by sending off a job application in July. Three days later we were standing in the reception area of Daedalus Mess at Cranwell waiting to book into the Mess to stay overnight as we were attending an Armed Forces Christian Union dinner. Phil received a mobile phone call from NetJets to undergo an initial screening interview then and there! It did seem a very bizarre moment to undergo something important, with all the commotion of a busy Mess foyer going on around him, but Phil remained calm and tried to conduct his interview in the professional way it deserved. I said a silent prayer for him to be able to succeed if it was God's will. He was invited to attend an interview three weeks later and we went into dinner with rather more than Christian military fellowship on our minds.

On August 8th Phil was officially offered employment with NetJets and, thrilled, we celebrated with a bottle of Moët Chandon. Bien-sûr! Two days later the preacher in church centred his sermon on "the unexpected" – at least two people were listening on tenter-hooks to his sermon! We chuckled in the car afterwards on the way home as we reflected on the sermon which might relate not only to Phil's future employment but also a rare sighting of a meteor shower of shooting stars which was forecast to be visible to the naked eye later that evening. Close to 11pm, before going up to bed, we popped outside and stood in the still of the evening to look up at the heavens and witnessed the incredible splendour of God's pyrotechnic display. What a culmination of our joy, our hope in faith, a celebration of Phil's new employment and a new future. A display which satisfied us in a way that champagne could never achieve.

CHAPTER SIXTEEN

I will lead the blind by ways they have not known,
along unfamiliar paths I will guide them;
I will turn the darkness into light before them
and make the rough places smooth.

Isaiah 42:16

At the end of September 2007, and after a year on the waiting list, I attended the first session of a Pain Management course in Peterborough. Its aim was to manage long-term pain effectively, to improve a patient's quality of life and to prevent disability. This all sounded promising, although I was sceptical as to how my situation could change radically, but the course advocated that shared care and collaboration between patient and course team would equip and empower me... so what did I have to lose?

The department was situated at what felt like the furthest point imaginable from the main hospital entrance. I walked slowly down a long corridor, which seemed to stretch on and on and on – not the most welcoming consideration for a patient with mobility difficulties. However, I focused on a point in the distance determined that this first hurdle, of actually getting to the course venue, wasn't going to defeat me.

The team consisted of a physiotherapist, occupational therapist and cognitive behavioural psychologist, who each led various parts of the session according to their expertise. The team seemed very positive and upbeat, which must have been difficult for them to aspire to when they met with eight uncertain and sceptical patients! The group consisted of all ages, each with very different medical problems, but we soon realised that we shared common factors in disability and poor quality of life through our shared suffering of chronic pain. The most encouraging part of the first session was when a past course member described the many positive benefits he had derived from the course and the enormous reduction in suffering he had achieved by carefully following the directives on the course. I think we all suddenly sat up a little bit straighter and listened to him plant the first seeds of hope.

We learnt from the team we would be very active in goal-setting, improve our posture (immediate straightening of backs and tummies pulled in) and would also learn how to breathe properly – that was intriguing on its own, as we knew we were already breathing! At the end of each session we would be provided with exercises for balance and mobility, learn how to manage the challenges of daily living, and change behaviour patterns, improve our personal relationships and also receive help according to our individual needs. Armed with a pack of course material and a list of tasks for homework it was apparent that this was a serious and purposeful course where no stone would be left unturned. I arrived home feeling very drained, exhausted, tired but not weary in spirit because of the excitement of change afoot. Then I spent most of the afternoon fast asleep, in spite of having read the course handout about positively trying to change sleep patterns by sleeping less during the day!

As the course progressed it became very challenging but it never failed to hold my attention. I did feel as if I was becoming more equipped and empowered to deal with my pain. A large part of the course was given to learning how to pace oneself, and as an introduction I had to reduce the number of steps taken in a day to four hundred and keep to this figure for the suggested three days. Try counting your steps from the moment you rise in the morning and you will soon discover that this number allows only the barest movement during the day! I followed this pattern absolutely rigidly in the hope that having been tried and tested I would succeed, and after each three day period I increased the number of steps, very gradually, and my pain remained at a low threshold. The task quickly became enjoyable as the number of steps increased threefold rather than twofold as I improved at a fast rate. I incorporated a daily walk and made it my priority above all else.

Supporting and encouraging one another in the group sessions was definitely the key to success; when we met for our six-month review the differences in each person's posture, demeanour and spirit were astonishing to see. No doubt the course team had seen it all before with other groups, but we were all staggered at seeing the changes in each other. We no longer looked like patients!

I had not suffered any flare ups during the latter couple of months, and I really felt as if I was making my escape from the grip of chronic pain. Even my sessions of acupuncture with my GP had reduced in line with the marked improvement in my health. I was offered top-up sessions instead, as and when I felt the need.

In further pain management course sessions, we continued with various other strategies to improve our lifestyle, including the keeping of a diary to note our feelings and actions, with emphasis on describing emotions, particularly when we experienced stress. This was the hardest exercise for me to attempt as I knew that my faith in God minimised my stress levels considerably, and I really struggled to write anything down. On many occasions on the course I felt like a fish out of water as I didn't experience the same struggles many of the others described. One group member was a lovely Christian lady, and during the latter part we both felt frauds for being on the course as we listened to others struggling whilst our solution would have been to turn to our Bible and pray for God's grace to restore us. I felt very blessed to have this lady in the group as we could share openly how we were coping, with our faith as an aid in the tasks we were set.

The course came to an end, and we were given a future review date for a year's time. The opportunity of having done the course, the help from a professional team and the promise of ultimate victory through faith had proved a powerful combination in my having achieved fast results. I could not see a need for me to attend a further review. God's timing is always perfect, and I gave thanks that even though I had waited a long time for a place on the course, I was blessed with being a part of a really encouraging group, with the added blessing of having another Christian alongside.

December 19th, 2007 was a very memorable day for Phil as he completed his last day of work in the RAF. Equipment and clothing had been returned to the various sections as he 'cleared' from RAF Cranwell and left the Queen's employment. He had a final discharge date of 9th April, 2008 but with the accumulation of his various leave allowances he had worn his flying kit for the last time, and the washing of thick, woolly, green socks and long johns were now a thing of the past. Hurrah! It was a little hard to grasp the fact that the military, which had impacted on our lives for years, had now been cast off.

Christmas was soon upon us, and we had the excitement of being en famille with Amy home on holiday from Pocklington Sixth Form and Rob, in his last year at Newcastle University, home too for the holidays. One evening, as we sat around the dining table Amy remarked that all four of us were now "not working"! We all roared with laughter yet also gave thanks for what was in store for each of us in the future. As the song lyric says, "What a difference a day makes," or in our case what a difference six months made! Changes beyond our imaginings had occurred, personally and as a family. Phil was changing employment but able to retain his love of aviation, Rob had been accepted earlier in the year for a graduate training position with a top accountancy firm, Amy had decided upon studying law at University, and I was fitter and healthier. The seemingly impossible had become undeniable reality. God had opened up opportunities, pushed aside barriers and made our way smooth.

The idea of moving to France had become a veritable option; the timing we had originally thought we were working to, of spending more time in France only upon Phil's retirement at fifty-five years, had been blasted away by God's grace and mercy on our lives. Phil and I were really excited for our future and continually thanked and praised God for his greatness and goodness in blessing us, although regardless of the number of times we did so it just didn't seem sufficient in comparison to what he had done for us. How could we ever repay his benevolence? What could we do? What should we do?

CHAPTER SEVENTEEN

Yet he did not waver through unbelief
regarding the promise of God,
but was strengthened in his faith and gave glory to God,
being fully persuaded that God had power
to do what he had promised.

Romans 4:20

With Phil being available to take holiday after Christmas and my improved health, in early January 2008 we grabbed the opportunity and flew back to the Poitou-Charentes region. We were keen to explore another part of the region, experience its winter climate and seek further opportunities for going to church. We knew that the Parthenay venue was linked with the chaplaincy of Christ the Good Shepherd, part of the archdeaconry in France, and that there were additional church service venues in the southern part of the region: St. Jean d'Angely (Charente Maritime) and Cognac (Charente). We had sent an email to the reverend in charge of the chaplaincy, requesting possible contact with a member of his congregation, and an arrangement had been made.

We flew in to the coastal town of La Rochelle, and in getting off the plane experienced that wonderful feeling of walking on French soil and the buzz from speaking French again, even if only to the Border Control staff checking our passports. Everything seemed so natural and familiar, despite the fact that La Rochelle was an unfamiliar location for us, and we commented on how it felt as if we had come home.

We chose to stay in Saintes, sixty kilometres south-east of La Rochelle; an attractive town of around twenty-eight thousand inhabitants, built alongside the Charente river, with the majority of the historic part rising up from its left bank. The first day we wandered through the town and across a narrow footbridge to the right bank to admire a formidable arch, the Arch of Germanicus completed in AD20, and into a wonderful open museum of Roman statues, artefacts and relics with the most awesome architectural sculptures, which furnished a fascinating vision of what ancient Roman Saintes had looked like. We liked the town's very pleasant surroundings, yet felt that Saintes might prove too large for us; there was a lot of traffic moving slowly through the town, even in winter, so we followed the Charente eastwards to Cognac.

We were immediately taken with this much smaller yet more intimate town. It had a decent-sized pedestrian centre with a wealth of individual shops, cafés and restaurants, and we delighted in a beautifully manicured public park with a maze of walks and English style gardens. We wound our way through the historic cobbled areas down to the river, in glorious warm sunshine, and we hung over its parapet to regard the fish. Across to the left was the Château de Cognac with imposing three-metre thick walls, and we learnt later that day it was the birthplace of François I, King of France in 1515. We later enjoyed a chocolat chaud in the open air in Place François I (clearly a place to see and be seen). How content we were in having found Cognac!

Over the next few days we drove several marked scenic trails in the vicinity of Cognac and fell in love with the scenery of vineyard upon vineyard. We were fascinated to spot small vans (mostly white, old and battered) dotted across the landscape with lone souls methodically pruning the rampant year's growth to leave two leading shoots of similar length which were artfully tied down in perfect hoops. As we scanned the hillsides, the rows of vines formed such incredible patterns. One vineyard abutted with another but not necessarily with its rows of vines in the same direction – nothing to do with the sun but for ease of access for a mechanical grape harvester. The vineyards were in good order, regimented and yet surprisingly pleasing and easy on the eye, especially with the addition of a bright blue, cloudless sky. We also loved the appeal of the ramshackle limestone farm buildings, the contrast of impressive chateaus, the modern, new build, cream-coloured, pavilion-style houses, the warm glow of the terracotta pantile roofs, the numerous birds of prey we saw sitting proud on the supporting stakes for the vines and the dearth of traffic.

We met up with two delightful couples from the chaplaincy and enjoyed a lovely lunch in Brizambourg, in a restaurant serving a delicious five-course lunch for the princely sum of twelve euros! It was very valuable to chat with them about church life and fellowship and living in the area, and to pick up lots of tips, hints and suggestions for making the transition from the UK to France easy. We were bowled over by our day and barely slept that night for the exciting times we had enjoyed during the past week; we were both sad when the short break came to an end. How miserable we felt as we taxied back to the terminal building at Stansted whilst those around us couldn't wait to rip their seat belts off and exit the plane as soon as possible. What a pair we were, especially as I was still not fully fit; but we so wanted to be in France and especially in the Cognac area. No wonder some members of our family threw their hands up in horror!

The next day reality set in as Phil left early for Luton and caught a plane to Lisbon to begin his ground training course with NetJets. I endured a difficult day – a dark, grey day with heavy rain – and tried to acclimatise to all things British. The realisation that I was going to have to cope alone for the first time in ages, and moreover for a whole fortnight, was a bit of shock to the system, but in fact my being alone worked far better than I had envisaged as I put the planning and pacing techniques from the course into practice. In future I was going to have to cope with Phil's roster pattern of six days away followed by five rest days so I had better get used to it.

On Phil's return from his training course, France featured a great deal in our conversation, especially as Phil explained that although his 'gateway' (start/end of workplace) was confirmed as Luton, he could actually change his gateway to one of five in France, of which Bordeaux was the closest to Cognac. Thrilled, we started to talk about "when we move to France" rather than "if". We strived to think of ways we might serve the Lord in France and discussed all we had seen in the Cognac area to try to determine the clues as to what might be God's will for us there. Now that I was feeling more capable I wondered at what I was actually capable of achieving. I am sure my parents felt that in our intention to move to France we were merely following our own selfish inclinations, were acting thoughtlessly with regard to the family and especially letting them down. We were not heartless to their anxieties and endured instead the consequences of stepping out in faith, resting in the assurance that our loving Father knows what is best for us in his ultimate plan.

We questioned whether we should run a Chambre d'hôte business and perhaps advertise through military journals. We discussed ways we might link up with ex-military Christians living in Poitou-Charentes too so that we could continue to pray for the safety and protection of our military, as we were already doing in our Associate Prayer group in South Lincolnshire, as members of the Armed Forces Christian Union. Could we even forge links with the French military, which had a presence in both Charente Maritime and Charente? We had inadvertently come across the French L'Armée de l'Air base in Cognac, and at the time I had categorically said to Phil that there was no way I was ever going to live anywhere which overlooked the military airfield. After twenty-four years of all things military my idea of rural France certainly didn't include a view of air force base buildings, high security fencing and green camouflaged hangars! Yet I asked myself, was I being selfish and missing the point?

Every morning I followed the same ritual, sitting in bed with a cup of tea and reading my Bible. On Valentine's Day the reading was Luke 7, which includes the inspiring story of the Roman centurion who had great faith in Jesus, believing Jesus could heal his dying servant without Jesus being at the servant's bedside. It made me rethink my own views about healing. The Bible story made me contemplate what an important spiritual lesson we can learn from the most unlikely people. In this instance the Roman centurion was from a different cultural and religious background, put in a position to enforce the Emperor's rule, yet he had become close to the Jews around him and had helped them build a synagogue. He must have been a very open-minded man, of great strength and character, who was prepared to risk his job and possibly his life in his pursuit of a different faith. He clearly recognised the importance of Jesus on earth and had absolute faith in Jesus' ability to heal. He knew that Jesus only had "to say the word and let my servant be healed". Jesus saw and recognised the centurion's great faith. What love to heal from afar – not romantic, fanciful, lovey-dovey or amorous Valentine's Day love but true, unconditional love. Did I have the same absolute faith in Jesus' ability to heal insurmountable problems from afar? Did I have the faith of the Roman centurion? Pause for thought...

The next day Phil received notification regarding his flying training (yet another flying training course) to fly the Cessna Citation Excel, which would be held in the USA, and he would be away for a month! Another huge test for me in coping alone but with all the preparation for his going away I had little time to think about it too much.

The following week he flew to San Antonio, Texas, and I was determined to manage, feeling really upbeat and capable... until 12.58am on Wednesday 27th February when I woke to feel the bed shaking and all the beaded fringing on our window blind tinkling eerily, which put me in the most frightful panic, not knowing what was happening to me. Our bedroom was on the second floor of a modern townhouse, the end of the row, surrounded by similar properties and all with the master bedrooms located on the top floor. As I have heart arrhythmia I had been convinced when I first woke that I was having a heart attack, until I fumbled to put lights on, pounded down the stairs to ground level, saw all the pictures on the two landings set at a jaunty angle and rationalised that I really wouldn't have had this much energy in a cardiac arrest! I rushed to a window to look outside, and my neighbours had similar thoughts, threw open their front doors and bedroom windows, and called across the street to people they had never previously spoken to. A sense of community was established that day, which hadn't existed before in our newly built homes. All had suffered similar fear and panic, whereas I was amazed to learn later that friends in their bungalow had slept through the whole incident! We had experienced an earthquake registering 5.2 on the Richter scale – definitely a fearful moment, which made my heart race. Fortunately, because of the time difference with America, I was able to speak to Phil; I also spoke to my parents who had been nearer to the centre of the earthquake. I used to joke with other military wives that as soon as the men were away the washing machine or car broke down, but had never envisaged something as dramatic as an earthquake.

By March 2008 I joined a Health Walking group, which walked a four mile circuit in the local area on alternate Saturdays. I also did five mile stretches myself during the fortnight in between the set walks and my pain reduced to a very low threshold. I felt very, very blessed to have been brought from the wretched situation of the previous eight years. Each day there was a greater and greater improvement, and each day I praised God for his steadfastness, for being my rock and refuge. I felt robust in body, mind and spirit, and the healing processes gathered speed and momentum. Just as in rolling a snowball to try to form the largest ball, I had rolled my 'snowball' of better health and fitness farther and farther along the way, and in doing so had gathered greater inner strength. I felt hale and hearty and knew that the past was firmly in the past. I made an appointment with my doctor and convinced her I was healed and wanted to stop my medication. She explained that it would have to be a sensibly slow process because of the complexity of the drugs – the only drawback to me wanting to throw all the packets firmly in the bin.

Just when I thought the victory had been won I started to have awful nightmares each night – very disturbing nightmares of blood and guts, maimed babies, people having been butchered; ugly, disgusting, frightening and horrifying nightmares. They were such a shocking revelation, and I felt very disconcerted, ashamed and embarrassed to tell anyone about them. I was someone who refused to look at anything violent or gruesome, rarely went to the cinema and then only to watch films largely targeted at a female audience, switched TV channels as soon as anything unpleasant was shown and returned any books unread to friends if I thought them distasteful. Therefore to actually experience these dreams really quite upset me. I would wake in the early hours fearful that I couldn't destroy these thoughts from my mind, perplexed as to why they even occurred, and longed for a peaceful, dreamless sleep. One might assume that it was the reduction of the medication which caused the nightmares, but during the day I remained as fit as a fiddle, suffered no side effects and felt utterly in control and driven by my faith. The problem seemed to be my subconscious state, over which I had less control. Eventually I became convinced that the Devil was trying to undermine my psyche and reduce my faith when I was at my weakest and most vulnerable: asleep.

As one matures in Christian faith, relying totally on God and visibly being so full of joy and euphoria, it is easy to forget that the Devil likes to attack and spoil things. He loves to create havoc in the world and wheedle himself into our lives to upset and diminish our abilities and our faith. We often underestimate the Devil's schemes to create evil and undermine goodness, purity, love, community, family and ourselves.

Jesus was tempted by the Devil as he spent forty days in the wilderness whilst he fasted and prayed. My fast was abstaining from medication, and once the penny dropped I knew exactly what my plan of attack should be to keep the Devil at bay. I needed to pray and cry out to Jesus. On waking during the night from a nightmare I would get up and go into our shower room, declare my complete faith in Jesus to rid the Devil from my subconscious, and pray for the strength to get through the night. For three nights the nightmares continued but I followed the same routine: I concentrated on Jesus, reached out to be near him and believed that his power would overpower all evil and reduce the Devil to a squirming, shrinking, miserable figure who would cease to have any hold on me.

On the fourth morning I got out of bed and walked across to the window to raise the window blind to allow the beautiful light and morning freshness to invade the room. I was suddenly aware I felt different and knew instantly I had been healed. The Devil had been well and truly ousted. I gripped the window sill, sighed deeply and looked across to the meadows and woods beyond. I felt a tremendous excitement and joy reverberate through my body, my mind and my spirit. What blessed relief! I felt completely vital... whole... cleansed... recovered... on top of the world!

Before I had had insight into what was happening inside me, but now I realised that I couldn't see below my skin and inside my body. The ability to do so was blocked. I can bring to mind the realisation of that moment in the fullness of clarity even today and relive the wonderful emotion which brimmed up inside me in knowing and receiving the absolute proof that Jesus was my Saviour. He was, is and will be undeniably capable of the most astonishing power to heal. Never again have I experienced such appalling nightmares or an episode of chronic pain; in fact, I have experienced no pain whatsoever. Did I really deserve such mercy?

I had no idea what the future held for me now, but whatever, wherever, I vowed I was going to put Jesus at the forefront of my every step.

Chapter Eighteen

Oh Lord my God, I called to you for help and you healed me.
Oh Lord, you brought me up from the grave;
you spared me from going down into the pit.
Sing to the Lord, you saints of his; praise his holy name.

Psalm 30:2-5

April was a monumental month, not least because the word 'healing' was constantly on my lips, but so many other reasons contributed to it being a great month. I celebrated my fiftieth birthday, which was a very poignant day with so many cards, presents, flowers and good wishes received plus the greatest blessing of having Phil, Rob and Amy with me too. We purposely kept the day low key and indulged in being just the four of us. We started with a woodland walk to include the incredible five hundred metre topiary avenue at Clipsham – one hundred and fifty yew trees clipped to depict historic events. I considered my half century and wondered how the rest of my timeline would map out. I couldn't imagine any event topping my healing! After a pub lunch, a good slice of Rob's skilfully crafted birthday cake (a badger as we lived in Badger Lane), and a lovely meal out in the evening at a favourite restaurant, I went to bed content, feeling honoured by my family's love and kindness.

Two days later Phil was confirmed by the Bishop of Grantham in our church, St. Firmin's, Thurlby. It was a beautiful, sunny day, and although much of the country had snow, Thurlby escaped a covering which made travel to the church easy for all. The confirmation service was supercharged with emotion as Phil publicly declared his faith in the Lord alongside other confirmands, and we had the added pleasure of gaining a goddaughter that day, as she was baptised and confirmed at the same time. Rob and Amy came along too which made the whole day absolutely perfect.

April 15th was another special day, because we stepped out in faith and signed an estate agent to market our house, having chosen them because they charged the least percentage on a sale and nothing at all to do with the fact that the agent's parents lived just north of Cognac!

The next day we celebrated our twenty-sixth Wedding Anniversary and that same day received Phil's terminal lump sum from the RAF into our bank account. Reasons for celebration continued coming and we celebrated the confirmation of Rob's accountancy graduate training position for September and his twenty-first birthday at the end of April.

One matter of concern that month was the global financial crisis, which had begun in 2007 and was expected to increase dramatically to rival the Great Depression in the thirties. We chose to remain calm and simply continue to trust God's hand on our lives, regardless of the doom and gloom surrounding the housing market and the fact that house prices were forecast to fall significantly. In healing me God had achieved the seemingly impossible so a dismal housing market wasn't going to deter our faith!

The world in crisis made us think about those households that were already suffering on only one salary due to a loved one being ill and now had the threat of redundancy to contend with. A job in the military had previously been regarded as safe but even redundancies in the military had been a reality since 1993 as a direct result of the end of the Cold War, and further defence cuts because of the financial crisis would directly affect personnel. Personnel detached to a conflict zone, with all the concerns that this generated, could now have to contend with the threat of redundancy hanging over them. How would their concern for their job in the future affect their capacity to do their job under conflict? The slightest distraction might cause them to misjudge or miss something vital in the circumstance, and the result might be devastating.

I imagined the scenes of conflict in Iraq or Afghanistan, and I thought back to our visit to the Somme battlefield sites and the horrifying photographs we had seen displayed of the effects of conflict. So many people severely injured and shattered by their experiences. How many people in the future would be in need of care, physically and emotionally? From our experiences of my suffering chronic pain we knew how essential it was to have a short break – to completely break away from home surroundings and look at life afresh in a new, relaxed environment. It was then that I had a 'Eureka' moment and knew without doubt the reason God wanted us in France: Phil's military background, wealth of experience and heart for all ranks; my experience of chronic pain and suffering; my social work experience of being a listening ear to many; and our Christian faith to share my healing with all who needed healing themselves.

When I explained this to Phil he agreed without hesitation. Now our way forward was clear: we would find a property with a self-contained annexe and offer short breaks to serving and ex-serving military personnel. It would be a pleasure to serve others in thankfulness for my healing, and with God as director of our project we felt certain we must provide a free holiday. We had managed on one salary throughout my years of illness, and with the children becoming more independent we could direct that money toward helping others. By disciplining ourselves to hold on to our money lightly we could be materially secure, but not greedy, and use the excess for a good cause. It was exciting to envisage the challenge of the whole project and the amazing way that it would evolve.

The month ended in a remarkable way because my GP signed me back to work and I was finally free from the stigma of being unemployable. What a terrific feeling I had as I walked out of the surgery, straight past the pharmacy which I had once been so reliant on, knowing I was regarded fit, healthy and able – and what is more, with the paperwork to prove it! No more a patient – not sick, not an invalid and not in need of benefits. I put in place the cancellation of future payments of incapacity benefit and disability allowance and cut up my Blue Badge for car parking with real fervour. Great feeling! Great day! Great month!

I really persevered with the French class even though it appeared more difficult each week. Just when I thought I had mastered certain grammar I simply forgot it a few weeks later. Quite frustrating! We were given a long list of avoir (to have) phrases to learn, which felt like wading through treacle. The only phrase which really stuck was avoir le cafard. Cafard has two meanings – 'cockroach' or 'to have the blues' – and it was very easy to envisage that if I saw a cockroach I really would have the hump! The trouble was I really needed to be among French speakers to improve my skill, but with no initial bite on the house sale hook I was going to have to knuckle down and learn as much as I could through grit and determination.

Fortunately the opportunity to be among French speakers popped up sooner than I had imagined because in June we were fortunate to fit a four day break into Phil's standard five days off. We flew into La Rochelle late afternoon and travelled across a drizzly landscape to Montour, a hamlet north-east of Cognac where we had booked three nights at La Closerie, a very pretty building of immense character and charm and in the process of complete renovation by its new owners, Jacques and Sylvie, of equal charm. At breakfast we discovered their Chambres d'hôte business had only opened that month to welcome their first guests – and what a welcome they offered! With the delightful array of breakfast items on the table we lost no opportunity in taking up their offer of an evening meal, and that same evening we dined superbly and thanked God silently for the blessing of us having discovered La Closerie. Jacques and Sylvie could clearly speak a lot of English but from the start we said we had to practice our French and wanted to avoid speaking English if they agreed correct us. We chatted easily in our enthusiastic but grammatically incorrect French – about our future plans, the interesting cultural differences between the UK and France, French politics, the ins and outs of house purchase in France – and they were happy to answer any of our questions and give advice. We gained confidence in speaking and picked up some very useful tips about life in France. Later we fell into bed exhausted but exhilarated that we had made our first real French friends. When another meal was offered the following night we jumped at the chance, and by the time we came to leave they had offered us accommodation at any time in the future, even for a longer period if we needed it. They basically opened their arms wide to help us, in any which way they could, and we were very moved by their warmth and friendship.

The morning of our departure we travelled west to Marennes and then routed north to Rochefort, on their advice, to observe the many storks nesting way up high on the electricity pylons – an astonishing sight and well worth the detour. We ate a leisurely lunch in the port and over coffee planned how late we could stay in Rochefort before driving to the airport at La Rochelle, when we realised that Phil's passport was missing. A moment of panic gripped us; we dashed back to take the car apart and soon Phil had both suitcases fully open on the tarmac of the car park with all their contents spilled out on the ground! Phil just couldn't remember having seen his passport at Montour, but he did recall having shown it to the car rental company. We returned to the airport with our hearts in our mouths, but the car rental salesman simply handed over Phil's passport calmly. In that situation, as the salesman, I would have made a quick phone call to the customer reassuring him of the whereabouts and safety of his passport, but I suspect the salesman did not envisage the need because French citizens are required to carry a card to verify identity, nationality and they can even travel within the European Union on that card. Far, far fewer people have passports – another lesson in national differences.

With us now knowing exactly our long-term plan in France, we had hoped that our house would sell pretty quickly, but there was a complete lack of interest in our property. We dropped the price by ten thousand pounds having already put the house on the market twenty thousand pounds below its supposed market value. There are many places in the Bible declaring that one should not put one's hope in money, and we felt this was a testing time for us to really consider where money ranked in our priorities. We needed a certain amount for material security, but how much above that was really greed? Our ministry of providing free rest and recuperation would require careful budgeting, but we knew we could achieve it through our resourcefulness and God's grace. There was no denying the vast number of 'For Sale' boards in and around Bourne but only a few 'Sold' signs in evidence, and sadly there were even 'Repossession' notices posted on the windows of some properties in our vicinity. It clearly was not a good time to sell.

On 15th September, Lehman Brothers investment bank collapsed – one of the oldest, richest and most powerful banks in the world. Regardless of how much people knew about banking, everyone knew that this demonstrated a bad worldwide economic situation. Panic gripped the stock market; one of the biggest mortgage lending companies in the UK lost a huge percentage off its shares, and the situation went from bad to worse. House prices in the UK were dropping fast, and many French houses on various websites were also slashed hugely (in some cases as much as forty to sixty thousand euros) so we took heart that even if our house sold for less we would still be able to buy in France.

Later that week we took Amy and all her worldly goods to Birmingham University then flew from Luton to Bordeaux: a city and port situated on the Garonne river, known as 'la perle d'Aquitaine' (the pearl of the Aquitaine region) which is south-west of the

Charente department. The city is the major capital of the Bordeaux wine area, of more than ten thousand wine-producing châteaux and thirteen thousand other grape producers. In fact there are even rows of grape vines planted ornamentally outside the terminal buildings at Bordeaux airport.

We caught the Jetbus into the centre, alighted at Place Gambetta and stayed in a nearby hotel, which had the smallest room and en-suite we have ever seen – 'small' being the dominant adjective for everything in the room and 'squeeze' being the dominant verb! It's not often one has to sit on the loo in order to close the door! However, the hotel served a great breakfast and was brilliantly placed to explore all the sights, with the city awash with students milling around – on bikes, skateboards, unicycles, pogo sticks(!) and scooters. We had left one university behind and joined Fresher's Week at another! We fell in love with the city. Its grandiose classical buildings reminded us of Paris[9]. Stunning riverside walks and developed quays alongside the Garonne, attractive boulevards, public parks, and its modern Mirror Water feature are just a few of the wonderful sights we touched upon. The only slightly puzzling feature, which we never resolved, was that wherever we looked there were people walking around with single long-stemmed, bright pink or orange gerberas... Intriguing!

After a couple of days of city life we headed north-east to Cognac and stayed once more at Montour with our friends, this time in a second room they had renovated. They also had Belgian guests staying, and we all enjoyed one of Sylvie's delightful menus, served outside on the terrace, and learnt that both France and Belgium were seeing similar difficulties with their housing markets. We spent a couple of days thoroughly exploring the area, visiting as many villages and small towns as possible and noting those we liked. We took details from an estate agent, located several properties and began to narrow down the type of property which would suit guests coming for R&R.

We returned to the UK a week later and found that the economic situation had worsened further. Mortgage lenders had put up their rates because the bank borrowing rate had soared, which further decreased our probability of selling. We went to the Sunday service at St. Firmin's and listened to a retired clergyman preach on the credit

---

[9] Next to Paris, Bordeaux actually has the most protected buildings.

crunch. He outlined how the world had become far too greedy and if people recognised that they had Jesus alongside them their imagined needs would be far smaller. The sermon further emphasised our thinking on the whole subject of "for the love of money is a root of all kinds of evil" (1 Timothy 6: 10). In October stock markets across the world plummeted and many household names and stores ceased to trade. To see so many major names in trouble was unsettling, and it made many wonder if the whole world was actually going to grind to a halt. Inflation rose, and with Phil newly 'in' at NetJets we imagined they must be having difficulties and wondered whether Phil might be one of the first 'out'.

We kept our trust in the long-term plan but decided that we shouldn't just sit around and wait for the house to sell but use our time more constructively. Phil joined the French classes and came to as many classes as his flying schedule allowed; we both became youth workers at church, helped with an Alpha group, started to cycle as well as walk; and I had piano lessons from a very patient friend. It was so wonderful to just say yes to all sorts of requests for help or explore a new hobby and to feel totally well, knowing that I was not going to let someone down by an attack of chronic pain.

That month I also received an invite from the Pain Management Course team to attend a review planned for December. I declined to attend the review but filled in the questionnaire to assist their records and took the opportunity to thank them once again for all their support.

In November we attended the Armed Forces Christian Union 'Day of Prayer and Worship' at St. Clement Danes church, Strand, London, which is the Central Church of the Royal Air Force. General Sir Richard Dannatt GCB CBE MC, who had recently retired as Chief of the General Staff, spoke as well as many others from all ranks, of their experiences in conflict. I spoke to three young widows who had bravely come for the service in the afternoon, and it was a humbling moment. We heard so much to confirm our plans to run our project in France, and we felt more than ready for all systems go – except that our house would not sell.

In the New Year of 2009 we decided to change our estate agent, reduced the house by another twenty five thousand pounds, and six weeks later welcomed the first prospective buyers through the front door for months. Within a fortnight we had two other viewings, but confidently left everything in the capable hands of our agent as we flew to Perpignan for an eight-day holiday.

Perpignan is in the far south-west corner of France, near the Pyrenees and close to the Spanish border. We arrived late afternoon planning to pop to our hotel, a mere four kilometres away, before going in to Perpignan for a meal, but it took us two hours to get to the hotel. It wasn't helped by the fact that everyone on the flight hiring a car had chosen the same rental company, but then once in the hire car we could not fathom the road network to get near to the hotel, even though we could see it! We did several parts of the network twice and got crosser and crosser with each failed attempt, especially when one route took us on the rough track of a dried up river bed!

The next morning we drove west to Quillan through the most spectacular scenery: a winding route, hugging the foothills of the Pyrenees, through a gorge with vast outcrops of rock rising steeply and jutting out menacingly along the route. More than once we thought we might lose a wing mirror! We stayed with a friend from the French class in Bourne who had moved with her husband to this delightful town, which is situated on the river Aude. It was really wonderful to listen to their hilarious tales of settling in France, and we could already identify with so many of their experiences.

Life in France seemed so full of vitality, and the next day provided a great illustration. We drove through the mountains, negotiating several hairpin bends to Mirepoix and were soon sucked into their terrific Monday market. A myriad of stalls spilled out from the central square and filled the streets, selling an immense diversity of goods, yet the most noticeable fact was the vibrant colours of the wares on sale – a mass of striking oranges, pinks, yellows and blue. It was a lively scene, with people swarming around in brilliant sunshine, a cacophony of sound as market traders raised their voices; people greeted one another and musicians played on street corners. It was a hectic yet captivating atmosphere, which was infectious and we wanted to catch it.

We moved on to Limoux to discover another sort of commotion occurring as it was the Fête d'Enfants, coinciding with Mardi Gras, and class upon class of tiny children were dressed up in superb costumes: Red Indians, Chinese, Africans, Animals, Clowns etc. They all proceeded to parade around the main square for parents, well-wishers and tourists whilst the town band played, to the best of its ability, the melody from 'Bedknobs and Broomsticks'. What a treat we had that day, and how much we so wanted to be part of this lifestyle! But as to when that would happen we were clueless.

We arrived back in the UK and were amazed to learn that there had been further viewings whilst we had been away, with one person having actually put in an offer. This offer we rejected, knowing that another buyer was also interested in the property. Finally on March 27th we secured a sale, and we learnt it should be a fairly quick transaction as our buyer did not have a property to sell. We would only have to wait for a mortgage to be put in place, and we had been blessed with none of the encumbrance of a chain and all the anxiety that can generate. The 'Sold' sign went up outside, and we felt euphoric every time we looked out of the front window.

We were so confident that everything would go through with the sale that we lost no time in organising a party, which in effect would be our leaving party; we called it a 'Celebration of Blessings'. We wanted to get as many folk together, who were near and dear to us, who had supported us faithfully in prayer and practically through my years of chronic pain, and who were behind us prayerfully in our plan to set up the 'rest and recuperation' project in France. To celebrate the many blessings we had received over the years was reason enough to party, but then there were all the lost celebrations which had passed quietly, including my fiftieth birthday and our Silver Wedding anniversary. I phoned up the local hotel detailing the sort of celebration we wanted with a three-course meal, and the manager immediately agreed to our request for the function. He sounded as excited as I was and rushed on to explain that he had recently received a phone call cancelling a wedding booking that weekend, so he was able to offer us the promise of a grand affair for a hundred people at a very reasonable price. Clearly it was meant to be, and once again how appropriate for our function to be called a Celebration of Blessings! Three days after our sale was secured, we secured the party date, and the next day all the invites were either posted off or hand delivered.

The day of our Celebration of Blessings was perfect – lots of sunshine, a lovely warm day, and a hundred guests filled a function room decorated festively on a French theme with blue, white and red helium balloons. After an aperitif everyone sang our favourite hymn, 'In Christ alone our hope is found; he is my light, my strength, my song' composed by Keith Getty (song) and Stuart Townend (lyrics) in

2001. No other words were more fitting for us than those from this emotive hymn. There were many non-Christians at the party, and I hope that their hearts were touched by the gusto with which those whose hope is found in Christ sang. Phil and I spoke from our hearts about my past experiences of suffering, my healing and our intentions of setting up the project of rest and recuperation in France. There were several serving and retired military personnel in the room who could relate to the need for such a project, and it was wonderful to have their support on the day. We thought it was a very happy day of love and fellowship, and we very much felt the presence of the Holy Spirit bringing people together as we enjoyed the fun of being in one place with so many dear people. It didn't seem like a Leaving Party at all – more an affirmation that we valued our friends and their prayers; we would not lose touch with them and indeed looked forward to welcoming them to our home in France. Distance between us just didn't seem an obstacle to us, especially as we were used to coping with distance in relationships. Phil's various postings up and down the UK had meant long hours of travel to family and friends, and the distance from Cognac to the UK could be reduced drastically with the choice of several low-cost airlines providing a service from four airports, all within two hours of Cognac. In addition, high speed trains regularly left Angoulême for Paris, with onward Eurostar connections to St. Pancras, providing another easy alternative without even having to consider the option of driving.

We were quite overcome by the many gifts we received either for the project or for ourselves, with many friends purchasing wonderful books to encourage us in our walk with our Saviour. We received many heart-warming thank you notes and were thrilled so many had considered the day really memorable. We praised God for their friendship, their faith, their support and their love. We had wanted the event to be a celebration of praise and worship as we thanked our loving God for the many blessings he had bestowed upon us, and the day surpassed all our expectations. Our God had once again been gracious in his blessing of our special day. At that moment we couldn't have been more ready or further prepared to leave our country of birth and move to France.

CHAPTER NINETEEN

See, I am sending an angel ahead of you
to guard you along the way and
to bring you to a place I have prepared.

Exodus 23:20

We wholeheartedly believed and trusted that the above verse from the Bible was true. We simply had no reason to doubt and thus concentrated all our efforts on 'leaving' the UK, rather than on 'arriving' in France. A massive chapter in our life was about to close and we wanted to bring all our personal interests, clubs, classes, finance, health issues to a conclusion, in the most correct and appropriate way, and inform the relevant authorities of our imminent move. In our determination to do everything according to the book we had read as much literature as we could on the Internet – a fantastic source of information for browsing the various forums for moving to France. It was a busy time as we worked methodically down a huge list, but very exciting. Fourteen months previously it had made good sense to open a bank account in France, particularly as Phil's salary was paid in euros, and we were now comfortable with French banking, having tested the use of our account on our recent holidays.

We paid for copies of our medical notes, and I spent a long time carefully translating twenty-three pages of mine! We arranged car insurance to get us through the first month in France and purchased a left-hand drive, used car from Hayes, Greater London – coincidentally my father's birthplace and a stone's throw from where my grandparents are buried. The car was in good condition, having only had one owner, with the added attraction of having been originally registered in France. This fact appealed greatly because of the imagined ease of importation back into France.

We ruthlessly cleared the house of our belongings, donating much to Rob, Amy and other good causes! We sorted and packed our possessions, sold both our cars to a local family – they had arrived to view one car and left buying both, praise the Lord! – and we enjoyed many memorable 'last suppers' with friends.

We exchanged contracts with our buyer, arranged removals for 2nd June (the day of completion), booked Amy a flight to Poitiers, to enable her to spend the whole of her University summer holiday in France, then in late May started to send a few emails to estate agents in Cognac asking about any rental properties when we learnt Phil's job could definitely be at risk. Aviation companies operating fractional ownership and renting of their private business jets had experienced a plunge in sales as a result of the global financial crisis, and now NetJets was not immune. We wondered whether Phil, having recently joined the company, would now be made redundant, and Phil was notified that a new option for employment with them would soon be publicised. However, we pushed that concern to the back of our minds, confident in the knowledge that an angel was watching over us and guarding each step we were taking towards the English Channel. Having come this far we simply had to keep trusting.

A beautiful day dawned on Tuesday 2nd June. We completed the house removals by 11.50am, exactly three years to the day when we had paid a reservation fee to purchase the house. After three years of metamorphosis through faith all that remained was to have one last look around and thank God again for his tremendous blessing on our lives. We drove away from Badger Lane at 2pm excited and exhilarated, with our Citroen packed to the gunnels including everything we thought we might possibly need for a month. Our furniture would not arrive in France for several weeks, but that gave us some weeks of grace bearing in mind we hadn't a clue where we might actually be living!

We headed south for Crowborough, East Sussex on a huge high, but by 4pm we had only made it as far as Heathrow due to exceptionally heavy traffic on the M25 and a spate of accidents. A normal three-hour journey from Bourne to Crowborough took us a total of six hours, and we were extremely relieved to finally arrive at our destination and spend what was left of the evening with Phil's father.

The next morning, the frustration had abated and the excitement had returned; we left Crowborough and caught the 13:00 ferry from Dover to Calais, and when we drove off the ferry ramp on to French soil, the thrill we felt was awesome, particularly knowing we hadn't a return ticket! We had planned the journey south-west to Cognac in two stages, heading for Lower Normandy for an overnight stay. We stopped on the autoroute near Rouen for a break at an Aire – a motorway service area with snack bar, refuelling and shopping facilities, which also had picnic tables. As we walked towards the entrance door, a larger-than-life gentleman came out whom I recognised immediately and said, "You're a long way from Lincolnshire." As is my wont, I chatted away amiably, while Phil looked bemused but joined in politely. The gentleman had been a hero of mine when Phil and I had been glued to the television screen in the 1980's watching many a tournament of The World's Strongest Man. Afterwards Phil asked, "Who was that? You didn't introduce him to me." I wasn't quite sure what to say at first, whether to be astounded at the fact we had actually met someone else from Lincolnshire en route or in Phil not having recognised Geoff Capes, the incredible strongman whose fame had begun with his prowess on the athletics field in the shot putt.

The next day, after a dream of a journey, we arrived in the Cognac area with a grand welcome from Jacques and Sylvie at La Closerie. They treated us royally with a delicious meal. We phoned the estate agent in Cognac to see if we could view a rental property the next morning, whilst our friends offered to put us up in their home for as long we needed, saying that they could also organise a barn to store all our furniture and possessions. We were flabbergasted by their immense generosity but simply couldn't impose on them in that way and instead viewed a property in the village of Thors just fifteen kilometres north of Cognac, which immediately ticked all the boxes. It had three good-sized bedrooms complete with bedroom furniture, some basic furniture downstairs, a laundry/utility area with washing machine and tumble dryer, a massive garage providing good storage space, which would later be more than adequate for storage of our furniture, an enormous courtyard area in full sun, a large covered area for outside dining (abri) and a small lawn area with mature fruit trees. Everything was more than adequate for our needs. We signed a rental agreement, paid our deposit and unpacked our belongings into the house. We could not get over how everything had fallen into place so easily and speedily. "Oh, ye of little faith!"

The house was right in the middle of the village, opposite the main Square with the church and boulangerie, providing fresh bread every day and rather nice pastries. Monsieur le Maire lived diagonally opposite so we had to watch our p's and q's, and eight cows ambled slowly, slowly, slowly across the Square twice a day so we had to watch our p's and q's in more ways than one! Next door but one was La Poste, the post office, very convenient as they sold papers and magazines as well as stamps, but two focal points in the Square became our lifeline in time of need. First, the village pump, because the water had been cut off inadvertently on the day we arrived, which meant we made a fair few trips back and forth with a bucket, until the water company put the water back on the next day; and second, an all-glass telephone box, because France Telecom could not connect us for several days. The temperature in the telephone box was like a raging oven, and to make a call you had to try to stand outside with the telephone cord stretched as tight as possible to avoid being completely roasted. The Square sported a very fine bus shelter with only a limited timetable for an occasional bus, including a fine map of local walks. We also discovered some quarry pits a short walk away, which had been turned into a lakeside campsite with a bar and restaurant, and around the corner from the post office was a very nicely kept village hall and landscaped municipal park with very attractive flower beds. We missed joining in with the locals for a slap up meal our first weekend as we had not subscribed by May 31st but we vowed to do so the next time.

In those first few days, as we were welcomed by many in the street and at local shops, and out of courtesy, we presented ourselves at the Mairie. We could hardly believe what we had achieved in such a short time with organising so many things French in order to settle quickly and easily in Thors during that first week. Migrating to France really was not difficult as some had negatively led us to believe. Agreed, we knew there would be challenges, but from the welcome we received from the inhabitants of Thors we felt very comfortable, at ease and at home in our surroundings. We had not gone to the moon – only a mere 1080km south – and we had not arrived in an unwelcoming place devoid of human existence or essential resources, but we were in a place promising 'riches' and abundance.

CHAPTER TWENTY

We went through fire and water,
but you brought us to a place of abundance.

Psalm 66:12b

Our first Sunday in France was an astonishing day. We drove to St. Jean d'Angely where the chaplaincy of the Good Shepherd used a function room in a gîte complex to hold their Sunday service. We were welcomed royally, meeting up again with the two couples who had kindly spent time with us when on our church fact-finding mission in 2007. We were introduced to other members of the congregation who were permanently domiciled in France and those who had holiday homes, some of whom hailed from two villages within spitting distance of Bourne including one gentleman whose brother had been a previous headmaster of a primary school in Bourne. To astound us further we met a couple from Helpston who we had met at Phil's confirmation service at Thurlby! It felt as if we hadn't actually moved to France!

We had offers of help to ease settling into our new life, were invited to join a house group in Cognac and received invitations to share a meal. We even discovered that some members of the congregation were members of the RAF Association Sud-Ouest France, and it appeared that not only was Lincolnshire not as far away as we had first imagined but neither, surprisingly, was the military community. We came away from a lively coffee time, on a high and completely overwhelmed.

Our first Monday in France was not so much astonishing as astounding. We awoke to drizzle and a heavy sky but decided to go ahead with our plan to drive to Saintes, despite the rain, in order to organise our health cover in France. With Phil due back at work inside three days we only had a small window of opportunity to go along to the relevant health authority. We could join the French health service, as Phil was in employment, once the relevant certificates issued from Newcastle had been processed by the French. We parked in a Leclerc supermarket car park, conveniently opposite the offices of the Caisse Primaire d'Assurance de la Maladie (CPAM), the public organisation for health, and marched confidently up their steps carrying a bulging dossier of papers, only to turn on our tail as they were closed on Mondays. We had made a typical British mistake of assuming that everything in France opens as in the UK. We soon learned through trial and error which supermarket was open for an odd couple of hours on a Sunday morning or which individual shops and offices closed from Saturday late afternoon through to Monday afternoon and in many cases even Tuesday morning.

With our main aim in Saintes thwarted I opted to do a food shop whilst Phil spent time in the café using the free Wi-fi and caught up on admin and emails. It seemed a fair exchange until the rain became ridiculously heavy as I struggled across the car park with a loaded trolley. The sky was inky black and great claps of thunder broke overhead, then a tremendous wind gusted as lightening shot across the sky. I slammed the boot down, leapt into the car and in seconds the rain intensified further to lash the windscreen with screeds of water, so that it was impossible to see anything ahead. Then a hail storm arrived with enormous hailstones that caused a great racket on the car roof and really frightened me to the point I was convinced our newly purchased car was going to look like a colander! I prayed that any damage to the car and me would be minimal, especially as I didn't wish to use the medical services until we had our health cover in place! Ten minutes later the sky cleared and I stepped out onto the flooded tarmac in my flimsy sandals. The car looked totally undamaged and I made my way back to the café in search of comfort and sympathy. Phil was in the exact same place, typing away on his laptop, mind on the job in hand and totally oblivious to the severity of the storm which had passed over!

With so many of our friends and family interested in our move to France and our proposed project to give R&R to military and ex-military personnel, we had to come up with a practical way to keep everyone informed of our exploits. I decided to write a monthly newsletter and dreamt up the title 'Confiance et Rejouir' (the sentiment of assurance in having faith and rejoicing in that assurance), producing the first newsletter on 15th June, twelve days after having stepped onto French soil. We wanted to convey life as it was – not a travel document but simply our day-to-day observations of our surroundings, relationships, challenges and results of having faith in a living God. We believed most of our friends and family would take our prayer requests to heart: to work through the administrative tasks with ease to finalise emigration and for God to direct us to the most suitable property to run our project.

I don't think either of us could have envisaged the number of friends we would make in those first few weeks: British friends in the chaplaincy and in Thors, and French friends. Within a few days we were on first name terms with many of our near neighbours, and we spent many a hilarious moment trying to converse with them, often falling back on the comparison of French customs with British customs as an easy topic of conversation. In discussing sport with our companions at the village Méchoui (sheep roast meal) we asked whether the French played cricket. Our question was met with blank stares and so we attempted to explain the concept of the game and tied ourselves in veritable knots trying to find the right phrases to illustrate the positions of in, out, on and off! After much confusion I thought the only way to get the idea completely across was to draw on the paper tablecloth a cricketer on a cricket pitch, including the stumps and a bowler. I have to admit I was rather proud of my effort. "Eh, bien," declared my neighbour sagely, "I know what you are talking about. I know. I know! It's ping pong." This emphasised the fact that I clearly have no talent for drawing, as I had told my art teacher in secondary school many a time when she had criticised my efforts.

Coincidentally we went to a well-known sports shop in Cognac two days later to order an outdoor ping pong table, ostensibly to keep Amy and her student friends happy during the summer holidays, and we seriously hoped that we had ordered a table tennis table and not a set of stumps and a cable knitted cricket sweater! We have since learned that France has an international cricket team!

We returned to the CPAM office in Saintes to put in motion the process for acquiring our health cards, and had an interview to verify our eligibility to join the French Health Service. Having been warned by British and French friends alike that when visiting any department of authority one must take along every possible important paper or certificate from the Department of Health & Social Security in the UK, UK tax office statements, French utility company bill, birth & marriage certificates, paperwork proving employment status as well as bank details, our dossier was close to bursting, however we were determined to succeed the first time around. After a brief interview and slight wait whilst the requisite photocopying was completed we shook hands with the smiling bureaucrat, who assured us that we would receive our carte vitale – an electronic health insurance card which enables direct receipt of medical treatment – in a few weeks' time (actually a ten week wait!) We were pretty pleased the interview had gone off without a hitch and we had completed the whole task within ten minutes, although Phil joked that he was disappointed that he had not been asked to show the pet hamster's birth certificate as part of the bureaucracy trail.

We were surprised how quickly the paperwork was concluded for leaving the UK and settling in France, and we were fortunate to be able to complete a great deal on the telephone as calls back to the UK were free in our telephone contract. Our post lady commented on the amount of post we received. We were clearly one of her better customers. One letter she brought had us in stitches. It was from South Kesteven District Council, and we had been waiting for several weeks for it to arrive as a result of chasing up a form to prove our eligibility to remain on the electoral register.[10] In a phone call Phil had carefully spelt out our new address in France, letter by letter – or so he had thought – but when the letter arrived several weeks later at our house in 'Rue du Centre' it was rather clear why it had taken weeks to wing/sledge its way to us: it was addressed to us at 'Rue du Santa'.

At the end of June, changing the registration on the car was intriguing too. We automatically drove to Saintes, as that had been the authoritative centre for health, and dutifully reported to the Mairie, only to learn that in this case the Sous-Préfecture in St. Jean d'Angely further north dealt actually with our area of department 17. Of course the usual occurred, and by the time we reached St. Jean d'Angely the Sous-Préfecture was closed for lunch. When it re-opened we produced the paperwork, but they sent us to another office in the town who dealt with importation details. We had no importation documents, but as the car was originally French the extremely nice gentleman said he would simply print off the detail on his computer to help us. Within ten minutes we were back over the road and the lady clerk was now extremely happy with all our documents, except

---

[10] This is possible for fifteen years.

that she couldn't quite verify the engine size of our car to determine the exact cost and, therefore, would we be happy to write her an open cheque? An open cheque to a government office was certainly a first! We were a little taken aback, but she explained that we could expect the cost to be around four hundred and fifty euros. Clearly she was not going to take "non" for an answer so Phil got out his pen and flashed his signature across the cheque. French administration is very different from British administration techniques… Be warned!

Amy joined us from 2nd July planning to spend the summer with us until mid-September. She had just finished her first year at Birmingham University, reading Law with French. We thought it would be really advantageous to have Amy join us in our search for a property, especially as we had already viewed nineteen properties and were convinced we had not seen anything suitable for our needs. We hoped she would be useful in discerning which property might be ideal for the project.

The next day we put this plan into practice and viewed a villa-style property at St. Fort sur le Né. It looked promising, but it did not have an obvious layout to provide a separate annexe for guests. However, Amy was extremely keen and whispered, "Buy it!" to us, which made us laugh aloud as we prescribed her enthusiasm to its attractive swimming pool! A swimming pool was not on our list of priorities, although with the temperatures we were experiencing we could very well understand why so many properties did have pools. However, we were unsure whether St. Fort was right for us, because although the village was located ten minutes south of Cognac, on the route to Bordeaux and the airport, there was only a small general food shop & service station, a doctor, dentist and pharmacy. Hardly the metropolis we had enjoyed in Bourne. There was a small restaurant opposite, but its shutters were down and there was no sign of life so we were convinced it had ceased trading.

Within a couple of days we had viewed twenty-two properties and Amy was heartily sick of the exercise. Yet Phil and I were being cautious, getting to grips with different styles of building, drainage and water systems, heating systems, becoming aware of the problems of keeping a property cool in summer but warm in winter, of termites and other possible infestations, the importance of having a good boulangerie nearby, and which villages were more community minded than others. By looking at many properties it helped us to consolidate our priorities for the project accommodation as well as our personal needs over the next twenty years. We had no desire to move for a very long time having already moved house so many times in the previous twenty-seven years. We came to a conclusion that having a private annex as part of our accommodation would be better than an independent gîte as a lot of our guests would already be experiencing feelings of social isolation, and we wanted to encourage them to socialise again whilst not compromising their need for privacy. God had given us gifts and talents in hospitality and care, and we prayed continually for discernment in recognising the right property to fulfil this ministry, as well as for wisdom and courage to act. God had brought us to a marvellous area, and we were both brimming with good health and fitness as well as feeling such a profusion of joy in our hearts from being so blessed. We did not want to err and let God down in our mistakes, after all he had done for us, by rushing a decision in our enthusiasm and therefore jeopardising the project and our long-term future.

CHAPTER TWENTY-ONE

"For I know the plans I have for you," declares the Lord,
"plans to prosper you and not to harm you,
plans to give you hope and a future."

Jeremiah 29:11

In our search for a property, one kind-hearted estate agent went out of her way to help us. She took us to visit her friends who had reconstructed part of their property to provide two studios in their sous-sol. A sous-sol is a lower floor which is not always immediately evident from looking at the front of a house. Access to the lower floor is either around the back or at the side of the house, normally with a steep drive. It incorporates the garage and a utility area which can also be accessed by an internal staircase.

We were very impressed with what had been achieved, especially as this sous-sol was accessed from the road level, with the main part of the house on the upper level. Such a property would suit the accommodation we wanted to provide, with ease of access for those with a disability. We felt encouraged and from then on factored sous-sols into our viewings.

France has public holidays (jours fériés) rather than bank holidays, on set dates of the year. Only those related to the Christian calendar are moveable; for example Ascension Day, when Jesus Christ ascended to heaven, is thirty-nine days after Easter, and Pentecost, the coming of the Holy Spirit, is forty-nine days after Easter. Easter is a celebration of the resurrection of Jesus on the third day after he was crucified, and Easter was established to be the first Sunday after the Paschal[11] full moon, following the March equinox around 20th March.

---

[11] Paschal or Pascha (and in Hebrew pesach) means Passover, and Jesus shared the Passover meal with his disciples at the Last Supper before he was crucified.

In the UK, if a public holiday falls on a weekend a compensating day is given on the following Monday, but in France no compensating day is set, which can be a cause of much disappointment for many. For example, if July 14th, Bastille Day (known as Fête Nationale) falls on a Sunday, when people do not work and virtually everything is closed, there is no compensating day. To complicate matters further, if a public holiday falls near a weekend many employees and businesses 'faire le pont', meaning they 'make a bridge' and they take the intervening days off work or shut up shop. Therefore a public holiday falling on a Thursday denotes that many services will then be shut for four days! The rules are more relaxed in tourist areas but not necessarily in cities as we have found to our detriment.

July 14th was first marked as a public holiday in France in 1880 by a military parade, and every year a large military parade is held in Paris, with all sectors of the military being reviewed by the President of France, with flypasts from military aircraft in the presence of thousands of spectators and with millions watching the event on television. There is generally a military parade in most towns too and a public recognition of the service the military provide. The date historically relates to militia storming the Bastille, a fortress and prison in Paris, as a pivotal event of the French Revolution.

Our first July 14th public holiday was quiet, and we spent the day pottering in the heat, then drove to the local town of Matha. We had seen a poster in the local supermarket, and from our translation expected a procession with flaming torches. In East Sussex we had gone to many a torchlight carnival in Crowborough with dressed floats and bonfire society members in fancy dress and so we were pretty excited about the forthcoming event.

We arrived in the town at 9.30pm in order to get a good view but were bewildered to discover that the streets were deserted. We sat on a bench wondering if the event had been cancelled, however anticipation mounted when a handful of people appeared and we heard marching music strike up. We went in search of the band, which seemed to be emanating from the Hôtel de Ville, to find a man carrying a boogie box, which he put inside a small white van and then drove off with his hazard warning lights flashing. Out of nowhere lots of children arrived, like a swarm of bees, with their families in tow, and formed a queue outside a garage. Soon each came out into the setting sun, with a colourful Chinese lantern and a flaming candle inside. In fact lanterns were handed out to all, and now we were part of a sizeable crowd. The proverbial centime finally dropped: we were the procession.

We processed through the streets in rather a haphazard fashion, following the stirring sounds from the boogie box of the National Anthem and other traditional marching songs. It became quite exciting as various lanterns went up in flames because the small children were not able to hold their lanterns steady – hence no doubt the flaming procession! With no apparent health and safety directives in operation, the lanterns continued to ignite as naughty boys mischievously set off jumping jacks and people's attention wandered from the danger at the end of their short sticks. Eventually we arrived at a large field where a large crowd were congregating and much to our amazement all sat down on the ground. When we asked why people were sitting down we were told phlegmatically it was necessary for everyone see the fireworks clearly – basically, wasn't that obvious?! We did indeed enjoy a stupendous display of pyrotechnics lasting thirty-five minutes whilst Matha's taxes went up in smoke.

One of the most noticeable, refreshing things which impressed us about the people we met in rural France was the courtesy and politeness afforded to one other. From day one strangers would greet us and say good morning / good day / good evening, whether we passed them in the street or entered a building. We similarly got used to saying goodbye as we left a building to all and sundry too, and soon developed the trick of having a quick glance around a room, mentally checking whether the room consisted of all men, all women, man and women, or men and women in order to get our greeting correct, either Monsieur, Madame, Messieurs (Sirs), Mesdames (Ladies), Monsieur-dame, Monsieur-dames, or Messieurs-dames! It's actually quite an art. Only once did the situation become hilarious when I greeted, unbeknown to me, a British gentleman and his wife correctly only for them to reply to me with gusto, "Bonjour, Monsieur!" and then heard them congratulating themselves in getting the words right!

It was also very apparent that women were women and men were gentlemen, which was refreshing, and the fact that everyone sat down at the fireworks should not have surprised us.

Mid-July we went to view a sous-sol in St. Brice. We had first been sent the details of this house eighteen months previously whilst we had been living in Bourne. Located just on the edge of Cognac, in a picturesque setting close to the Charente River, the layout seemed attractive, especially as the sous-sol was accessed from ground level without a slope which would be ideal for a wheelchair user. We met the agent at the house but the electric gates refused to open, even though the agent changed the battery on the remote control. We made another arrangement to view the following week and met again with the agent who assured us she had easily got the gate to open and close before we arrived. She pressed the remote control but the gates refused to budge. By this time I was convinced that God was warning us away from the house and I wasn't keen to view it, but Phil was and he must have had his hero T-shirt on that day, as he volunteered to scale the wall and try to open the gates from the other side manually. After much ado he succeeded and we went inside. There was not a good atmosphere in the house; it felt cold and unwelcoming, it gave us the shivers, and frankly we could not wait to leave the place quick enough, much to the agent's obvious annoyance – but we were sure God was steering us away.

Once back in our car we decided immediately to see if we could view the house in St. Fort sur le Né, south of Cognac, again. Amy of course was delighted and most keen to have another look at its inviting pool. The owner was home so we 'hotfoot it' to St. Fort. Reassessing the interior, it seemed possible that we might be able to incorporate the large garage, small utility room and a single bedroom to form an annex, still leaving ample accommodation for ourselves. We sketched out the floor plan to consider at home.

We were delighted to see the restaurant opposite was open (it had been shut for a holiday), and not only did we enjoy a delicious lunch but the lady proprietor was extremely friendly and warm in her welcome. As we drove away from the village, Phil and Amy were full of praise for the property and were convinced this was the property, but I suddenly developed real misgivings. The village looked a little tired, and later in discussing the day's events I remarked to them that none of the houses had any flowers, making the village colourless and foreboding. They looked at me in astonishment and vehemently denied that had been the case, and both were staggered with my misgivings. So we continued our search and viewed yet more properties, all of which proved to be non-starters, with the exception of a lovely house which was situated in St. Brice, beautifully decorated and maintained inside and out, with an ideal space to divide the property and form an annex. Oddly its grounds backed onto the 'cold property' with the malfunctioning electric gates. However, the drawback was cost and only a miracle would have allowed us to purchase it, and it really didn't feel as if this was a miracle waiting to happen. From the outset we had set an upper limit for a purchase and nothing would push us over our limit, especially as we needed to incorporate the estate agent's fees (paid on buying in France) and the notaire (solicitor) fees into our sums, which in our case would be 10% of the purchase price. Quite a hefty amount to consider, and we felt beholden to God to be sensible, discerning and mindful of how money was spent.

On the last day of July we viewed the property at St. Fort for a third time. Phil and Amy were convinced it was worth another viewing, and although I was reticent no other property had yet compared with all it offered. Our agent organised a builder to attend the viewing so that he could advise us whether the changes we would want to put in place were feasible and to give us an idea of the cost involved. As we drove into the village the flowers were blooming in profusion, and I didn't feel apprehensive or any bad vibes; on the contrary I felt at ease, and as I walked around, a tingly feeling of anticipation and excitement brewed. The builder was encouraging too.

I believe I can quantify why I was put off the St. Fort property: the Devil was trying to thwart our plans. I am sure he had a hold on that home in St. Brice, and the fact that we began to be interested in the house next to it, which was clearly far too expensive for us, was part of his scheming too. When we are confused, undecided and hesitant, the Devil loves to further his opportunity of wheedling his way into our lives, to upset our equilibrium and faith, tempting us to doubt God and step away from Jesus, to stop listening to the Holy Spirit and to go our own way. Moving closer to God, Jesus and the Holy Spirit keeps the Devil at bay, and then he is the one who withers and fails.

We went home to think seriously about the option of putting in an offer. We collected our post from the postbox and found a letter detailing Phil's new contract with NetJets related to the downturn in the aviation market. He was not going to be made redundant but instead had a new contract: to alternate between having a 'year off' and a 'year at work' for the next 4 years. He would begin his first year off on 1st October and, albeit a substantial drop in his salary, at least he retained a salary. We refused to become anxious about the situation which we could not control and instead regarded the change as a blessing because Phil would have a year off now in order to move into a new home, throw himself into the DIY and set up the project. The timing was perfect.

We put in an offer for the St. Fort property and it was refused. We upped the offer by five thousand euros and the owner stated he was not prepared to accept a lower offer than the asking price, which was just outside our budget. We trusted that if God wanted us to have the property for the project then we would eventually be successful in securing it, and we remained steadfast and calm. What transpired over the intervening days was that the estate agent agreed to take a 'miserable drop' in their percentage so that the sale could be agreed. We and the owner were very happy but the estate agent was crestfallen, yet in any financial crisis a sale is a sale.

We signed the initial paperwork (promis de vente) on August 8th (with further paperwork ten days later and a final exchange detailed for 12th November) and celebrated that afternoon with a visit to the splendid château of La Roche Courbon, north-west of Saintes. Amy took a photo of Phil and me in front of the château, which we later placed alongside an article in our Confiance et Rejouir newsletter with the caption "Right property found at last". We were flabbergasted to receive several emails from people who had been duped into thinking we had bought a château! In our hearts and minds our new home would be Château Jones, but grand floral flowerbeds, spiral staircases and turrets would not be in existence, and moreover we would welcome all without paying an entry fee!

CHAPTER TWENTY-TWO

"Be joyful in hope, patient in affliction, faithful in prayer.
Share with God's people who are in need. Practice hospitality."

Romans 12:12-13

August was extremely busy with house guests. Amy's friends took up the opportunity of ridiculously cheap flights to Poitiers, and we followed a pattern of returning friends to the airport to meet a flight on which more arrived. We had always been used to having lots of visitors at home, however having guests in a foreign country was a different scenario. Yet it was a perfect initiation for continually producing meals for various food intolerances, dislikes and diets, as we might be providing for our future project guests. It also gave the excuse to visit as many local tourist sites as possible as from November onwards (completion of our house purchase) there would be very little time to indulge in such pleasures. We signed up for tours with all the main Cognac-producing houses, visited museums, parks and open spaces, and really got to know the local area within twenty kilometres of Cognac and further afield on the west coast. We particularly wanted to search out a whole variety of activity to suit all tastes and pockets, and collected information leaflets from every source possible to fill a box file.

Each time we went to Poitiers our route bypassed the centre of Melle. The 'Welcome to Melle' sign intrigued us as it promised medieval buildings, much historical interest and a silver mine. Intrigued we took a day out of packing up the rental property to visit this small town. Straightaway, as is our want in every town we visit, we went to the Office de Tourisme to ask for a town plan and enquire whether a walking route existed with marked points of interest. We were handed a colourful brochure detailing a six-and-a-half kilometre circular walk around the town, and the enthusiastic tourist officer explained we had struck lucky in coming to Melle:

there were three beautiful Romanesque churches in excellent condition dating back to the 11th-12th Century, fountains, wash-houses and thousands of trees and shrubs lining a circular trail, with unusual plants every couple of metres which looked particularly stunning in their autumn colours. Thus enthused we went and sat on a bench outside in the sunshine to read the brochure. The opening paragraph in English had us in stitches:

> *"To all nature enthusiasts. Here is served on a bed of greenery, the most delicious puff pastry: the Discovery trail. Pleasures of the senses and pleasures of the essences, as well as pleasure to learn because each species discloses it's identity, for you not to forget. When a leaf tells you about its life it is exciting!"*

Someone had made a valiant effort to convey the sense of wonder and in so doing had mixed up feuilleté (puff pastry) with feuilles (leaves) or feuillu (leafy) and delightful with delicious. With such an introduction we couldn't wait to explore, and we calculated that thousands of euros must have been spent on setting up such a charming walking trail and heritage for the inhabitants of Melle. Half way round the route we did remark that it was a shame the puff pastry was absent because, peckish, we could easily have enjoyed a sausage roll!

Although we were only renting for a few months in Thors we had made the point of introducing ourselves at the Mairie, which we had been told was the correct thing to do. For the same reason I took myself off to St. Fort one morning to pave the way of introduction into the community. Monsieur Dihé le Maire kindly listened to all my questions regarding planning permission for the work we wished to do on the house and gave me a gift of old photographs of the village from the 1960's. I then went into the shop cum post office cum petrol station which was empty on entering but I soon managed to cause a queue of six people by requesting several stamps to send to the UK. The postmistress was unsure of the cost, read through reams of notes in a file and then phoned another branch to ascertain the cost. Everyone was obviously curious and queued happily with ears pricked up when I explained we would be moving into the village next month. Six cheery souls were happy to stand aside patiently and say, "Au revoir!" as I left. I sincerely hoped that the message would get across that it might be a good idea for the shop to order a stash of airmail stamps for future sales.

We were delighted to be surrounded by vineyards, all set out in regular patterns with the vines neatly trimmed and each laden with long, compact and heavy bunches of white grapes – varieties we learned were called Ugni Blanc, Folle Blanche and Colombard – perfect for distilling for the production of eau-de-vie (water of life). Eau-de-vie from many vineyards is mixed to produce certain blends of cognac. The black grapes – far, far fewer in quantity – were related to the pineau production, vins traditional and a refreshing, sparkling, low alcohol grape juice. We purchased a bottle of red pineau from our neighbour, Raymond, and were immediately hooked on its appeal.

Pineau is an aperitif made solely in the cognac-producing areas of the Charente and Charente Maritime. It is a fortified wine made from eau-de-vie and the juice of grape varieties such as Merlot, Cabernet Franc or Sauvignon and aged for fourteen months, with at least eight months being aged in oak barrels. There is a white pineau which resembles sherry, equally delicious, and both pineau are served chilled from the fridge. The grape harvest was expected during the third week of September and we really looked forward to the event, particularly as a neighbour had told us that the noise of the grape presser had to be heard to be believed.

Meanwhile we received yet more paperwork from our Notaire to translate and sign, including a map of all the distilleries close to the property in St. Fort, in order that we were aware of a possible danger of explosion! Rather different from our Bourne estate agent having pointed out flood warnings as Bourne was right on the edge of the Fens.

The grape harvest officially began on 28th September, and many a grape harvest trailer passed the drive full of glistening beads of grapes, from the early hours until late into the night, and the intoxicating aroma from bruised grapes hung in the air. Phil began his year off on 1st October, and what a day he had to mark the occasion, with the highlight being riding on top of Raymond's grape harvester, along with my seventy-nine-year-old father. The excitement on their faces was brilliant to witness, although my mother and I watched with a little trepidation as the machine lurched under an oak tree and they only thought to duck at the last moment. The grape harvester was thirty years old and particularly noisy as it 'picked' the grapes; an impressive machine consisting of metal rods which shook bunches of grapes and caused the grapes to fall off onto a catching tray. Rubber scoops then lifted the grapes off of the tray, then by a conveyor belt into a large hopper, which when full was lowered carefully into the grape harvester trailer. The stems of each bunch remained on the vine with most of the leaves too. The grape harvester sifted out any leaves or debris as part of its mechanical operation. After a couple of trips up and down the rows the grape harvest trailer was brimming to the full and it returned to the farm to transfer them to a pneumatic press which gently pressed them under low pressure to extract as much juice as possible. Gone are the days when the grapes were trodden vertically by bare feet!

Raymond also showed us how he tested each row with a refractometer to test the sugar content in the liquid of a squashed grape in order to determine the optimum specific gravity for being ripe to harvest. He proudly passed us the refractometer so that we could hold the meter up to the light and read for ourselves how successful his 2009 harvest was. Later that afternoon Raymond's wife brought across to the house a huge basket chock-full of four variety of grapes for us to taste and also a two-litre bottle of red grape juice, straight from the press, for us to savour. We poured a glass and toasted the harvest, having first decided to put aside the memory of a snail we had seen chomping happily away inside the harvest trailer before it left for the press!

Phil hung up his uniform in the wardrobe for the year and lost no time in acquainting himself with the various DIY stores; he compared prices and began a list of what we would do first in the house after we had moved in. There seemed an array of tasks to organise but we were not daunted. We started the process of arranging advance appointments for various contractors to come to St. Fort during the week after we had moved in and provide quotes on the work we envisaged was required. We asked our faithful prayer warriors to pray for the right people to be involved with the project and that they would be fair in their estimates, honest in what they could achieve and more importantly to turn up when they said they would.

We visited bathroom showrooms to ascertain which designs would suit someone with mobility problems and decided on having a wet room. Although there were few statistics regarding amputees as a result from conflict, we knew that over fifty armed forces personnel had been given amputations in 2009, which was more than the total figure in the last three years. With the conflict having no apparent end the numbers were likely to increase rather than reduce in number.

We wanted to be able to offer anyone a holiday, regardless of their injury, and spent hours looking at suggested plans to enable a wheelchair to move around the annex easily.

November 12th arrived at long last – the day of the final signing and for receiving the keys to Château Jones. We met at our Notaire's office at 6pm for the appointment with the estate agent along with a work experience colleague, and the current owners whom coincidentally the Notaire was acting for. We all sat around a large oval table whilst the contract was then read verbatim, and we all signed as if we were dealing with an international treaty! There was one slight hiccup because the contract stated:

"Monsieur et Madame Jones-Bowey mariés à la Mairie de Uckfield (Royaume-Uni) le 16 avril 1982."

This states we were married in the Mairie in Uckfield. Umm... actually we could have sworn that we were married in the Registry Office in Crowborough, six miles away (although in the district of Uckfield). However the lawyer explained registry offices do not exist in France, all are married in the Mairie (with some choosing to have a church blessing afterwards), therefore we would have to defer to the law in France. Not wanting to create a stumbling block for the house purchase we agreed to have been married in the Mairie in Uckfield, not wishing to point out that actually it didn't matter as the Registry Office had been demolished to make way for a supermarket!

Eventually the deal was sealed, once we had written a cheque to the previous owner for the equivalent of council tax they had already paid for the last two months of 2009, and the Notaire had passed over a cheque for fees to the estate agent. There was even a clause in the contract stating that the Notaire had not received any back handers from us or, as the Notaire said in English because we were unsure of the phrase, "black handers"! We also signed a prenuptial agreement for the princely sum of seven hundred euros with regard to inheritance law, which was a king's ransom compared with the amount paid to the Registrar in Crowborough in 1982. Finally, after an hour and half, the keys were passed across the table and 3 Impasse de Saint Pierre, St. Fort sur le Né, in the department of the Charente was ours.

CHAPTER TWENTY-THREE

"Remember this:
Whoever sows sparingly will also reap sparingly,
and whoever sows generously will also reap generously."

2 Corinthians 9:6

It was quite extraordinary to reflect on the past eighteen months; how far we had come from my disconsolate life with chronic pain, Phil's rapid change of career, and the birthing of a project. All due to our having moved nearer to God, from our determined attitude to read and listen to his Word, having welcomed Jesus into our hearts with our arms opened wide, and from asking the Holy Spirit to drench our thoughts and actions with his insight. God's comfort and peace had surpassed all human contact and relationships. He had surprised us and delighted us, once we had wholeheartedly acted to deepen our faith and do all we possibly could to share our own experiences with everyone we met. Some I'm sure regarded us as boring in our exuberance to share our joy in the Lord, but to not pass on our experiences would have been selfish. Why would we want to keep such access to unconditional love, forgiveness and power of healing to ourselves? Would you, too, not want to shout it from the roof-tops?

The day we moved into our property, Friday 13th November, was a beautiful, sunny day. With God on our side we didn't need to worry, as many in our culture might have been concerned about the date. We simply prayed for God's safety and protection on our lives and our families, as we do every day with no regard for superstition.

We had hired a large van for the weekend, to move the lighter items and made many trips back and forth to St. Fort from Thors. On one trip we collected a new pool house shed from the DIY store, to replace a large wooden, vermin-infested shed in a very poor state. The beautiful, azure blue swimming pool we had admired in early summer now resembled a stagnant, menacing green, filthy pond. The previous owners had ceased to treat the pool, once they knew we had signed on the dotted line; it was full of leaves, debris and frogs, and pernicious weeds had grown across the terracing up to the pool edge. Later that week we took a sample of the water to be tested and it was so dire that if we had been a public swimming pool we would have been permanently shut down. We didn't fancy putting our hands in the water even with rubber gloves on, so it was pleasing to learn that the testing kit regarded our pool as not suitable for swimming! One only had to look at it to realise that one would not pay to swim in it. After pumping out thirty-five thousand litres from our very acidic pool, which flooded the bottom of our garden, we refilled and added the first treatment which improved the chemical constitution markedly, although the water still remained attractive to wildlife and we were forever fishing out mice and frogs. Our vocabulary regarding all aspects of a swimming pool snowballed and thrived as did Phil's career change – from pilot to pool boy.

Our list of jobs grew lengthy as some items had been taken from the house which we had expected to remain, or they were broken – such as the shower and a part on our only toilet – and then to cap it all, the electric water heater gave up the ghost. Within ten days Phil had bought new shower fittings and dismantled the whole cabinet and rebuilt it from scratch, found the part for the toilet by driving to various DIY stores with half of the toilet in the boot to demonstrate to DIY staff the problem, and he had much success in stopping the leak on the water heater. It was a great day when all three worked and we could reap the benefit of comfortable ablutions!

By the end of November we had worked our socks off with a great deal of basic cleaning and tidying up of the garden. We had cut down fir trees which had been left to grow unhindered and laid weed suppressant around the pool and existing terrace to eventually increase space for relaxing (whatever that meant). Purchasing the pegs to hold down the weed suppressant effectively had been a task in itself as we thought tent pegs the easiest item to do the trick. I had trotted off to the outdoor shop but could not find what I wanted at all and had to resort to miming putting up a tent before the assistant finally reacted by hopping up and down with glee and cried out, "Sardines!" I must have looked deflated as he quickly explained that a tent peg is the same name for a fish. I wasn't utterly convinced especially as he further explained that they were only in stock

140

between March and April. This incident was our introduction to seasonal shopping, and we also found the same was true for frozen – yes, *frozen* – peas!

Gradually we ticked off all the tasks on our initial list, having received endless visits from various builders, plumbers, electricians, chimney and wood-burning stove installers and window fitters. All kept their appointments, although not all produced speedy quotes. All were wonderfully helpful and informative and moreover extremely patient to cope with our limited vocabulary of construction terms. 99% had a great sense of humour, which helped when the dialogue became taxing and our drawing on paper incomprehensible.

In addition we painted inside the wardrobes in three bedrooms and had a very funny incident in trying to purchase an inner shelf unit for one of the wardrobes in our favourite DIY store. The unit in question was boxed up behind a strong link chain, presumably to stop the overlarge, heavy boxes falling and crushing someone. We found an assistant and pointed to the shelving unit asking if we could purchase "cette étagère". He looked at the box, nodded at us and promptly disappeared into the back room, presumably to get the key to release the chain. After a good while passed we went in search of the assistant and found him in his back room staring intently at his computer screen. He looked up and asked us to be patient for a few more minutes. So we went back to the unit, to guard our desired purchase from other customers! Eventually the assistant appeared and announced that he was very sorry to disappoint us but our purchase would not be possible as he could only locate five units, having searched stock in the other stores local to Cognac. We stared at him aghast and stammered that we only wanted to buy one! "One?" he said in equal astonishment. "But you said you wanted to buy seven!" We had used the word 'cette' meaning 'this shelving unit' and he had heard 'sept' which is 'seven'. The two words have nothing to distinguish them in pronunciation but everything in quantity. With a dismissing flourish the assistant flicked the chain back with one finger – embarrassingly no key needed at all! He then walked off back to his room to deal with his computer screen – probably a game of patience – and we struggled to balance the unwieldy shelving unit on top of the trolley, then proceeding to terrorise customers with our inability to steer the large object to the cash desk. Even the simplest French word can cause mayhem!

We chose to treat six days of the week as if we were working for an employer and rose early each morning to get to work on time. We were obviously keen to get the project up and running as soon as possible, hoping in fact that we could be ready for the next season. It was a tall order and the time needed each day to locate DIY materials was totally unforeseen, plus time spent comparing prices from different suppliers. We had not factored in how weary it would make us each evening. Progress was hindered too by our phone and internet not being connected as we had expected it to be. In this age of technology it never ceases to amaze me how tardy the installation of communication services is. We spent a whole month utilising McDonalds in Cognac so that we could hook up to their fast-connecting, free Wifi, often purchasing small coffees rather than spending out on a Big Mac to justify our being there. Also we went to support the local Cybercafé – a time-consuming option as their keyboards were not qwerty but azerty, which changed my fast touch-typing into complete gobbledygook and was terribly frustrating when time was of the essence. However, the internet was a faster way to research products on store websites rather than trekking from one town to another.

In between all the hard work, we were determined to take some time out, and one morning when we checked the letterbox found a leaflet publicising an event to support the Téléthon – an annual fund-raising event in December to raise money for muscular dystrophy, which is broadcast on television. The support of radio stations and community events across France raises millions of euros. St. Fort was doing its bit by holding lotto in the Salle de Fêtes. For the uninitiated, lotto is the equivalent of bingo, and if ever there was a pair completely uninitiated in the realms of bingo, we were that pair, leaving the French poodle to run rings around the British bulldog.

Firstly we made the mistake of arriving ten minutes late as all other French village events we had been to in the past had begun at least half an hour later than advertised. However as we struggled to park the car we realised that this was quite a different event. We elbowed our way into the overcrowded hall, where nearly two hundred bodies of all ages were jammed together on wooden benches and with barely a dividing space between one bench and another. Monsieur le Maire was responsible for selling the lotto cards priced at two euros, and as it was a charity event we splashed out on six cards each. His next question caught us off our guard as he asked us whether we wanted a packet of 'jeu de puce'. We recognised 'puce' as the word for 'fleas' but were very confused as to what Monsieur le Maire was alluding to. With more people waiting to buy their cards, he quickly came to our rescue and showed us a packet of tiddlywinks. Still the penny did not drop, and I asked him in bewilderment, "Do we really need to buy those?" By the looks on the faces of the French around us the Brits were clearly gormless. When we finally understood that the tiddlywinks were for covering the numbers we quickly paid up another two euros for the requisite counters and slunk off to find a space on a bench. We were momentarily embarrassed, but with six cards each we thought we would get our own back and win a prize.

We spread out our cards in front of us haphazardly and sat back to regard our lotto comrades, rather surprised to see that no-one had purchased more than two cards each. That fact should have sounded a warning bell, but before we could give it much thought the lady caller on the stage started to explain the rules. We missed a lot of what she said but understood that we would begin with a line and then afterwards go for a full house.

The whole hall hushed to silence, all eyes down, and she began to turn the antiquated contraption to release a numbered ball. "Soixante-neuf," she called, and with the heat of excitement it was difficult to translate quickly. Phil covered his sixty-nine with a counter and we were off. What we hadn't appreciated was the speed with which the numbers would be called, plus the fact that sometimes traditional calls for various numbers were used which left us pleading with our brains to comprehend. It was then we realised that we were trying to play with too many cards, but we couldn't lose face and soldiered pitifully on.

Suddenly a loud shout broke our concentration and someone had called a line. At last we had a breather whilst the numbers on the winning card were systematically checked aloud by Monsieur le Maire's wife. This at least allowed us to add any counters to our cards which we had missed the first time around, especially as no nicknames for specific numbers were used in the checking process. A line was agreed and a stupendous prize handed out. There was an array of superb prizes, including electrical white goods, food and home appliances, even a weekend break, many food items and therefore nothing but a fervent, competitive atmosphere in the room.

We both felt stressed and our brains were red hot from trying to translate and get the counters down on the relevant cards in time before the caller fired another number at us. The whole proceedings were not helped by the fact that the caller had a dreadful cold and had to stop every now and again to blow her nose, cough and clear her throat, which frightened everyone in the room and made us all jump out of our skins, as she forgot she was millimetres away from a booming microphone. Whilst rather unfortunate that she had a cold, it was to our benefit as it allowed further seconds to try to cover up the right numbers before another number was called. After three hours it got to the stage we could place the counters down in time but were so mesmerised on the task in hand we actually forgot the true object of the game. It was only brought to our attention when our friendly neighbour pointed out that Phil had just missed calling a line! He made it known to all those in the room and the lotto elders came and explained as slowly and loudly as possible that we could not have a prize as we had called late and we really must get it right next time! We could only see the funny side and dissolved in giggles, putting our heads in our hands, which they mistook as disappointment. Another lengthy explanation and apologies given, and the evening resumed with us not even coming close to winning again.

What a fantastic evening though; we won nothing but by the close of play at 1am we had learnt French numbers to perfection. We had sown generously and reaped a bountiful harvest of language skill and new friends. It was a joy to have been among fellow villagers of all ages, from the very elderly to the very small who were wrapped in sleeping bags and bedded down close to the wall, and to see tables of teenagers having a wonderful time without bemoaning the fact they had to go out with their parents and grandparents. We vowed that we would have our wits about us the next time the village staged Lotto!

CHAPTER TWENTY-FOUR

"Therefore I tell you, whatever you ask for in prayer,
Believe that you have received it, and it will be yours."

Mark 11:24

Many non-Christians know that prayer is a part of the Christian faith, especially having heard prayers being said at some time or another in their life. In all probability they learnt the Lord's Prayer at school or perhaps attended a church parade with Scouts, Guides or a similar youth organisation, and have heard specific intercessions in church, when they went to a carol service at Christmas, a baptism, wedding or funeral service. The act of people becoming quiet and still in preparation for prayer would not have passed them by, and on one occasion they might have enjoyed the moment of reflection rather than keen for the moment to be over. They might not be aware that prayer is not just an action carried out by someone in authority (church minister, head teacher etc.) but an individual opportunity for a Christian to communicate with God, in an individual way and at a time of choosing for that individual. For those of us who pray regularly it is a natural continuum from morning until night rather than an add-on or application for occasional use – a major part of the operating function of our faith.

When we come to prayer we come before God completely as ourselves, unique and worthy, just by simply existing as a child of God. It doesn't matter if we speak incoherently, bungle our lines, lose our thought or even fall asleep, because even in the act of falling asleep God is answering our prayer by giving us peace from the burden we are praying about. We can be silent, shout in anger and cry out in anguish, sigh or weep. We can sit, walk, lie down or even stand on our head to pray, whether that is in a purposeful place or simply just where we are at that very moment. God accepts us completely as we are, how we are and where we are. Moreover he wants us to be open, honest and sincere; he wants us to believe in what we are doing and never to feel shy or guilty in asking for help for our own individual needs, as well as for those of other people.

When we begin to pray for the first time it is natural to feel rather embarrassed, conspicuous and a little scared to put ourselves on the line, but if we persevere in praying we learn to listen and to pick up God's direction and his guidance in our hearts. Once prayer has been tried and tested, it readily becomes natural, spontaneous, customary, and instinctive, and then the answers to our prayers materialise! There is no greater encouragement for living or embarking on prayer than having prayers answered. Sometimes we have to wait a very long time for our prayers to be answered, as my experience has shown, but often the reason is because of asking with the wrong motive in mind. Then an individual needs to do some fine tuning to their request, which in addition might require him or her to make a change in attitude, lifestyle or within a relationship (with another person or simply with God himself) before an answer and direction is received. Prayer requires persistence, perseverance and patience, yet make no mistake, when the answers come they are phenomenal, pleasurable and positively encouraging.

With this in mind, as well as us praying ourselves we asked as many people as possible to pray a blessing on our forthcoming project, for the work in the house and the garden to progress well and for our health to remain strong and vital. We prayed for wisdom in organising our work schedule, for honest and hardworking contractors, for the safety and protection of our property, for the stages of planning and building work to run smoothly, for us to master rapidly the complicated vocabulary for the building terms and always to do everything in a respectful and godly way.

One prayer was rapidly answered in the shape of the owner of the sous-sol we had visited back in July. Mel offered his help and support with our renovations, and being an ex-military man he understood our idea for such a project, empathising fully with the need for rest and recuperation. From the word go Mel gave a hundred per cent and was a fantastic encourager for all our plans by his own attitude to follow a job through and succeed in any which way. He taught us all sorts of tricks to various trades and each day we made great strides. We were a good team and had many a laugh, especially in regard to Phil's list and Paulette's list: the extra jobs I added each day as I came up with more and more ideas to complete each room. After a work day had finished around 4.30pm Phil and I would drive off to the local DIY store armed with a long list of essential resources for the next day's schedule so that we could complete the maximum. It was a tiring pattern of events yet we remained healthy and able to cope in every way – further prayers answered – and felt we received praise indeed when Mel said that he "hadn't known folk get on with things so fast".

In the New Year 2010 our request for permission to change the garage into a bedroom and wet room was submitted to the Mairie at St. Fort and, with the project depending upon its success, we began a waiting period of a month to await the outcome of our application. We were confident that all would go well, yet extra prayers were inevitable. That month we could have easily swapped places with the workers on Changing Rooms, DIY SOS or Ground Force because of the scale of dust, dirt and achievement as well as sourcing necessities. As the work continued we became increasingly stronger and fitter, and such was our confidence in keeping healthy we even refused our Grippe A jabs for the swine flu epidemic which had hit Europe with a vengeance.

We decorated two further bedrooms, broke through and destroyed a wall between the kitchen and a bedroom to form a large kitchen / dining room, built a wall between the kitchen and sitting room (which had previously been open plan), removed another wall in a study to form a dining area within the proposed new annex, moved a loft hatch from the garage to the hall, stripped the walls in the cloakroom, and built a frame to mount a corner wash hand basin, as well as moving several electric radiators and adding further sockets and lights. We shifted barrow-load upon barrow-load of turf and soil in readiness to construct a private terrace for our future project guests and to erect a large shed (euphemistically called a pool house as it housed the pool pump and plumbing) on the newly constructed concrete base. We had a very amusing time destroying the old wooden shed, despite some parts being a beast to take down, because in nearing the end of the task Phil enjoyed a Buster Keaton moment. Whilst I gripped tightly to what Phil thought was an unsecured side there followed a huge crash and bang as the other side of the shed smashed to the ground, fortunately narrowly missing by a whisker all the delicate parts of the pool pump and pipe work. The instructions for the new metal shed clearly stated it would take two men six hours to complete; however, realistically it took two men and one woman eight hours to erect. The task of adding hundreds of fiddly screws and washers fell to one woman, and that morning turned out to be an experience I wouldn't wish to repeat. Whilst I was on task inside the shed, a fast jet practicing combat manoeuvres high overhead went through the sound barrier. The bang was frightening from inside the metal shed, and I was convinced for a second that all our fine work was about to be destroyed in a second as the shed walls appeared to suck in and then explode outwards. My fiddly nuts and bolts were scattered across the shed floor.

Four stère (1 stère = 1 cubic metre) of oak logs were delivered by a local woodman, and we proudly built a neat wood stack to rival our neighbour's pile, which must have looked extremely strange to them and any passers-by as we had no chimney or fireplace. We cut down two lengthy, tall leylandii hedges, reducing them by a half, and began to dig a thirty-five centimetre trench across the lawn for the pool electrics which had previously been set only a few centimetres below the turf. We removed several diseased ornamental trees and planted a selection of fruit trees – apricot, peach, greengage, cherry, apple and pear – and dreamt of the laden crops we would harvest.

We had little success though with a rotavator we had borrowed to turn over a large area for a potager – a vegetable garden which includes ornamental plants. Due to our heavy soil, a mix of clay and limestone, the neat furrows Phil had envisaged producing with ease remained a pipe dream because the rotavator was impossible to manage; the difficult, glutinous soil clung relentlessly to the blades. Phil gave that up as a bad job, and instead we set to work with a spade and dug over a small area to at least begin the semblance of vegetable garden. Our vision for a smart-looking potager bursting with organic vegetables, to boost the diet and health of our guests, would become a slow advance. We sensibly decided to leave the major work until the spring and instead turned our efforts to decorating our bedroom. We could put up with a potager looking as if it had been trampled by a herd of cattle, but to rid one bedroom of two hundred galloping horses, which had been the last occupant's choice of wallpaper, seemed a far greater achievement.

Phil also purchased a mini filtration unit, to plumb in at the point of entry for the water supply into the house, and he was awfully glad he had taken the trouble to look up the word for 'scale' and 'to fur up' and had learnt the correct pronunciation. The word for 'scale' is 'entartrage', which is only one letter more than the word 'entartage' which means 'custard pie attack'!

Phil and Mel were keen machine operators – it is said men like their tools – and the machine I came to loathe was the angle grinder. It was a necessary tool in order to remove floor tiles so that partition walls could be added or removed. The property had been tiled throughout before any of the interior walls had been constructed, and the angle grinder was also useful in removing damaged tiles before re-tiling. One corner of the garage was stacked with an assortment of leftover tiles and building materials left by the previous occupants, and for the first three months of our renovations we were able to use up every spare tile. This was a huge blessing as we didn't have to spend time sourcing or purchasing new tiles, and it never ceased to amaze us how the right number of tiles were always available to finish a job.

One day a week we chose to have a day off from the physical work and selected a location to do a day's sightseeing, not only for our interest but to become more accustomed with what our area had to offer future guests. Some days we just got to know Cognac better or used the day to deal with the various French authorities, such as the occasion when we went to the Sous-Préfecture in Cognac (the building which houses the administrative offices) to swap our UK driving licenses for French ones. On entering the building people were standing around the room, looking worryingly resigned, so we hovered in the background at what we thought was the end of the queue. Suddenly a voice bellowed at us from behind a glass-fronted counter and a stern looking Madame demanded for us to come forward. We applied our usual cheery smiles and happy voices and thus reduced the 'scary monster' to a pussycat, filled in endless forms in triplicate, surrendered our European British licences and eventually paid her colleague a stash of euros for the privilege of receiving another European driving licence. Many of the same people were still sat around but somehow we had managed to beat them to the finish by getting our paperwork back first. In return for our confiscated English licenses we were given a handwritten note to show a gendarme if we should be stopped. As this happens frequently in France, we were not utterly convinced a handwritten note would suffice a strict control check of our car; it didn't seem very official or adequate in comparison to the reams of paperwork we had just completed! Our new driving licences arrived in the post a week later, and what was undoubtedly official was the fact that they had been stamped up, authoritatively, for us to drive not only a car but twelve tonne trucks, smaller lorries, coaches and minibuses! In view of the work we were undertaking, to be able to drive a large truck might prove very useful. Our driving licences were a great source of amusement for many of our French friends, including one elderly gentleman who had once been a police officer and who was astounded with our preferential treatment when he had only ever been allowed to drive a car!

We finally got around to buying a TV aerial and hooked up to the French broadcasting stations. Most of our ex-pat friends could not believe we managed without British TV stations, yet we argued it would improve our French by leaps and bounds... and so it did. We soon got into a habit of watching certain geography programmes with Thylassa, all about the sea and coast – a great favourite as there were many beautiful places to admire and little description to manage. By chance we discovered a weekly gardening programme and became quite fanatical about a quiz programme just before the evening news. We always turned on French subtitles and this enabled us to learn the pronunciation of words as well as the written form. Bizarrely, one afternoon I flicked on the TV to accompany a pile of ironing and watched Countdown broadcast at a similar time as in the UK and in a similar format. When I explained to my neighbour how pleased I was to have discovered a popular British programme, I learnt to my embarrassment that 'Des chiffres et des letters' – 'Numbers and Letters' – is the original version of Countdown and had run on French television continuously since 1965!

More egg on our faces, although not as much as when I popped into our village shop and, chatting cheerily to the owner's wife, enthused that we only came into the shop to see her lovely smile (sourire). She suddenly stopped still and stared at me very blankly and in embarrassment explained that I had just said it was a joy to come in the shop and see her lovely mouse (souris)! Typically a couple of people were in the shop to witness my faux pas. We continued to make our mark on the village in many ways, big and small.

We were so blessed with excellent weather to get on with all the jobs. We were even able to lunch on the terrace from the beginning of February, which was a lovely welcome break away from chaos, dust and more dust. Although the winters are cold in the Charente, often dropping as much as -10, the early morning skies are generally clear so that a sunny day ensues and the temperature pulls up to something bearable. Being a much drier climate than the UK, ice on the roads is a rare occurrence and therefore there is no gritting of roads or pavements in our area. This does of course mean that on a rare occasion when there is moisture on the roads and it freezes, only a mad man would venture out.

On February 11th we received a hand-delivered letter from the Mairie which I opened with trepidation, and rightly so, as what I read filled me with doom and gloom. The form inside the envelope was to do with our application for constructing the annex, and the letter began with the word 'ARRÊT' in bold capitals. I knew very well that meant 'STOP'! Oh, what despair and despondency! I felt as if the wind had been snatched from our sails, and I sank into the armchair feeling suddenly really downcast and miserable. I called out to Phil the awful news – how very dreadful, and what on earth were we going to do now? Fortunately Phil is far less reactionary – laid back – and when he looked at the letter in full the back page seemed to suggest we had actually received the permission to proceed. So why arrêt/stop? We pulled our trusty friend out of the bookcase – the heavy and cumbersome dictionary – and learnt to our absolute relief that a second meaning of 'arrêt' is simply 'judgement or decision', and judgement had been made to proceed.

We celebrated with some bubbly and got straight on the phone to our family to tell them the good news. We even started the process of booking a trip back to the UK as we didn't expect to hear from the builders for ages, especially as many people had painted a negative picture of getting work done in France. However, God's perfect timing pushed the idea of a visit back to the UK aside because Claude, the building firm owner, phoned that evening to say his men would be with us the following morning. Oh ye of little faith! After the initial panic of taking on board this fact, we set to work in the dusk and dark to clear the garage of all our belongings, only just managing to shoehorn everything into the new pool shed.

On February 12th the builders arrived at 8.15am, as promised, and by the end of the day they had most efficiently blocked up the garage doorway and the previous entrance into a small utility room and opened up a new window and doorway in the back of the garage. Three days later they returned and prepared all the new plumbing for a wet room in the annex and the outside drainage to join up to our current septic tank system, as well as similar work for a toilet we were adding to our own bathroom. We were thrilled at the speed and progress of work so soon after the judgement had been received.

Each day the builders worked until 6.15pm and expected nothing from us. They followed a very committed work ethic and thought it very odd when we offered them a hot drink, explaining that it was not customary for a French worker to have a break other than their authorized longer lunchtime break. However, they quickly became used to homemade soup and fruitcake being brought out to their truck at lunchtime to supplement the meal they cooked up on a camping gas stove balanced precariously inside on the dashboard of their truck!

By 17th February a window was installed in the bedroom area in place of the previous garage door, another in the wet room and also a glass entrance door. The following day they put in patio doors to replace a window, our side of the house, where we had incorporated a bedroom into our kitchen / dining room. The effect was superb, and practically we now had a backdoor leading out to a terrace where previously the back garden could only be accessed impractically through the sitting room. We felt really elated on 23rd February when the builders broke through from the bedroom / wet room area into the main part of the house, which meant that the former study and utility room were now part of the annex. The main building work had been completed in five days, and Phil and Mel could begin to start work putting up the frames for the plasterboard walls. The builder had originally quoted for all the finishing work but he was perfectly happy for us to pick and choose which parts we wanted to complete ourselves, which kept costs down. We informed everyone who came on site why we were doing the project and they were all interested and gave their support to our idea. The French military had suffered eighty-eight losses in Afghanistan and our workmen knew about the dreadful injuries and psychological traumas associated with combat, which had been well documented in the media.

Before we had moved out to France we had been members of the Armed Forces Christian Union and an Associate Prayer group made up from members living in the South Lincolnshire area. Once a month we met in a member's home and prayed for all three services of the British military, as well as a number of serving personnel who had asked to be linked to a group for prayer. Phil and I were keen to set up our own group in France, and the first meeting of the Poitou-

Charentes Associate Prayer Group went ahead mid-February. We were thrilled that it was so well supported. Many of our members had no direct contact with the military, with only a couple of ex-servicemen making up the group, others with family members serving in the Armed Forces, but most importantly the common denominator was a willing heart and mind to pray. We also shared fellowship afterwards over a two-course lunch, which Phil and I happily provided as many travelled a long way to join us each month. We all felt as if we were doing something positive, using spiritual potential to assist in situations which were beyond our comprehension and experience.

Later that month 120 km/h winds were forecast for the evening of 27th February, and a terrible storm hit most of France, as it motored north-east from the Bay of Biscay. The sea whipped up into a frenzy, and tremendous waves, coupled with an exceptionally high tide, breached sea defences, flooding three thousand homes in a quarter of an hour. We had taken the trouble the previous night to batten down as much as we could, but the noise of the wind kept us awake from midnight until 4am, when we finally lost electric power. The following morning we had escaped damage, but our neighbour's rotary washing line had been twisted in the wind to resemble a wrung out dishcloth and their shutters had been damaged. With power not being restored until 5.30pm the next day, we were unaware of the full extent of the destruction and tragedy. Only when we were able to switch on the news did we realise that we had paid a very small price compared to the coastal areas of the Charente-Maritime and the Vendée. Cyclone Xynthia was so violent that fifty-one people had lost their lives and President Sarkozy declared it a national disaster. Across much of the coastal region there are hectares of oyster beds, and it was a double tragedy for them, with flooding and damage coming on top of low yields due to a virus which had attacked the oysters. Huge areas of reinforced concrete on some of the low-lying islands, such as Ile de Ré, had been ripped apart and reduced to rubble, and we could not imagine the fearful time those inhabitants had suffered.

Two days later we spent a wonderful afternoon in the garden, planting onions and herbs in the potager and finished off the paving for the guest terrace. The terrible events at the coast were forgotten whilst we worked in glorious sunshine until we watched the evening news on television later that evening and all the horror the victims continued to experience was evident before our eyes. La Tranche-sur-Mer had been flooded with water levels rising to 1.5 metres, and we found it difficult to envisage the lovely seaside town where we had enjoyed two family camping holidays scarred by the tragedy. As survivors tried to fathom the devastation to their homes and the environment, they also faced the threat of eviction orders and an order for demolition, whilst we were building up our home and enjoying the pleasure of doing so. Their loss of home and livelihood was a huge contrast, and the small donation we sent to the victims' fund seemed a pathetic gesture. The largest gesture we could offer was a commitment to pray for them.

CHAPTER TWENTY-FIVE

"When Moses' hands grew tired...
Aaron and Hur held his hands up –
one on one side, one on the other –
so that his hands remained steady till sunset."

Exodus 17:12

In our monthly newsletter we had suggested that if anyone would like to come out and support us in our work to set up the project we would welcome them with open arms! The February team (Diana and Hywel) and March team (Sue and Chris) both came for a week, and it was great to have lovely friends visit us and encourage us. We were thrilled by their enthusiasm to come across and help us, and thanks to their marvellous effort a great amount of sterling work was achieved. The sitting room was stripped of wallpaper in readiness for painting, a tall hedge reduced in size, a large awning fixed, outside lights put up, walls and ceilings painted, a previous grassed area dug up and prepared with weed suppressant for an area of gravel, and the dreaded trench finally finished housing the pool cable. That particular job had taken weeks as the heavy, sticky soil proved a nightmare to work with whether wet or dry. The tatty-looking electric heaters in the sitting room were removed and saved from the scrapheap by cleaning them up and, following Chris's excellent suggestion, re-sprayed successfully. We aimed to work hard and play hard, and therefore planned sightseeing trips every other day in the hope that our guests would not feel they had to go home for a holiday!

On one of our days off, we took Sue and Chris to the Repas de la Chasse – the annual hunt meal – to experience local hospitality at its best. The menu consisted of vegetable soup, seafood platter, huntsman's stew (venison and wild boar), roast beef, cheeses and coffee accompanied by a selection of three small gourmet desserts all washed down with copious amounts of cognac, wine and champagne.

We had to admit defeat when the champagne was being opened, and staggered back home slightly inebriated and definitely fit to burst. Chris decided that this sort of event could only be weathered once in a blue moon. We could only laugh, and explained it was typical of any French meal. (We can only emphasise that training for such an event is essential, which consists of going to as many meals as possible!) Our friends had been astonished by everyone's friendliness even with the language barrier, as people had made a real effort to introduce themselves and include us in their conversation. Such events were broadening our circle of acquaintances and made us feel very much a part of our village.

Each town, village and hamlet has a hunting fraternity and a national federation closely guards all the activities of the hunters with stringent rules and regulations. The documentation pertaining to the law is published on the noticeboards outside every Mairie, and the seasons for hunting are governed by the ecological needs of an area.

The hunting fraternity hunt in small white vans, wearing combat gear or in fact anything green for camouflage, on top of which they add a vibrant fluorescent orange vest, so generally the wildlife can see them coming! They mostly all have a scent hound and seem to spend a lot of time standing around chatting with their guns unprepared but shooting the breeze about the one that got away. A partaker of the hunt meal had asked us, "What do you get when you add ten fishermen to ten hunters?" We hadn't known and he was thrilled to answer: "Twenty liars!"

By late March a local firm had constructed a chimney and fireplace in the sitting room and the result was a joy to behold. The mantelpiece looked the perfect height in proportion to the room, despite our previous reservations when we had looked at the plans prior to signing. The owner of the firm explained at the time that it had to be the perfect height to be able to lean an elbow on whilst standing by a warm fire with a glass of cognac! Now why hadn't we thought of that?! We couldn't use the fire for fifteen days, to allow it to set and settle, but it felt really good just to sit beside it and imagine a roaring fire in the wood-burning stove. At long last the large store of wood on the drive looked purposeful for the impressive new chimney rising above our roof.

With the fireplace completed I finished decorating the sitting room – a large room of 35m² with a ceiling of equal size. I struggled and struggled to paint it to my satisfaction. With two sides having patio doors the light showed up all my imperfections and I just became more and more frustrated with every attempt. My arms ached and ached from being in one position all the time, whether I painted with a paintbrush or a roller. After my fourth attempt (I don't give up easily) and 140m² of dissatisfaction I arranged for a professional to do the job, which was a huge improvement.

Our April team was made up of family helpers: Amy and my parents, who simply would not go home at the end of their stay! On their desired date of departure they were stranded without a flight home, due to the effects of two volcanic eruptions of Eyjafjallajokull, in Iceland, on 14th April. The ash cloud caused large-scale disruption to flights across Europe and closed air space until 20th April; such an extent of disruption had not been experienced since the Second World War. The April team had to wait five more days to return home but their flight cancellation was our blessing as they rallied to help us.

Just before Easter, Amy had learnt that her third year of reading Law with French would consist of an Erasmus year (a European student exchange programme) at Montesquieu University (Bordeaux IV). We were delighted at the thought of her being able to study so close to us in France for a whole year, and we were amazed to think how she would be closer to us at Bordeaux than we had been to her at Birmingham when we had lived in Lincolnshire. It was another wonderful blessing for us, and whilst she was with us in April we were able to take her to Bordeaux and look for student accommodation in preparation for her starting the first term in September. She and Phil toured various dubious digs whilst I took my parents on a tour of the public parks, which included the impressive garden of the Hôtel de Ville, Bordeaux's city hall. Just inside the western entrance we were surprised to see an enormous sculpture of the opening jaws of a crocodile (by Guillaume Renou) which reached eight metres high towards a brilliant blue sky. The sculpture was made of fifteen thousand iridescent stainless steel pieces of green, purple, blue and orange, and fifty huge white teeth gleamed menacingly in the sunlight. The crocodile rose out of pond, and we sat down on a bench to admire the splendid sight. I explained to my parents that the current Monsieur le Maire of Bordeaux was Alain Juppé, a former Prime Minister of France under President Jacques Chirac, and just as I was finishing my explanation a suited gentleman passed by and acknowledged us with, "Bonjour Monsieur-dames!" It was none other than the aforesaid Monsieur! Open-mouthed we watched him walk up to a TV crew, which we had completely missed seeing in our wonder of the crocodile, and an extremely smart, young lady presenter, who looked every bit the part of Mademoiselle Efficiency, began an interview with him. All ran smoothly for a couple of minutes until an elderly dame hastened on the scene and pushed between the Mademoiselle and Monsieur Juppé, and shook his hand with much enthusiasm. This clearly knocked the young woman off her stride, and she was left stranded with her notes whilst the elderly dame launched her points and had her say. Monsieur le Maire of Bordeaux, with many years of office behind him, didn't seem fazed in any way, and he remained courteous and patient until the elderly dame tottered on her way. The young lady, with far fewer years' experience, having lost her moment of glory, seemed more than a little cross and looked as if she could envisage the perfect victim for the snapping jaws of the crocodile.

By the end of April virtually all the contractors had completed their work, whilst Phil and Mel had worked really hard putting up plasterboard and building an interior wall to separate the wet room from the bedroom. Having made so much progress we took time out, on a public holiday, to go across to the restaurant 'La Pierre Levée' in our road, to celebrate Brin d'Aillet, which is the custom of welcoming in the new garlic in the Charente, with eighty-six other villagers. Aillet is immature spring garlic which is eaten raw in a starter accompanied with grillon, a local regional dish of minced pork and ham which resembles a rough textured paté. We enjoyed a super meal, including steaks BBQ'd superbly which Chef Michel cooked over the embers of grapevine, which imparted a delicious flavour. We sat next to a family who owned a vineyard, and they shared their hard-working lives with us. We had so many questions regarding the pruning of the vines that we ended up covering the white paper tablecloth with drawings to get our questions across. It was so much fun and the whole afternoon wonderfully convivial, until Michel decided to offer a kilogram of homemade grillon to the person present who had travelled the furthest that day. Because everyone was local there followed noisy discussion, chunter and argument as to who lived further away, until Michel in desperation said, "Forget that; who lives the closest?" We sheepishly put our hands straight up, and the room stunned to an unnerving silence as the Brits claimed the treasured, prized grillon.

A few days later Phil jetted off to the UK having learnt his father was seriously ill in hospital. We were extremely thankful that he could get a flight at a moment's notice, although it meant that the Deputy Project Manager immediately gained unwanted promotion! The time Phil was absent passed quite well, except I wished I had heeded more notice in my French lessons. The plumber was unimpressed with having to deal with a clueless Madame, but I was pretty sure technical plumbing vocabulary had not been covered in my lessons. On Phil's return he fitted loft insulation over the whole roof space, and because our roof is low pitched he became very adept at removing roof tiles in order to place the insulation in the roof from the comfort of being on top of a stepladder, instead of trying to squeeze in between the rafters in a difficult attic space.

We purchased all sorts of aids for the wet room to assist people with mobility problems, which took a great time sourcing exactly what we wanted to provide. We had no wish to exclude anyone from being able to use the annex facilities and considered every possible need. It was our constant prayer to get everything right; we couldn't bear the thought of marring our future ministry. I'm sure we wasted time discussing minute details, and God was probably shouting down, "For my sake, get on with it!"

By the end of May five rooms were decorated in addition to all the progress we had made in the annex. To completely finish a room gave us tremendous satisfaction, although it was always the achievement in mastering the niggling, smaller jobs which gave us the wow factor, as they were madly responsible for impeding the progress of the bigger tasks. We searched and searched for an interior door for the wet room, the right size to allow the use of a wheelchair yet also light in weight for someone to open easily. The choice seemed very limited with perhaps only one door being on display in the DIY stores, but that mystery was solved when we went back to Mr. Bricolage and interrupted two assistants having a gossip in one of the aisles: "Bonjour Mesdames, where can we find interior doors please?" Much to our consternation they giggled uncontrollably and then said in unison, "Exterior! Outside!" Yes, indeed, interior doors were outside with the exterior doors... French logic is often very perplexing.

On 3rd June we celebrated living in France for a whole year – an immense year of joy in a new country, with a new aim for the future and exactly two years from having had an appointment with the Pain

Management team to attend a pain management course. How our lives had changed! It was a beautiful day – a pleasant 26°c – but work was planned as usual. In the morning I painted our kitchen a bright yellow with one wall brilliant Tuscan orange, to reflect the warmth of the sunshine and with the orange glow to make the room feel warm in winter. Then we spent the whole of the afternoon laying out a vast sheet of pool bubble cover to try to cut a perfect shape to produce a bespoke pool cover. A pool cover has the benefit of keeping in the heat as well as reducing the loss of heat overnight as the air cools, so it made perfect sense to have one, but our swimming pool is a strange shape and very irregular; therefore to have a bespoke made would have been very expensive. It was difficult to measure the shape of the pool; our impatience rose with the heat and we soon struck off making bespoke pool covers as a sideline, despite the fact the finished product saved us a whopping two hundred euros. Our aim was to keep the water temperature at an optimum so that we, and our visitors, could enjoy the pool fully.

A forestry team arrived from Aslackby in Lincolnshire, ably and enthusiastically led by our friends Chris and Jacqui, the third team to answer the call for help with our project. They worked incredibly hard. Chris worked tirelessly and expertly in very hot weather, thinning out part of our bottom boundary and felling several extremely tall trees. He showed great skill in managing to bring down all the trees exactly and perfectly, which particularly thrilled Phil as our ugly and badly constructed wood store remained intact. Phil and Chris then chain-sawed the wood into suitable length logs for the wood burner, and the remaining brushwood grew and grew to a pile taller than the house and thirty feet across at the base. It looked a little as if we had gone one step forward and two back because the mountain of brushwood was now a greater eyesore than the dilapidated wood store. Phil spent hours cutting branches to produce thinner logs for burning, not wishing to waste any of this bountiful resource, but the huge pile refused to reduce much in shape or form. Fortunately for us, the indefatigable Shoobridge team came in July and axed, sawed branches, filled the wood store with kindling and fed a borrowed shredder for days until the enormous pile was merely a memory. They sensibly worked early in the morning as the temperatures rose quickly (one day to 35°c); we fitted in sightseeing and many lazy hours under the awning on the terrace or in the pool as if we too were on holiday. We were very glad and humbled by the amount of work all our helpers had accomplished, especially when they had chosen to have a holiday helping us instead of jetting off to a more interesting location. All the teams' help allowed us to make great strides forward, forced us to take some time out and served to involve more people in our ultimate goal of getting the project up and running. Even those visitors who were not up to heavy manual work were a wonderful help with a number of jobs to improve the garden, watering the vegetables each evening in our potager and the many pots around the house, helping to prepare food in the kitchen or simply just clearing up. This meant so much to us as more items were ticked off our lists. We thanked God for our good Samaritans, for the way they supported us and kept us going when our hands and arms were weary, and not least for the fun and laughter we enjoyed in being together. We really couldn't have been more blessed, and we prayed that they would be equally blessed in their own ventures and also thanked God that all our helpers stayed safe and avoided accidents, although rather tongue in cheek we produced a photograph for the July newsletter with Sandra, the shredder queen, pretending her arm had been pulled into the shredder with grave consequences. We did add a proviso that "all our guests go home rested and in one piece".

Our potager had metamorphosed from a miserable sight into a large area of impressive growth with French beans and runner beans galore, spring onions, peppers, courgettes and numerous tomatoes. We even had a fine looking row of parsnips and hoped they would last into the winter as parsnips are rarely obtained locally and never the size of root we used to enjoy in the UK. Why we were dreaming of roast parsnips when the temperatures refused to budge below 30°c makes little sense! Our elderly neighbour, while admiring the lush vegetation, told us that our plot of land had been sold for building because it was deemed unproductive, even for vines. That fact made us even more determined to beat the odds and succeed. We dug trenches in between the rows of vegetables and filled them with our kitchen waste, garden cuttings, vacuum cleaner waste bags, fabric trimmings and paper we had shredded for security, in an attempt to lift the fertility of the soil. Everything went straight into the ground and, warmed by the sun, decomposed quickly. We dismissed the use of a compostor in a bid to cut down on the amount of effort that was required in managing a good heap. Our time was constantly in short supply and, once the project was up and running, would continue similarly, so the more we could plan garden management to the minimum the better.

A lot of time was also spent in travelling to various airports to pick up or return our visitors – not that we minded in the least and it was excellent practice in readiness for our project guests. One trip to Poitiers (two and a quarter hours' journey north) proved that it really paid to go to the airport. Just as we were in the process of saying goodbye to our friends we were taken aback when a traveller, wishing to avoid an excess charge on his baggage, thrust a bottle of rosé into Phil's hands. The gentleman was adamant his well-chosen bottle should go to a good home, and thanking him we laughed all the way back to the car park at our good fortune. Later we sat in the sunshine, toasted the mystery gentleman and admired the beautifully clear expanse of garden down and across to the wood store, which Phil had smartened up by replacing some of the dilapidated planks and treating it to preserve its life. We recalled a visit to a DIY store and an enquiry to the smiling, seemingly untroubled female running the customer service desk where we could locate wood preservative. She became very red in the face and quite incoherent of speech, which left us very confused, so we asked the question again as clearly as possible and loudly. She immediately rang a bell and her supervisor quickly arrived. The blushing lady mumbled our request to him and then he turned to us and said that we had just asked for a wooden condom! Who was blushing now?

The same DIY store clearly didn't hold the faux pas against us because the same month when we discovered we were short of one wall tile for the wet room, a shop assistant helping Phil to locate the correct design of tiles unearthed a box from the shelf, ripped open the top of the box and allowed Phil to have just one tile. Phil should have paid for a whole box of sixteen but instead he came away with a free gift and much astonishment. We could not imagine this turn of events in England.

Our joy for our amazing life in France had taken us to a new level and we felt we were living in Eden, when we were struck by an immense sadness: the heartbreaking news that Major James (Josh) Bowman, commander of A Company, 1st Battalion Royal Gurkha Rifles, along with two of his colleagues, had been shot by a renegade member of the Afghan National Army. We had been praying for James in our Armed Forces Christian Union Associate Prayer group; his aunt and uncle are members and through them we had been getting to know him. It was difficult to get on with everyday tasks when this tragic news was constantly in our minds. We thanked the Lord for James' love of the Army, his recent role in Afghanistan and career, his trusty Gurkhas, his keenness to serve Queen and country, and for all he had achieved in his short thirty-four years. We prayed diligently for his whole family, not only for their upset and loss but also for them to be able to cope with all the invasive media attention surrounding their devastating bereavement. Our prayer group gained strength in the special bond of fellowship Christians share, and we turned to our Bibles, especially the psalms, to help heal saddened hearts and be restored with hope. Before Jesus died on the cross he spoke of the grief and despair his followers would suffer in his absence yet he impressed upon them to keep in mind the ultimate purpose of spreading the Good News, in continuing the work he had begun. Grief has its purpose, and by talking with God the burden and anguish can diminish. God is the ultimate provider of peace and solace, and in becoming close to him it is possible to see a way forward, to carry on living and working. We became closer as a group, more unified in purpose, perceiving like Moses that our brothers and sisters in Christ can be at our side to hold us up and to keep us focused on the Lord, the one who knows our burdens inside out.

CHAPTER TWENTY-SIX

"May the favour of the Lord our God rest upon us,
establish the work of our hands for us –
yes, establish the work of our hands. "

Psalm 90:17

We really struggled to work in the July heat; it was draining, exhausting and frustrating. Tiles refused to stick fast to the wet room wall; they slipped and slid in all directions, assisted by the extra heat given off from the ceiling spotlights. Outside work was just as fruitless; we tried to lay down slabs to continue the path around the house, for ease of access if a guest visited with a wheelchair, but it became a race against time to try to heave them in place before the foundation mixture dried out. Defeated, we thought there was no other alternative but to accept our schedule would slip a few weeks and get right away from the work. Therefore, a few days later we headed north-west to the Marais Poitevin region, a vast thirty five thousand hectares of marshland, crisscrossed by numerous small canals, dykes and ditches, with pockets of drier land forming island areas for cattle and sheep to graze. The French call the area 'La Venise Verte' (Green Venice), and very green and picturesque it is with attractive villages catering for tourists wishing to hire bicycles, rowing boats and flat-bottomed boats resembling punts.

One afternoon we visited Coulons, the capital of Venise Verte, a remarkable village with many historical buildings dating back to when it was the centre of busy navigation, transporting of all manner of goods. Now many of the old buildings are restaurants and quaint shops selling regional fayre, including the specialty crystallised angelica, which has been cultivated in the area since 1602. We were fascinated by the area's history, and instead of hiring a punt, booked a ride with a guide. He punted us plus two other couples along a route under low bridges along a network of waterways for over an hour, and we not only learnt a great deal about the history of the locality but also the care which was being undertaken to preserve the region. Some of the dykes between the main waterways were extremely narrow with overhanging branches of trees swooping down across the water. It was a relaxing and fun trip with all the ducking and diving beneath the vegetation, as well as there being a surprising moment when we were asked to peer closely over the edge of the boat, our chins level with the water, whilst the guide stirred it up with his punting pole and then struck a match to set light to the air just above the water! The quick flash of flame was surprising, probably due to the presence of methane from the stirred up rotting vegetation in the shallows, and the trick detracted a little from the beautiful scenery as we wondered whether we might lose our eyebrows or topple into the murky water!

The weather was perfect and we decided to try camping. We owned a small dome tent which had only been used over the years for the children to play in the garden, but we couldn't foresee any problem in using it with such lovely dry weather. Phil's reduced salary and our 'giving' to get the project up and running meant we could not afford to spend out on expensive holidays to far off places. We thought that if we discovered a love of camping to suit our taste for the outdoors and a holiday to suit our budget then we would be very content.

The campsite was peaceful and strangely quiet bearing in mind it was July when virtually the whole of France went on holiday (according to the number of shops and businesses running on a skeleton staff, with many businesses closed for three weeks).

It took us no time at all to set up our itsy-bitsy tent, a folding table and chairs. With less than 4m² floor space in the tent, virtually all our belongings had to stay in the boot of the car. We must have looked very amateurish with few camping extras, but we had a lovely few days in the open air and three superb nights' sleep. The only problem we encountered on the first morning was our inability to get up and out of the tent! It wasn't easy to develop enough spring from our blow-up mattress to catapult ourselves out through the small entrance flap of the tent, especially as the tent was only a metre in height. Each morning we suffered awful cramp trying to get up and out, and our feeble attempts resulted in many an ungainly position on the damp dewy grass. Our cramped camping experience highlighted the difficulties guests might have in getting in and out of bed, reaching for things once in bed, turning lights on and off, and getting up and out of the furniture we planned to provide in the annex. In considering all the practicalities, we realised we had to cleverly manage where guests might want to put their possessions, have everything within their reach, and minimise clutter and the risk of an accident.

On our return we visited the camping shop and purchased a two-room, easy walk-in tent, with a spacious bedroom and adjoining 'kitchen-diner' – a superb tent for any self-respecting nomad – in readiness for our next camping adventure, and also collected brochures from mobility shops for equipment and accessories for the annex. We had enjoyed a wonderful, beneficial break and recharged our batteries, as well as having developed a greater sensitivity and awareness of the difficulties our guests might have in using our accommodation. This emphasised that time is not wasted by stepping off the treadmill; on the contrary it was imperative.

When I produced our September newsletter we asked our readers (friends and family) to suggest a name for the project. We wanted to begin work on a flyer, to distribute to contacts in the military, advertising our project facility. Naturally we shied away from considering any form of Internet publicity because we imagined offering a free holiday might open the floodgates for people to take advantage of our benevolence. We were convinced that word of mouth should be our main form of advertising, and anyway we were overtly confidant that God had our guest bookings in hand. After all, we had come to France by way of his direction, we had been blessed enormously while the project was coming to fruition, so why should there be a need to advertise? We were prepared to rest in the confidence of our faith. We knew that many of our friends thought this attitude naïve as we didn't seem to have drawn up any assessment of the project's viability or estimated the costs involved; instead we simply stated there was a need, we would fulfil it, and it would work! I don't think we would have been given two minutes in the Dragon's Den, but then we were not in the business of making money and lining a portfolio with investments but in the business of investing in people and spending our money to treat and spoil them.

A friend in France listened carefully to our plans and asked, "But why be so altruistic?" I suppose what he actually meant was, what are the benefits? It says in the Bible that Christ did not please himself on Earth but did his Father's will in order to save God's people. If we planned to put our project guests first, at a cost to ourselves financially, physically and emotionally in caring for them, then our guests would not only benefit from rest and recuperation but experience a benevolent way of life and faith, which might in turn encourage them to put other's first – and so the cycle of care and love would gather momentum.

'Time Out' was the first suggestion we received as a name for the project, and as our readers rallied to the call we were inundated with suggestions, including favourites 'Rest Assured', 'Fortify', 'Eden' and 'Joie de Vivre', of which a second newsletter poll resulted in the last of these being selected as the name for the project. The French phrase 'joie de vivre' is used in English conversation and encapsulates joy in everything, whether that is derived from practical living experiences, philosophy or faith. However we shortened 'vivre' to 'vie' as it was less cumbersome in pronunciation for our guests whilst not losing the sense of the phrase as 'vie' translates as 'life' in any case. It was super at long last to switch to using 'Joie de Vie' in all our conversations, and the name fitted perfectly for what we would achieve.

Now that we had a name, we wanted to have the project up and running, but DIY progress seemed interminably slow. The area outside the annex looked far from ready, with various piles of sand, gravel and rock waiting to be used for the foundations of the ever-continuing path around the house. All piles were protected with various bits of tatty scraps of polythene sheeting and situated right on top of where the guest courtyard was supposed to be taking shape. It was an intricate process working in such a confined area. I dug down to remove turf, plus twenty centimetres of soil, in preparation for laying many more metres of weed-suppressant as a base for the shingle courtyard. Just as I thought I was winning in reducing the sand, gravel and rock, having laid a few more metres of path, I hit a stumbling block in the shape of an enormous, heavy, thick canvas with some mysterious eyelets and lengths of bungee attached. When we finally freed the monstrosity, what was unveiled was a complete side of a military marquee which we could only hope was army surplus and not stolen! Phil's eyes lit up when he saw it, and he purloined it for the perfect cover on our stockpile of winter wood. All forms of canvas had featured over the past two months, tent to marquee, and yet again we commented that God certainly had a sense of humour, as well as providing us with all sorts of practical things to keep our costs down.

Part of our joy in living in rural France was continually seeing the whimsical side of life, and often we were amused by the general lack of regard for health and safety, more akin to a bygone age when people had fun whilst living dangerously. One such event was the St. Fort equestrian event which took place on the old football field – a piece of rough ground with two bent and rusty football goals in memory of the era when St Fort had a thriving and winning football team. The equestrian event was well supported, in anticipation of the jousting which was to take place later in the afternoon by professional knights; but first off were demonstrations of horsemanship by youngsters from the local riding school. They performed a series of acts, in a similar way to the White Helmets (Royal Signals Motorcycle Display Team), in that they charged towards one another in a daredevil sequence which looked equally dangerous. We were pleased that they reined in short of attempting the finale pyramid act! Then we held our breath as other riders superbly executed circus stunts, atop of their mounts, standing bareback on their galloping ponies without the provision of riding helmets or fall nets. It made my slow trotting riding lessons appear very tame by comparison.

A lovely young lady dressed in a long flowing gown, resembling Maid Marion, was the next act; she carried a leather bag of arrows on her back and a long bow to her side as she tried to control her frisky, all fired up steed. A modern target was placed on the ground, and because it was set very close to the crowd line we could easily see the many arrow holes where Marion had successfully hit the target on previous occasions. The crowd hushed as she trotted away to the right and then thundered down the crowd line, struggling to control her steed as well as pull back on her unwieldy bow... *tchi...* She sadly missed. Nerves, we assumed, but in each attempt the arrow fell short... *tchi...* wide... *tchi...* long. We were willing her to get at least one arrow home, especially as the disappointed crowd were beginning to ignore her efforts and look fed up, but then something occurred to improve all our interest. Directly in line with the target a middle-aged lady, in high heels, was picking her way through the grass towards the crowd, clutching a large handbag and camera. As she came level with the target Marion asked her politely to move back out of her firing range, but the lady, whom we immediately recognised as the avid reporter/photographer for a local newspaper, insisted on standing a mere couple of metres to one side, clearly determined to get her journalistic shot. Well, now all attention was on Marion as she galloped full pelt down the crowd line, dropped the reins and quickly aimed the bow whilst the audience were on tenterhooks to see which would get their shot. With our immense relief both did, and how enthusiastically the crowd clapped Marion in recognition for her courage as she rode nobly off into the greenwood, whilst the lady reporter trotted off in search of a knight. I was equally delighted as I got my scoop for September's newsletter.

One inspiring spinoff from writing a newsletter was that wonderful words of encouragement and support were received by return, especially appreciated when Phil returned to work on October 1st. His year off had flown by, and it seemed strange not to have him around, while he switched comfortably back to 'pilot mode' and quickly got back into a routine of six days' work followed by five rest days. The aviation market for private air travel had not made any significant upturn and we hesitated in purchasing another car in case Phil was made redundant and also because the cost of used cars was far greater in France than we had been used to in Lincolnshire. We were in a quandary as to what to do, when Phil spotted a car rental scheme in a local supermarket, which seemed far too good to disregard: five euros a day including insurance! He signed an agreement to lease a small Fiat for one year. No one could doubt we were telling the truth about the costs involved because the car sported technicolour stickers advertising the super deal, plainly visible at twenty metres.

My elderly neighbour, Josette, started calling me 'la pauvre Paulette' as she couldn't imagine how I would cope when Phil was down route for six days or how I would keep myself occupied; this comment from a seventy-nine year old lady who started work in the restaurant, La Pierre Levee, at 6.30am preparing all the desserts for a menu listing over twenty-five desserts each day! Her sterling efforts forced me to work even harder, and I dug up the turf in the front garden to extend our driveway right across the front of the house. Her kitchen window overlooked my efforts so I hoped to change her opinion of me. At the same time, to ring the changes of muscle fatigue I carried on with the slab path around the house and, after another ten metres had been laid, decided to call it God's path. It was an amazing miracle that I could even contemplate getting on with such a heavy manual task, let alone actually doing it, and what's more, enjoying it to boot. Every time I finished another metre I thought about our future guests who would be treading God's path towards their recuperation and I was spurred on to do a little more.

We often took the opportunity to go to the restaurant each week, not only to support the owners who lived opposite us but because we could always be guaranteed an excellent meal and a great atmosphere. During the weekday lunchtimes it was frequented by workers in their heavy protective boots, overalls or paint-splashed clothes, and our presence there in our rough working clothes was not out of place. Michel produced a cracking meal of starter, main course, cheese, dessert, coffee and a carafe of vin rouge or rosé for the princely sum of thirteen euros. Not only did this suit our pocket but we thought it would admirably suit the pocket of our future guests, giving them a flavour of local life just yards from their accommodation.

The family had virtually no English, but if we didn't understand an item on the menu they always pointed out an example of the dish on another table or brought it out from the kitchen. Michel managed to say on one occasion, "I good boy," and later, "I pretty boy," which wasn't a great starter for a conversation but very amusing.

We particularly enjoyed Michel's entrecote steak, and one day when we congratulated him on the quality, Michel replied surprisingly in English, "Me? No... it zee cow." So with this new addition of cow to his vocabulary he could now say "pretty, good cow"!

Meals out and lunch with friends were the sum of our social life, and we began to look around to extend our entertainment in other ways. We joined the RAF Association (RAFA) Sud-Ouest[12] France branch because two friends were very heavily involved with running it and very persuasive in their encouragement for us to become members.

The RAF Association is a charity helping serving and retired RAF personnel, as well as being a member organisation of which there are many French members. We saw this fact as another opportunity to practice our French, and at the beginning of November we drove down to Cestas-Gazinet near Bordeaux for a lunch with eighteen members, which included four former Free French forces airmen who had served at RAF Elvington during 1943-45. Elvington was close to our heart as it was in spitting distance from where Rob and Amy had

---

[12] South-West

been at school in Pocklington, near York, and they both had played in a Swing Band event at Elvington. During the war more than two thousand Free French airmen passed through its gates and were involved in Handley Page Halifax bombing missions. In May 1944 their numbers had allowed them to form their own bomber squadrons – 346 Guyenne and 347 Tunisie – and in October 1945 they had left Elvington for Bordeaux-Mérignac airport. It was a real privilege to lunch with these elderly gentlemen and listen to their amazing stories and anecdotes.

On our way to the lunch we had stopped for coffee in St. Emilion, famous for its fine wine production and a Unesco World Heritage site because it is an outstanding example of historic vineyard landscape. It is a quaint town, much smaller than we had envisaged, with a maze of extremely steep and narrow cobbled streets and many striking architectural buildings, including a monolithic church which had evolved from a cave where once an Eighth Century monk named Emilion had lived. We were lucky to have a quick walk around the town and admire the views of the pristine vineyards before the clouds darkened and it began to rain heavily. Heading for the car park I pulled my hood down and kept my focus on the tarmac to avoid the puddles when I happened to spot a postcard floating in a puddle. I picked it up and Phil put it straight into his pocket to dry it out. We didn't give it another thought until we got home that evening and remembered our find, which was a great pity as we had missed a great opportunity in sharing it with our lunchtime comrades. The postcard would have interested them, because it was dated and stamped September 1945 and portrayed a pen and ink drawing of the rear view of a wealthy lady standing on her doorstep, wearing a smart hat and dress, sleeves rolled up, apron on and her arms extended so wide in front of her that they were hugely out of proportion to her body. The lady was welcoming across the threshold of her home a young, timid mother with four young children clinging to her skirts. We presumed the mother had lost her husband in the war and that now the war was over she was seeking a roof over her head and assistance. The words across the front of the postcard were 'Soyez les bienvenus' translated not just simply as welcome but conveying a real feeling of care, warmth and answer to provision of their need. Our discovery of the postcard made us contemplate another confirmative sign from God for us to open our door to strangers and to make sure our welcome would be no less wide, demonstrative or unprejudiced as the lady's welcome on the postcard.

CHAPTER TWENTY-SEVEN

*"Meanwhile, the people in Judah said,
'The strength of the labourers is giving out,
and there is so much rubble that we cannot rebuild the wall.'"*

Nehemiah 4:10

January is a traditional time in France to receive a visit from an éboueur (professional of hygiene and the environment or, less elaborately, refuse collector) and a sapeur pompier (fireman). They usually call at the gate, during a weekend, to hand over their cheap and cheerful calendars in return for a large gratuity. Naturally we feel very obliged to be generous, because we wouldn't wish to risk rubbish festering in the lane or the paramedic / fire service missing our emergency call. One cold Sunday afternoon, I was digging out yet more barrow-loads of sticky soil to extend the driveway, when the calendar duty fireman popped his head over the wall and I nearly had a heart attack – at least I was in the company of a paramedic!

"Where is your husband?" he asked flabbergasted. "You really shouldn't be doing that!" Now that isn't a bad line in order to win the mistress of the house's favour, and the keeper of the purse when the master is away. I quickly dropped my spade and went inside in search of euros, with an idea brewing in my mind as it struck me that the fifteen or so barrel-loads of soil needed to finish excavating the site might just provide the fireman with the perfect training for fireman lifts. Disappointedly he didn't take up the opportunity of manly exercise, preferring to keep his hands and nails clean, and instead wrote out my receipt in his best handwriting. As he left I hoped that the refuse collector, whose title in French literally means 'one who works in mud' might later show his face over the wall… He wouldn't fall shy of getting his hands dirty.

Both Phil and I were laid very low in January with a rotten cold/cough virus, the first time we could recall suffering an illness at

173

the same time. We did feel grim and it was a toss-up as to who felt sufficiently well enough to make a cup of tea. Our stamina took a real knock, which proved how virulent and ghastly the virus was. We were left with persistent hacking coughs, and we huffed and puffed as we worked, when normally the task would have been effortless. At one point in the month I wondered whether I was even going to drum up anything newsworthy to write in our January newsletter, but eventually we felt enthused to tackle a self-assembly bed and wardrobe unit in the annex. We really should have listened more to the groans of our weak bodies though and left our tool belts hung up on the hook a little longer.

Phil and I are slow to learn from our mistakes because when we find the perfect solution in a furniture store, then learn it is self-assembly, we instantly forget all the hassles we have had in the past and continue with the purchase. Why do we do this, instead of sensibly fleeing from the shop? I smile inanely at Phil, he nods encouragingly and we act as if the task will be easy by dashing back home and ripping the flat-packed boxes apart with enthusiasm – why do we do that? We clearly are slow learners... very slow learners.

As usual, with instruction book in our hand and pages of ambiguous looking diagrams, we wondered who the comedian was who decided the timing of its assembly. The combination wardrobe/bed unit was supposed to take two people two hours and thirty minutes to make up into something attractive and desirable, which did not include the time to unpack five ridiculously heavy and cumbersome boxes and fathom which parts corresponded with which in the instruction manual. Three and a half hours later we had made progress but only after we had coerced Amy to help manhandle upright one half of the combination. The instructions had omitted to mention that the two people assigned to the project had to be weight lifters because of the excessive weight of the mirror or even that one needed a psychology degree to increase the manpower when the only candidate available preferred revising her law notes. Four hours into the task there still remained eighteen main features to assemble, which excluded the time required to fit thirty hinges and six door handles and two hours for Phil to re-site all the electricity sockets so that we could centre the unit perfectly, also making it easy for wheelchair access on both sides of the bed. Hours later, after some tense and dangerous moments, the combination wardrobe/bed unit stood proud and we were delighted with our efforts. All self-assembly hassles were forgotten in our admiration of the finished product... until the next time.

Progress continued to be slow into the next month too, and to add to our frustration, instead of advancing slowly we slid backwards as tasks would not go as we wanted. At the same time pressure increased because we were asked time and again when the work would be finished or when we expected the arrival of the first Joie de Vie guests.

Phil spent a long time working in the annex kitchenette to build a plasterboard wall around the hot water tank, which reached to the ceiling, and to hide an ugly array of water pipes not dissimilar to a ship's boiler room. He made several attempts to fit a concertina door to hide his work and was bitterly disappointed when I complained the finished outcome was well below standard for the first class deck. "Surely, Phil, the only solution is to rip it all down and begin again from scratch?" didn't go down well. Understandably Phil was very despondent, particularly with his time at home limited, and he thoroughly despaired with my idea to the point of refusing to give it another go. Oh dear, how irritable, ill-tempered and exasperated we were with one another! Foolish of us – and instead of getting on with something completely different we took out our frustration on one another. Discouragement and fatigue had overwhelmed us, and coupled with the after-effects of the debilitating virus we had forgotten to pray and leave our chagrin and vexation in Jesus' hands. As I said before, we can be slow learners.

We had been on such a high for so many months, and failure to do a task had not been our normal experience. For sure, tasks were hard, but we had overcome them. This particular failure was a huge disappointment because not only had we spent weeks trying to source an affordable door but also we had completely wasted our money, which hurt. Eventually we brought ourselves back to focus on the big picture, to accept there would be disappointments and to praise God that our disappointments thus far had been so few. We prayed for his mercy on us, sorry for the hurt we had caused one another.

In a better frame of mind, we searched the DIY stores for a replacement door, quickly sourced a much smarter design, more substantial and far easier to fit. It was a reminder to us not to be complacent but to continue to grow in godliness and grace.

Phil packed his suitcase for six days' work, went to bed early and rose at the crack of sparrows to head down the N10 to Bordeaux. His brief, always received on his work Blackberry, had shown he would be taking a commercial flight to Rome, connect with another to Milan and then meet up with his captain and the company plane around lunchtime. Surprisingly, he had only driven for thirty minutes when NetJets contacted him to explain the planned Air France flight had been postponed; therefore they would send another pilot to Milan. Phil returned home on standby and, determined to make the most of the time available, laid out his uniform in readiness for a quick getaway, donned his work clothes and set to removing all the broken and collapsed drive edging with his trusty angle-grinder. If he had been called out that day, a very white-haired pilot would have turned up for duty!

Standby is a rare occurrence and rarely continues for more than one day, yet remarkably Phil stayed on standby for the whole six days! With his usual five days off tacked on at the end we managed to accomplish more in eleven days than we had achieved in the previous two months. We were on cloud nine... How God had blessed us when we had drawn closer to him! Our achievements included edging our drive with new border stones, having sixteen tonnes of gravel delivered then spreading it across the whole of the drive (we worked like navvies), and we barrowed several loads around the back of the house to finish the guest courtyard; all completed in the nick of time before the next day's delivery of six cubic metres of seasoned oak, which had to be stacked quickly, extending our wood store, to make way for a huge pile of sand and more pallets of slabs. God's timing could not have been more perfect.

With the driveway finished, the paving across the front of our property progressed much quicker than expected, and we laid an area in front of the entrance to make it easier for wheelchair users. Every day was the same routine: donning threadbare gloves and worn knee pads (for worn knees), beefing up the muscles to mix the cement mixture, struggling to manhandle the large slabs in position and keeping to the task... with the exception of Wednesdays.

Primary school children in our region do not go to school on Wednesdays, although a change will be implemented fully by the end of 2014 for all state schools to revert to full education on a Wednesday.[13] Wednesday is the one day I try to avoid going shopping

---

[13] The idea of having one day off a week dates back to 1882, when actually Thursday was the day set aside for time to receive religious instruction

because it is a busy time, with harassed parents and grandparents dragging their bored children and grandchildren up and down the aisles of the supermarket. Next-door's delightful children were out in the garden early on Wednesdays and wanted to chat all the time. I thoroughly enjoyed their company because they were always keen to find out what we were doing, sing us a song, share what they had been doing in school and correct our French. They are always extremely polite so we didn't have the heart to tell them we were busy and really didn't have the time to chat, and in spite of desperately wanting to attend to my slabs, I kept stopping my work and walking over to the gap in the hedge to give the children my attention. Finally after several disruptive episodes, Anaïs (9) declared, "Well, Paulette, I can't stand here talking to you all day. I have a game to play!"

On another such occasion when asked what I was doing, I explained, "We are laying slabs," and then asked Anaïs the correct conjugation of the verb. I thought I had it right, but our young teacher exclaimed with much derision, "Non! You cannot say, '*We* are laying slabs,' because it is always Paulette who is laying the slabs. You keep going away, Phil!" It is not often a teacher is left bemused by her pupils laughing out aloud.

Incidentally Wednesday is a traditional day for many other reasons: when seasonal sales set by the government traditionally start, weekly cabinet meetings are held in the Elysée Palace, the release of new films (historically begun in the 1970's to coincide with the children's day off school), and on Wednesday evenings long feature films are not allowed to be shown on the free television channels in order to benefit the cinemas. Last, but not least, the first Wednesday of the month heralds the 'signal de national alert', the day when France's 4,500 emergency warning air-raid sirens are tested at twelve noon. When we heard an occasional siren sounding nearby our immediate thought was that we must be living close to a factory and assumed the siren heralded the start of the two-hour lunch. What on earth made us imagine that a factory might be situated in the middle of the vineyards?!

---

instead of classes. In 1972 Wednesday became the mandatory day off and children were encouraged to spend Wednesday afternoon doing sport and other active leisure activities. They also attended school on a Saturday morning until 2008.

By the middle of March we were definitely back to full fitness; feeling full of vitality. Our being below par in the previous months must have reached the ears of those far and wide as one morning I took a phone call from a local 'Maison de Retraite' (retirement home) inviting me to go and spend the day with them! The lady enthused about me using the day as an opportunity for a trial run and described the substantial lunch to be included. It was true that in the past month I had felt a bit 'past it', experienced reduced physical and mental functioning, hearing loss, dizziness, infection and reduced lung capacity – all symptoms of ageing which I could genuinely admit to, courtesy of the virus. A free lunch was appealing, but with my hopeless inability to act the role of an elderly, frail Madame, I came clean and admitted to being only fifty-three years old. I could sense the panic at the other end of the line as the lady gasped in astonishment and quickly ended our conversation.

A couple of weeks later, when we were driving near to the river Charente, we were curious to locate the retirement home and couldn't believe our eyes when we looked through its entrance to admire a vast, elegant, brick and stone rectangular château, with many attractive features: towers, turrets, polygonal pavilion, beautiful landscaped gardens fronting on to the river, plus a tennis court! I had missed a good day out; perhaps a club involving acting would be the next leisure pursuit to investigate.

Now in good health, we dug flowerbeds to edge the guest terrace and courtyard, planted fragrant plants, a magnolia, apricot and fig tree, plus a variety of herbs for our guests' culinary skills. What a difference we had made to this part of the garden in comparison to the unsightly rubble and rubbish-strewn area which we had inherited with the purchase of the property. We reflected on the past two months and how we had pulled ourselves up from the illness and despondency to refocus on our faith, without which we would have slipped further from our ultimate goal.

Christians are not exempt from feeling demoralised; we suffer the same feelings of being discouraged or defeated, but by worshipping and praying with other Christians each week we do not feel alone in our struggle. Jesus is always at our side, our faithful friend and teacher, but with the added bonus of our church family showing us love and concern we receive further comfort, strength and encouragement. It has a snowball effect. Our brothers and sisters in Christ praying to uphold each other keeps everyone on track whether for daily living or a long-term project. Worship and praise in the name of Jesus in a group is joyful and blessed as each individual in the group comes to know God through Jesus, intimately, uniquely and naturally; as Jesus said, "For where two or three come together in my name, there am I with them." (Matthew 18:20)

In worship the words, phrases and verses we sing are a revelation and inspiration for our lives, for healing, forgiveness or deliverance, and a wonderful release from our burdens. As we concentrate on Jesus reaching out to us through our praise and worship, we can fathom our living God at work. This enables a physical, mental and spiritual cleansing of our bodies. We feel much more pure of heart and much more able to improve the way we should think, love and behave towards others in the week ahead. Church services are very different according to denomination, congregation, leadership style and musical accompaniment, and it is worthwhile to go to a variety of services before determining which suits your taste at any particular time in your life.

Since the beginning of 2010 we had been travelling to Jarnac, another small town on the river Charente, to worship at the Eglise Evangélique twice a month. We felt the need to integrate even more with French people, and we had heard from friends that it was a lively church with lots of families. It also appealed to us because the church was only a twenty minute drive away compared with the fifty-five minute drive north we had been doing twice a month to worship at a chaplaincy church. The Eglise Evangélique worshipped in a cramped hall, which was in need of much maintenance and redecoration, but the welcome we received from the pastor Johann Del Zotto, and his equally welcoming congregation, was extremely warm, verging on hot. It was clearly apparent the Holy Spirit was alive and at work here, and the fact the service was an hour longer really suited our thirst for praise and worship.

There were a few English-speaking members, and we were impressed the church had bothered to set up a system to translate the sermon into English. A music band, with members of all ages, played brilliantly, and within a few weeks we felt very comfortable and at home. We were especially thrilled how much we could comprehend before the sermon and teaching – definitely more than half of what was being said or sung. We had thought it might be many years before we could be spiritually fed by worshipping in a French church, but instead at each service we were overwhelmed and inspired.

Unsurprisingly, not many weeks passed before we were attending the Eglise Evangélique every week, and as the pastor taught a six-week session on the book of Nehemiah, in the Old Testament, we listened attentively. Johann eloquently and masterfully made Nehemiah come alive and illustrated his relevancy to modern living superbly. Nehemiah, a man living between 445-432 B.C., rallied the people to rebuild the walls of Jerusalem which were in shambles, in the face of much opposition and heartache, yet this man of God acted wisely and used various measures to keep the wall-building project moving. He prayed regularly, persevered to get close to God, thus succeeded in achieving God's vision, trusted wholly in God's help to accomplish many seemingly impossible tasks and managed to build the wall in an astonishing fifty-two days! Nehemiah's example of character motivated us and we equated much of his experience to ours. We tried to imitate his example.

To celebrate the building of the wall, Nehemiah describes a lively service of dedication: a joyful sound of celebration with two large choirs assigned to give thanks with cymbals, harps and lyres. The sound of rejoicing was carried from Jerusalem to the surrounding area. We, too, were jumping for joy when we finished our 'wall' and we felt inspired to celebrate with songs of praise too. We sent out invitations for a date in early May for lots of people to join us in a Celebration of Thanksgiving, to dedicate Joie de Vie for God's glory and to announce at long last we were ready and awaiting our first guests.

Cue: Trumpet fanfare!

CHAPTER TWENTY-EIGHT

"Come, let us sing for joy to the Lord;
let us shout aloud to the Rock of our salvation.
Let us come before him with thanksgiving
And extol him with music and song."

Psalm 95:1-2

Thirty-nine people accepted our invitation to join us on May 7th, two years virtually to the day since our Celebration of Blessings and Leaving Party in Lincolnshire. We received many good wishes from our dear friends and relatives who had attended that event when we had shared our hopes and plans to set up Joie de Vie. We very much felt that our Celebration of Thanksgiving was not only for those who had supported us in France to bring Joie de Vie to fruition, but for those who had encouraged us and prayed from the outset.

The day began with bright sunshine and a clear blue sky. We enjoyed refreshments on the guest courtyard and terrace before going inside for a Service of Dedication and much rejoicing. We sang many of our favourite worship songs, including 'In Christ alone my hope is found', the hymn we had chosen to sing at our Celebration of Blessings. We also included a favourite reading from John 15, in the New Testament: Jesus explains, "I am the vine; you are the branches. If a man remains in me and I in him, he will bear much fruit; apart from me you can do nothing. If anyone does not remain in me, he is like a branch that is thrown away and withers; such branches are picked up, thrown into the fire and burned. If you remain in me and my words remain in you, ask whatever you wish, and it will be given to you. This is to my Father's glory, that you bear much fruit, showing yourselves to be my disciples."

These verses speak volumes to Phil and I, and they are particularly pertinent to our lifestyle in a village surrounded by hectare upon hectare of vineyards. Since arriving in France we had lived through

181

two seasons of viticulture and had watched our neighbours carrying out the various tasks to maintain their vines: pruning out the dead wood to maximise its fruitfulness, carefully going about their work to create a strong plant, training it to grow upright, expertly tying down the branches, cleansing its roots of weeds which might strangle growth, and speaking with passion about their job of nurture. By choosing Jesus as our rootstock we were intent to be as fruitful as possible.

For our service of Thanksgiving and Dedication we had asked our special friend Chris to say prayers towards the end of the service. As she took her place at the front she explained she first would like to read out an email I had written in reply to her when she had wished me well with all the food preparation for the proposed feast.

> *"I'm spending the day cooking tomorrow. What a joy that will be! A spoon in my hand instead of a trowel; a whisk in my hand instead of mixing cement; doing lots of washing up and hoping that my hands will be as soft as the adverts suggest and not like those of navvies; and listening to the radio instead of hearing the constant sound of Phil drilling. And lastly, I've just bought five loaves and two fish and asked God to do the rest, because I intend to put my feet up and watch TV!"*

God certainly provided an unforgettable day. We toasted his project with champagne but then ate the buffet lunch crammed together, cheek by jowl inside, because it rained splendidly. Did we care? Not a jot, because to enjoy fellowship with one another was much higher on our list of priorities than the weather.

Our friends did us proud by rising to the occasion, in more ways than one. We didn't want to receive any personal gifts for providing lunch and we had suggested instead that our lunch guests might like to bring a book or perhaps a CD for the enjoyment of our Joie de Vie guests. Their generosity in giving was staggering: books, CDs, DVDs, jigsaws, games, art materials, ornaments and all manner of wonderful things for the kitchenette. We were quite overwhelmed.

Putting our feet up after everyone had departed we realised we had reached the springboard to the real work ahead and we decided it was time to have a holiday. We chose to have the next three weeks away, and where better to spend the holiday than in our lovely home in the sunshine. The alarm clock was put away in a drawer, the work clothes were washed, ironed and pushed to the back of the wardrobe, we discovered books again, lazed by the pool and occasionally took ourselves off to eat out.

On one of the days we drove out to a restaurant Phil had spotted on his route to Bordeaux. The prominent stone building had caught his eye more than once, as it was in the middle of nowhere, yet the car park was always packed with cars or vans. Originally we planned to try the restaurant on Valentine's Day, but as usual something had cropped up to cancel our plan so to enjoy a romantic meal now would make up for having missed out in February.

Our first surprise was how large the restaurant was inside, consisting of several dining rooms, already buzzing with a cacophony of voices and waiters and waitresses, dashing hither and thither. A waiter led us through the first room to a more sophisticated à la carte dining room which looked lovely, and I began to eye up where we could sit. However, always one for a bargain, Phil told the waiter we would much prefer to eat their standard formule – a fixed priced menu consisting of starter, main course, dessert and not à la carte. I winced at the lost indulgent opportunity, forcibly smiled at the waiter, who in turn grimaced and explained the other dining areas were fully booked but if we so wished we could of course eat in the bar. Nice one Phil, I thought, and ungraciously considered that a sandwich at home with stale bread might be more appetizing!

Anyway, we retired to the bar area, the least attractive room in the whole restaurant, and the news was showing on a large TV screen, where no doubt I could soon look forward to Phil's attention being directed to Saturday sport! The lunchtime treat was getting better and better...

One large table had been basically laid for twelve, and a retired couple was sitting at one end seemingly content with one another's company and their aperitifs. We naturally headed to the opposite end of the table, but the waiter absolutely insisted we sit directly next to the other couple, who now looked slightly apprehensive at the thought of anyone being foisted into their comfort zone, let alone an English couple!

After a couple of minutes, while both couples tried to conduct a whispered conversation, I thought this lunchtime cannot get any more ridiculous so I broke the ice and asked them about their meal. They thawed instantly, smiled broadly, chatted and explained they lived near the coast but had stopped off at the restaurant to break their journey, after having dropped their grandchildren at the train station in Angoulême.

La pauvre Madame was quieter than her husband but she explained she was at present afflicted with awful toothache. The pain could only have increased in intensity when she learnt that the English man was a pilot, as was her husband. Robert had learnt to fly in his latter years and owned an ultra light aircraft. The stories came thick and fast, and his wife, Arlette, and I nearly lost the will to live, at zero feet above sea-level, while Robert and Phil soared to the dizzy heights sharing flying moments, discussing engines, flying parameters, instruments, take-offs and landings. The hours passed, but not the toothache, and Robert sensitively knew when to quit – but not without generously offering to take Phil for a 'spin' in his plane. We took their phone number and promised to phone in a few weeks' time to arrange a date, thinking at the same time, "We've only just met these people... Surely they will regret such an offer once home." We decided not to rush in phoning them.

Several weeks later the phone rang at 9am. Amazingly I recognised Robert's voice on the other end of the line. "How did you manage to find our phone number?" I asked, incredulous. "Easy," replied Robert, "I hired your Inspector Barnaby!" The TV series Midsomer Murders is incredibly popular in France, titled Inspecteur Barnaby, and at the time was being broadcast every Sunday evening. We arranged a date for Phil's flight, and I enquired after Arlette's dental health. "Easy again," chortled Robert, "she has had the crown of your Queen Elizabeth fitted!" What a character! We blessed the day our proposed 'romantic meal' had brought us new friends.

Whilst lazing around the house we received several enquiries from people interested in coming out to stay in Joie de Vie. We were pleased to have chosen a holiday at home, otherwise we would have missed many enquiries. Over the months Phil had made various calls to military welfare organisations, charities, and military units across all three services, to chaplains, social workers, as well as emailing our brochure to previous RAF contacts, and all had seemed enthusiastic to pass on the details of Joie de Vie.

Particularly we were interested in Combat Stress, the Veteran's health charity, which cares for British ex-servicemen and women suffering from mental health conditions including post-traumatic stress disorder, depression and adjustment disorders. They were currently supporting over 4,500 men and women. I had touched on

184

some of the veterans' problems in my training as a social worker, and therefore I was intrigued to learn more. I purchased several books, written by sufferers divulging their nightmares and flashbacks relating to their own suffering of military trauma. We thought Joie de Vie would be an appropriate facility for rest and recuperation in their recovery phase, especially as we were situated in quiet and calm surroundings. It was concerning to read of the number of veterans suffering, not only those from experiences in the Second World War, Northern Ireland and the Falklands, but when considering the recent operations in Iraq and Afghanistan the numbers would increase dramatically over the forthcoming years... a time bomb ticking away.

Many of those currently suffering had financial problems because psychological disorders impede on people's ability to work and often result in loss of employment, adding the social stigma of unemployment to their troubles. We wondered how our offer of a free holiday would be accepted. A friend suggested that it might be an idea to ask for a small donation, to cover Joie de Vie's utility costs, because people were justifiably proud and if they knew there was a small cost, it would help preserve their dignity. We could see his point and decided on five euros per day, to be left as a donation at the end of their stay. However, in our conversations promoting Joie de Vie, we spread the word that if anyone was in financial difficulty we could fund all their travel costs. Friends, relatives and our church friends in Thurlby had been absolutely terrific in helping to fund-raise for Joie de Vie, and all funds received had gone into a savings account for such an eventuality. We had to trust God that he would have his hand on every facet of the project and help us in our discernment so that our altruism would not be abused or Joie de Vie funds wasted.

Each morning we said our prayers, asking Jesus to lay his hand on those people who were the neediest, give them the confidence to email us and for them to have the assurance that our offer was genuine and sincere. We thought our people skills sufficient to be able to convince them that they would not be left high and dry in a foreign country. Meanwhile we tried hard to be patient whilst we waited for a firm booking and prayed the time on our hands now would allow us to get to know our neighbours better.

One should never be surprised by the speed in which God answers prayer, but two weeks later, after praying for more contact with our neighbours, I was gardening in our potager when an attractive, pleasantly spoken lady called across to me. She introduced herself as

Maryse and she lived at the end of our road alongside the river Né, which was a surprise as we hadn't realised the road extended beyond the farm and barns we could see from our gate. Once we had driven down to the farm, out of curiosity to see how long the road extended, but on seeing a 'Propriété privé' sign had turned around not wishing to trespass. Maryse seemed equally surprised at our lack of knowledge but kindly invited us to venture further than the private sign and join them for an apéro.

Apéro time is assumed to commence at 18:00-18:30 when an aperitif is served, plus various nibbles which are normally substantial enough not to require an evening meal. The trick we have learnt is to always have a main meal at lunchtime in case one is invited for an apéro. The French, it goes without saying, love to eat so it is no surprise that the smallest snack offered is always considerable. Putting out a few nuts or crisps as we might have done in the UK will not suffice. It is also expected guests will leave by 20:00, and no gift is necessary for the host/hostess, unlike when invited to dinner when the floral gift might exceed the cost of a formule lunch in a restaurant for two! We love apéro time because it is fun to taste all the delightful, tasty and varied finger foods people create as well as the time not being too long to concentrate on getting our grammar and conjugations correct. At the lengthier dinners the brain can easily be pickled by the amount of alcohol offered, so that the resulting fatigue in turn rapidly disables one's concentration on any language!

Maryse, a former school teacher, and Jean-Pierre, an ex-engineer, had moved into the village recently from west of Bordeaux, and their home was a vast restored watermill with stunning river features and water gardens fronting the River Né. Originally the watermill had two vertical waterwheels: one for the production of walnut oil and the other to mill flour. The wheel in situ was probably a hundred years old and an impressive sight looking through a gigantic glass panel in their sitting room. Maryse had been brought up in Verrières, the next small village east of St. Fort, and Jean-Pierre in Pont Abbé in the next department – Charente Maritime. They were very interesting people with a wealth of knowledge for our local area, which was like a red rag to a bull and we must have bored them rigid with all our questions. Immediately we struck up an easy relationship and they were patient and corrected our French. We walked back up the road very happy in having found them superb company, knowing we would become close friends.

186

To conclude the end of our long three-week break we had three wonderful days in the Tarn-et-Garonne department, about four and a half hours' drive south-east of St. Fort, to celebrate Phil's fifty-fourth birthday. Having watched a programme on the television about the Aveyron valley and gorge and been fascinated by the impressive scenery, we booked two nights in a Chambres d'hôte specifically entitled Escapade de charme, close to the picturesque and medieval town of St. Antonin-Noble-Val. Also enjoying a long weekend and staying with us in the Chambres d'hôte were four amiable couples, and our breakfasts with them were lively and fun. The proprietors were chatty, particularly with the French couples, but strangely distant with us. We could only presume that British guests were not their ideal choice of houseguest, which might explain why we were accommodated in a very poky room with a disconcerting five foot, two-man, deep bladed, cross-cut saw screwed to the wall above the bed! 'Escapade' means 'to escape or getaway' and to be fair, at first sight on being shown into the room, we very nearly did, but fortunately the advantage of perfect location overrode the fear of nightmares.

One evening in nearby Nègrepelisse we chose to eat in a truly authentic North African restaurant, owned by a very friendly Moroccan lady. It was surprisingly quiet in the restaurant for a Saturday evening, but the interior was very appealing. We delighted in the interesting photographs of her homeland around the walls, the heavy pungent smell of spices wafting from the kitchen, the bright colourful crockery to match the equally colourful tagine she served and the twangy, twangy traditional music coming from her CD player. With such authenticity we could easily imagine the bustling activity of the souk outside rather than the actuality of a quiet French square.

Just as we were in the middle of eating our deliciously fragrant meal, the restaurant door opened and a middle-aged lady with long, jet black hair, wearing a vibrant blue, velvet, flowing djelleba made an unforgettable theatrical entrance. With forks poised in mid-air our attention was focused not entirely on her but on the extremely large falcon perched on her arm, which sat haughtily upright, showing off its magnificent plumage. The falcon wore a small leather hood. It was one of those moments when we really did have to do a double take on the whole scene and cursed the fact we had left the camera in the car. Isn't that always the way? Our meal was momentarily forgotten and, intrigued, we called the lady over. We learnt that the raptor was only one year old and she daren't take off its head cap as it would become extremely aggressive! We immediately drew back from the menacingly sharp beak, knowing that a raptor has rather a penchant for chicken, and we surreptitiously pulled our plates nearer. We couldn't help but look down at our tasty meal and wonder whether we had discovered the reason for our being the only guests in the restaurant that evening.

Returning to St. Fort we checked our emails and were thrilled to have an enquiry from a couple wishing to book Joie de Vie. We were so excited by the prospect of welcoming our first guests. We made contact and chatted to them at length on the phone and afterwards had a glass of fizz to celebrate. We couldn't wait for the weeks to pass and were impatient for their arrival. Three weeks later they cancelled and our bubbly enthusiasm and fizz fell extremely flat.

CHAPTER TWENTY-NINE

"Lord, you have assigned me my portion and my cup;
you have made my lot secure.
The boundary lines have fallen for me in pleasant places;
surely I have a delightful inheritance. "

Psalm 16:5-6

After the disappointment of a cancellation, feeling discouraged was thankfully short lived, as further enquiries leapt across the ether. Finally we welcomed our first guests in the beginning of August; a tired, frazzled, slightly nervous couple arrived, but by the end of their stay they were refreshed, energized, confident and hugely sociable. They had been blissfully unaware they were our very first customers – our guinea pigs. We listened to them enthuse about their recuperation from sleep deprivation, worries, problems of stress and depression, and our hearts were filled with joy. It was such a pleasure for us to witness their physical and mental well-being visibly improve, and although a busy and tiring time for us, immensely rewarding and an unequivocal success. We thought that if they were to be the only guests ever to cross the threshold of Joie de Vie, all the effort and sacrifice had been well worth it. I wrote in my diary, the day they departed:

"I woke today thinking if I died today what a simply wonderful
life I have had – the twists and turns of earthly existence and yet
the amazing comfort of faith and the promise of eternal life. "

I felt secure, loved, rewarded, blessed and at peace. Our hearts' desire was to bestow generous hospitality on our guests, in the hope they would experience the same feelings.

We entertained more guests that month, and it was apparent how much people yearned for a refuge of calm and tranquillity. We realised that our location might not suit everyone, but our guests kept emphasising how much solitude and being in a safe place was a priority for them, also that being in a foreign country had a healing effect. We presumed that the atmosphere of a different culture, away from all the trappings of familiarity, was refreshing and stimulated a different way of looking at their personal situation and lifestyle. Our locality was considerably different from what they were used to, which helped to distract them from their problems, and the warmer climate clearly lifted their spirits and their feel good factor. Guests were amazed at how many hours they slept and we explained how the air is much purer in this region. With our prevailing wind from the west, there is little industry between us and the United States of America! Our air naturally induces sleep, which surprised the guest who doggedly declared, "Ooh, I won't sleep. I never do!"

We were astonished how quickly our guests settled and moreover how they were prepared to share their personal situations so honestly and openly with us. We hadn't experienced their individual traumas but we could sympathise, and empathise knowing we had many common denominators from shared military experience, knowledge of conflict zones, suffering and chronic pain, resolving education problems for 'military children', feelings of isolation when husbands were detached, knowledge of many posting locations, and in some cases the surprising discovery of having had mutual colleagues. It was absolutely essential we would preserve our guests' confidentiality and we were very careful not to disclose information to others, to maintain privacy.

Often we had a chance to share our faith and explain how God had been our saving grace, which was a great privilege and we were surprised how many were interested to hear our story. Although, should we really have been surprised? It was all part of God's master plan – He who desires everyone to benefit from a full and rich life through knowing Jesus.

The beginning of September heralded 'La Rentrée' – a word on everyone's lips without exception. Many businesses, restaurants, bars and shops had been closed for their long annual summer leave, but now there was an air of expectancy as folk returned home from vacation and life returned to normality. La Rentrée literally means 'the return to work' after the slack period of the summer break, but it encompasses so much more than that, making an impact on all ages and facets of society.

Schools return during the first week of September but not before parents have become worn out from traipsing from one shop to another to seek out the best bargains, as they have to purchase all the stationery, equipment and books for every subject their children shall be taught that school year. A large area in each supermarket is given over to La Rentrée. Money-off vouchers are handed out, so the aisles are full of parents grasping dog-eared school lists, trying to fathom the best deal in the hope of avoiding a scolding from the teacher for having failed to do their 'homework' properly!

For the discerning, the shopper without children, it is a great time to stock up on stationery and bargain-priced printer paper. It is well worth putting up with the nuisance of searching unfamiliar areas of the store for familiar products such as swimming pool chemicals, which have been sidelined to allow another aisle to be given over to La Rentrée. There are exercise books and file paper galore, of every size, with attractive covers to tempt girls or boys, although we are baffled by the impossibility of purchasing lined file paper as we were accustomed to do in the UK. All French file writing paper is squared, and we can only surmise the small squared design is useful for keeping one's handwriting neat and uniform, which might account for the fact that all our French friends, young and old alike, have the same handwriting! Our handwriting looks very slapdash by comparison, and I have had some French friends sniff at it in rather a disparaging way. I have explained that my individual style reflects my character, but they seem unconvinced and wonder at my ability to use lined paper! It is the little things which forge such a gulf between one country and another.

The end of summer is also the time of year when our favourite hypermarket has a very colourful and tempting display of gourmet food items from Brittany, such as biscuits, cider and chocolates, as well as competitively priced Breton hoop shirts[14]. Shoppers have to be quick off the mark to make their purchases because within a few days the items are rapidly pushed aside for La Rentrée, to display every size of backpack imaginable, to fit every size of child, from major, minor, to minimus.

---

[14] Incidentally the Breton shirt, in traditional blue and white, originally had twenty-one stripes in recognition of Napoleon's victories and it was introduced as part of a naval uniform for all seamen in Brittany. In 1858 the shirt had to be worn by law in order to make it easier to search for seamen who had fallen overboard. The boat neck design quickly gained popularity and the shirt became a must for any mariner, worker, fashion follower and film star!

It is a mystery to me why all things Breton are fêted each year in the hypermarket when the famous local 'pantoufle charentaise' (Charentaise slipper) is not. The slipper evolved back in the Seventeenth Century from wool felt offcuts left from the making of naval uniforms, at Rochefort, and was slipped inside a wooden clog to keep the feet much warmer. A shoemaker created the contemporary Charentaise in 1907 at La Rochefoucauld near Angoulême. The slippers were made using the recycled paper felts from the paper industry, and traditional styles often had a Scottish weave design! Since the 1950's a huge range of designs in every colour, becoming more innovative every year, has ensured exports around the world. We see people wearing them everywhere and anywhere – outside, mostly, in all weathers – and we can only deduce they are extremely comfortable and long-lasting.

La Rentrée is also the time when clubs and associations reconvene. At the end of September we saw a poster in our village shop for line dancing classes and plucked up the courage to join the Sun Dance Country Club at St. Palais du Né. It was a small group of débutantes of all ages and included some familiar faces: the couple who owned the shop in our village and Phil's hairdresser.

Line dancing has its roots in country music, but we were surprised, and pleased, to learn that many of the dances had been choreographed for most styles of music including popular, Irish, disco, Latin and Spanish to name but a few. The evening was a tremendous hoot as we fluffed our steps and found ourselves turning in the wrong direction, finishing by facing the wrong way or simply glued to the spot not knowing which way to turn. The greatest test was language comprehension – not so much French but our mother tongue! The teacher struggled to give us the English dance titles – extremely brave of her as she couldn't speak English – but her pronunciation was incomprehensible. We had more chance with the steps because she called those in 'Franglais', and irrespective of our poor ability to dance, a passion for line dancing was born.

We really looked forward to dancing on Tuesday evenings and tried to find time in the week to master the various steps from the instruction sheets which we had been given. One morning Phil went down to the shop for our breakfast baguette and took ages; I nearly organised a search party! On his return he explained he had been dragged into the back of the shop to watch YouTube videos of line dancers demonstrating certain dances we were struggling with. One doesn't get that sort of service from a supermarket... Village shop rules OK!

After a couple of weeks of a trial period, all new members were asked to pay their fees. We had assumed the class would run similar to Further Education classes we had joined in the UK, i.e. for six to eight weeks, three times a year, with no classes in the school holidays. Not so in France. In general classes begin at La Rentrée, continue without a break for a full ten months and cease only for the long July/August holiday. Classes are cancelled only if the class falls on a public holiday, which is sacrosanct as people do not want to miss out on the opportunity to 'faire le pont' or relax with family and friends, and of course the dance teacher isn't keen to work on a public holiday, even though French law dictates that all work should only stop on May 1st[15].

In previous years we had made many a mistake in not checking the diary as to whether a Jour Ferié (public holiday) was due that week. The only clue if it is a public holiday is the absence of HGV's on the road, which are banned between the hours of 10pm the previous evening of a public holiday to 10pm on the day itself, unless carrying perishable or refrigerated produce. Our guests had enough difficulty coping with French shop/restaurant opening hours in general, without the addition of a public holiday, which seemed doubly incongruous to them; firstly as the shops were closed and secondly because the public holiday wasn't on a Monday. Nowadays it makes sense to us for public holidays to be always on the day of the week the historical event occurred. We often explain to our guests that although it is a mere twenty-one miles from across the Strait of Dover to Cap Gris Nez, near Calais, the differences in culture between the UK and France are vast.

Getting back to line dancing, we paid our fees for the year, started to say our au revoirs and put our coats on, aware out of the corner of our eyes a couple were setting up chairs around a small table in the middle of the floor. Phil gave me a nudge: "Hey, pity the poor souls who've got to stay late for a meeting." Literally as the words had parted from his lips, our dance teacher called over for us to pull up a chair and sit down... for the Sun Dance Country's AGM! A bit of a

---

[15] This public holiday is called Fête du Travail (Labour Day), and no one works except in certain industries where it is not possible to stop, such as in a hospital.

blow when we had been looking forward to putting our feet up and enjoying a cool lager to refresh our weary legs, but we showed willing, believing an Assemblée Générale for such a small club could only possibly last half an hour at the most. One hour and fifteen minutes later, at 21:45, we excused ourselves, having developed a headache from sheer thirst whilst trying to keep up with the rapid flow of conversation between Committee members! Such conversation as the design of a club logo, the forthcoming December dance workshop followed by the Bal (dance) in the evening, a lengthy decision about how many bottles of pop to purchase, whether to provide sandwiches, and the captivating discussion regarding the price to charge for six cold crêpes! We later learnt that the stalwarts of the club, whom we salute with imaginary Stetsons in recognition of their fortitude, remained for another hour but at least were fortified with cognac before departing – recompense indeed.

With one club under our belt we looked around for something else to join and started to research the clubs and associations in Cognac. Courtesy of our neighbour Maryse we learnt that St. Fort had a Sport and Leisure club with more than eighty members walking and cycling regularly. As we love walking and cycling we could not believe how on earth we had missed a local opportunity to keep fit.

The cycling section of the club, though, was far out of our league as their racing bikes were lightweight, as was their Lycra apparel, enabling them to ride many tens of kilometres at speed, whilst we, with our heavy, old, ill-oiled bikes, were capable of cycling only a leisurely thirty-nine kilometres. On our ride we liked to include a coffee and cake in a Pâtisserie, stop and enjoy the views, admire vegetable gardens en route and, if need be, get off and walk up any 'serious' hill! One day when we had been out for such a leisurely cycle, we had been overtaken by a group of retired male cyclists, and one speedster had shouted at us to get a move on and tag along with them. We have a pretty good idea now whose voice it was that day – the very same person who is a member of our walking club and relates imaginative tales of Phil's movements across Europe for six days, none of which include him flying! All good fun – and even better now to be able to have the French banter and get our own back.

The St. Fort walkers are an amiable group and generally meet on the third Saturday afternoon of each month, walking about eight to nine kilometres, with their rate of walking dependent on their rate of

194

talking and the number of times we stop for a group discussion on any subject from telephone nuisance calls to how to cook a certain meal!

Phil was very pleased to discover that two members were ex-French Airforce and another has a great deal of knowledge about aviation from his previous job. Healthy exercise coupled with flying stories is a difficult combination to beat! I was thrilled that both new activities – line dancing and walking – meant I was not dependent on Phil for my social life. Both clubs kindly welcomed our Joie de Vie guests and friends to join in with their activities.

Phil's Rentrée began on 1st October with the start of the third year of his new contract and his second year off (not working). We considered this year off another blessing and started by being thankful for the chance to make further changes in our garden. We wanted to have an attractive garden for our guests, as well as keeping the maintenance simple. We also wanted to be able to tidy up quickly once guests had left and not become a slave to the garden, as had been the case with our large garden in Lincolnshire. There was not a great deal of time during a Joie de Vie booking to do the garden, and also we were very conscious of not wanting to make any unintentional noise or have machinery disturb their relaxed atmosphere.

Phil looked forward to improving his French in his year off and being able to join in with all our club and church activities, as well as working a full season together with Joie de Vie guests. If there were to be any problems we would be able to iron them out together, share the pickup of guests from the airport or railway station, as well as the trips to local beauty spots for those who had no transport and, importantly, pray together for our guests' safety, protection and healing.

In November we experienced another type of Rentrée – a reconsideration of our faith and entering into full membership of the Eglise Evangélique by being baptised by immersion in water. The denomination of the Eglise is Pentecostal, derived from the Pentecost event in the New Testament when the gift of the Holy Spirit descended on God's people. Baptism by immersion is an outward symbol of living in Christ. We were already saved by our belief in Jesus being our Lord and Saviour, but we wanted to testify to others our confirmation and commitment to have God, Jesus and the Holy Spirit imprinted within our body, mind and spirit as the writing is seen in a stick of rock. Nicodemus, a member of the Jewish ruling council asked Jesus, "How can a man be born when he is old?" Jesus answered, "I tell you the truth, no-one can enter the kingdom of God unless he is born of water and the Spirit." (John 3:4-5).

It was a very moving service for us, and we were entirely astonished at the number of people who came along to witness our baptism – so many members of the church and a great many dear friends from the Anglican Chaplaincy in France too. We stood and gave our testimonies in French and then were baptised in the water tank at the front of the church. As I came up and out of the water it was the most extraordinary feeling and I truly felt renewed. We quickly got changed and joined the rest of the congregation to sing our hearts out in praise and glory. The pastor's wife, Vanessa, and her friend Constance performed a beautiful worship song in English, as a surprise, and we were very touched by their thoughtfulness. After the service we continued to celebrate in the usual French way: by eating!

Great day, great year, great God!

CHAPTER THIRTY

"For the Lord your God is bringing you into a good land
– a land with streams and pools of water, with springs flowing
in the valleys and hills; a land with wheat and barley, vines and
fig-trees, pomegranates, olive oil and honey."

Deuteronomy 8:7-8

Following Christ has given us a completely different attitude to daily living. Our eyes have been opened to appreciate the nuances of life and to delight in the smallest blessing or experience. Some say we are contented with our lot, but the feeling we have inside is far greater than contentment – more akin to delirium! We yearn for very little, except to deepen our relationship with Jesus.

Materially, we have far less than we had before; in fact we have developed a disregard for materialism. We do not worry about being financially secure because we are safe in the knowledge that even if we were reduced to nothing we would have everything. We are thrifty, careful and love a bargain, but our focus is not on wealth but on giving and investing in people. Such a change in our attitude has been awesomely liberating and has allowed us to concentrate on living, working and loving without the encumbrances of doubt, uncertainty or anxiety. Some might say we are slightly deranged because we have willingly thrown away the mould of accumulation and speculation and replaced it with a reliance on God's mould of provision. God's provision is unfathomable, never-ending and rich. If you invest in him, his return and promise far exceeds any appealing percentage of interest on the account.

In Deuteronomy, a book in the Old Testament, Moses prepared a new generation of God's children to leave the wilderness and possess the Promised Land, the land of Canaan, situated on the other side of the Jordan River. God promised his people "a land flowing with milk and honey" which existed for their taking, if only they were prepared to put off all selfish desires and live by faith in him. Sadly the people were disobedient and suffered trials and tribulations because of their lack of faith in God; they persisted in clinging to their old ways. This caused a lengthy delay in them entering the Promised Land, of many years, which resulted in many from that generation missing out completely on the fruits of abundance across the river. Many had not had youth on their side and in wandering aimlessly they missed out on a great opportunity.

Before we became Christians we thought our life was pretty perfect, but then chronic illness, accidents and incidents were our wilderness years. Once persuaded to follow a Christian lifestyle, we focused completely on God, Jesus and the Holy Spirit, and our lives were filled with a tremendous spiritual, emotional and physical abundance. We became rich from the outpouring of blessings on our lives. We crossed a metaphorical River Jordan by being prepared to be obedient, humble and bold in faith, and discovered God's kingdom, "a land flowing with milk and honey". We never could have imagined the sweetness of complete healing.

God created us. He has a role for each of us in his kingdom – a role which might very well be in the locality where we reside already or perhaps in another locality in the same county or country. It might even be a call, as we experienced, to move to another country. Get close to God and that role will become apparent. God is gracious to those who are humble and willing to trust him, and in so doing one must be prepared to change course. The result is well worth the effort!

The Bible verse heading this chapter could not be more apt for our situation in France. We live near a river, wheat and barley are grown on one side of our property, there is a vineyard on the other side of the road and all around our vicinity, fig trees and a pomegranate tree in the garden... We cannot but walk in the way of the Lord and revere him. This good land and its people never cease to amaze us – a land, which has cordially welcomed us and whose inhabitants have befriended us without discrimination. Many of our French friends and acquaintances say they cannot but reciprocate our open and friendly nature, especially because we make an effort to speak their language. Word has got around the locality that we are 'sympa' (kind) and have a heart for people irrespective of income and situation, and such expressions give us hope that we are making some progress in living as Jesus desires.

It took us three years to build relationships with our neighbours and other villagers, yet it only seems like yesterday when Monsieur Rollin, living next to the village shop, called out to us from his garden and introduced himself. We struck up an instant friendship. He would wait at his gate for us to come down the lane to collect our baguette and paper, and he was the first Frenchman who honoured me with nine kisses! Three kisses are very common when you get to know someone well and four not uncommon, but nine has to be a record. One afternoon we were very shocked to learn he had unexpectedly died in his sleep, and we were doubly upset to learn we had missed his funeral. Funerals are carried out extremely quickly because French law declares that although a funeral cannot take place within twenty-four hours of death it must take place within a maximum of six days, not counting Sundays or public holidays. Only a special dispensation granted by the Préfecture, the appointed government representative for the area, will allow a funeral at a later date. I remember a neighbour telling me she read the obituaries section without fail every day in the local paper and at the time I thought it strange, but now I scan the pages too. We walked up to the cemetery, situated on the limit of the village, to pay our respects to our friend. I still imagine him in his garden.

Customs and etiquette are different in France, and one custom we particularly enjoy observing is Epiphany on 6th January, to celebrate the coming of the three wise men who visited the baby Jesus in Bethlehem bringing their gifts of gold, frankincense and myrrh. In later Christian writings the wise men were regarded as kings, and throughout France in January it is possible to buy a cake called 'Galette des Rois' – cake of kings – a flat cake, traditionally made out of flaky pastry filled with a delicious dense layer of frangipane, to be eaten in celebration of Epiphany. The cake is sold with a paper crown and somewhere inside the cake lurks a fève – a trinket, originally a broad bean! – and whoever discovers the fève has the honour of wearing the gold crown and becoming a king. Monsieur le Maire traditionally invites his subjects for an aperitif and slice of Galette des Rois soon after New Year at the Salles des Fêtes, as a token of community spirit, and each association or club have their own celebration too. Each year we have managed to notch up at least four celebrations of Epiphany in a few days and consumed rather a lot of pastry!

Adults delight in finding the fève as much as children and we promptly sport the crown with pride. People are usually quite careful in eating the cake as calls of "Watch your crown!" are passed across the room. They are not referring to the jaunty way the gold crown is worn; rather, dental surgeries deal with more emergency calls due to broken teeth in January than in any other month.

Our line dancing teacher divulged she had a collection of over three thousand fèves, each made out of porcelain, wood or plastic. After broad beans, fèves were originally figures of kings, but nowadays the figurines embrace not only Bible characters but also cartoon and television characters, in fact any theme the artisan baker chooses. Of further interest perhaps is that a traditional Epiphany reception is held at the Elysée Palace (Presidential Palace) for the President and around one hundred and fifty guests, but the pastry chef never puts a fève in the Galette des Rois because it would not be correct for a king to be found in the palace of the French Republic!

The St. Fort walking/cycling club hosted their own celebration for Galette des Rois alongside a film show of scenic and hilarious moments from our monthly walks. We firstly paid our ten euro annual subscription and then a member of the committee explained the statement of funds which included a whopping credit of 1500 euros. We were surprised that a small annual subscription could generate such an income, until it was explained that various state bodies hand out grants to clubs with 'sport' in their title. The projectionist had some difficulty in trying to organise the image on the screen and he was groping around for anything to raise the projector. In an aside to me Phil suggested that several wads of euro notes from the cash box might do the trick!

Certainly we had a sporting time the next day, 14th January, 2012, when sixteen walkers turned up to do the circuit around Moings, near Reaux. There was a carrot on the end of a stick to complete the walk a little faster: a glass of sparkling grape juice and a slice of Galette des Rois, laid out beautifully on a picnic table dressed with a red gingham tablecloth. We love French customs and etiquette!

We share many fun times with our walking group, not least because one of our leaders is famous for walking briskly, chatting animatedly and deviating unwittingly from the proposed route. Several members carry portable GPS's and one member a traditional compass. These walkers are often in a huddle to trying to ascertain the correct path while the rest of us chat or watch their antics. There is always a lively discussion, friendly disagreement with many an "eh bien", "bah" thrown in, and then with many demonstrative French shrugs we ... umm ... always ... retrace our steps to seek the correct path. The rest of the walkers act remarkably stoical, turn around and plod on with their conversations. Our custom before a walk is to gather in front of the church and have our photo taken – presumably a useful record of how many were present when we started off, in case we lose a few on the way!

At St. Preuil, near Segonzac, a certain circuit had been attempted twice before – the emphasis particularly on *attempted*. We hadn't been walking for more than five minutes before the group was brought to a halt for our leader to consider the map then explain he was correct, telling us to stride on upwards between two vineyards. After a mile of ascent we stopped to admire a vineyard owner's large, rambling property, attractively positioned to take advantage of the glorious views across the valley. At that point our leader realised he had missed the track which skirted around the property, but as usual undeterred and used to implicating Plan B we carried on up to a narrow minor road, followed it for a short distance and then headed back into the vines again to pick up our route. As we neared the edge of St. Preiul forest a large hound came straight towards us, lolloping along but looking tired and exhausted. It flopped down beside us and with doleful eyes passed a glance around the whole group, as if seeking out an animal lover to take pity on him. Fortunately one lady's heart melted; she instantly put on her badge of responsibility and seeing a phone number written boldly around the dog's collar she reached for her phone, speed dialled and when the person on the other end answered she announced with authority, "Bonjour, I am the wife of the President!"

She had to repeat herself several times to the owner, whom I presume was stunned to silence whilst standing to attention in the presence of one so intimately close to the President! Finally she admitted she was "the wife of the president of the Chasse," the hunting and fishing fraternity, and, from the variety of hound, guessed he also was a hunter who now had lost his hound. Indeed he was, and he agreed to rendezvous with us in a nearby hamlet. The president's wife wisely asked for the name of his dog, and when she repeated the name to the walking group we were completely helpless with laughter. On the other hand, Diplomat raised his head up to all the strange people and wagged his tail with great affection.

Eventually dog and owner were to be reunited, but not before the 'President's wife' had persuaded an altruistic local resident to secure Diplomat in her garage and had had her photo taken with the dog for our annual film show. Meanwhile another walker fitted her vivid gloves on the end of walking sticks to wave at height for the benefit of a white van coming across the hill. Fortunately it was the dog's owner, who nevertheless got out of his van looking slightly nervous to meet a President's lady and her entourage of ten. Finally the group re-mustered and we walked off chortling at the turn of events, especially when someone said it might be a good idea for us all to wear a collar with our telephone number written in indelible ink, in case we were lost.

We turned into the woods and the smell of mushrooms was amazingly pungent. Several walkers frantically pulled plastic bags out of their haversacks and rummaged around among the fallen leaves and undergrowth, in great anticipation of finding a delicacy. A shout went up when a pied-de-mouton was spied (translates as mutton's foot but known in Britain as the wood hedgehog mushroom) and others raced to the same area, breaking through the undergrowth as if gold had been discovered. Soon there were more whoops of glee as many rather nasty, toxic-looking specimens were examined rapturously and placed with great care into bags, whilst the rest of us murmured quietly to one another that surely the perfect mushroom was the champignon de Paris – the common, easily identifiable, white, risk free, supermarket button mushroom!

Unfortunately, the smell of fungi in the woods had an intoxicating effect on people's sense of direction as we ambled haphazardly through the woods from someone's choice picking to another. Eventually we joined a proper path which took us straight back to the large vineyard property we had passed over an hour ago! Unperturbed we walked back up the track and came into an opening, where there was clear evidence of wild boar having searched the ground for mushrooms. I secretly hoped they were having a siesta and not preparing an attack on my fellow walkers who had commandeered their mushroom rights. Apparently it was the exact spot where the group had become lost in the previous year.

We retraced our steps and discovered a promising track which, however, narrowed after a hundred metres; it led us deeper into the dense woodland... until it completely petered out. Ah, now we were truly lost, but were we concerned? Certainly not the fungi experts because once again mushrooms were in huge abundance, but others had begun to lose interest in the natural world as dusk approached. The air had chilled and thoughts of a warm fire or the TV coverage of a rugby match were making them impatient. Our leader blew his whistle, head-counted ten, then eleven as one came out from the undergrowth, rucksack bulging, and with renewed purpose we set off climbing over fallen tree trunks, negotiated tangled undergrowth and sought a feasible path. With immense relief the walking became easier, a path was discovered and we hastened on down coming out beside the very same vineyard property! If the owners were looking out of their window that afternoon, they must have seriously wondered what on earth was going on in the woods that day, for the same group of people to keep arriving at the same spot at regular intervals. I was ready to head straight back to the car park, a mere mile away – but no chance. Once the French decide on a mission they resolutely, or some might say stubbornly, refuse to give up... unless of course the aroma of mushrooms pervades the air.

While on the subject of mushrooms, Phil and I suffer moments of inquietude when dining with French friends, particularly when the hostess brings the main course to the table, the lid of a serving dish is removed with a theatrical flourish and a mass of strange-looking fungi are revealed to accompany the meat on our plates. Outwardly we smile and murmur our appreciation; silently we say a prayer and proceed to eat as few fungi as etiquette allows. In the morning on waking, when it dawns upon us that we are actually alive, we remark to each other how blessed we are to have survived yet another French meal without being poisoned!

At the beginning of February the doorbell rang and we opened the front door to find an envoy from Monsieur le Maire on the doorstep who presented Phil with a gift bag of homemade chocolate chip cookies! It transpired that Phil was on the list at the Mairie for being of a certain age, and therefore as a retired resident he qualified for the annual custom of receiving a gift. Hugely embarrassed, Phil tried to refuse it, but the envoy insisted that he could not under any circumstance return it to the Mairie. It appears that when an envoy is tasked with State responsibility, any mention of failure incurs thoughts of the guillotine! Once he had left, Phil leapt into the car, headed straight up to the Mairie and requested an audience with Monsieur le Maire, who graciously accepted that his office was entirely at fault for adding Phil to the list, however, for the sake of 'entente cordiale', would Phil kindly accept the gift?

We enjoyed the excellent cookies baked by the Maire's wife with our morning coffee before he changed his mind and asked for them back! That same evening we were back up the hill for a public meeting to hear the Maire's plans for putting a large part of the village on mains drainage and he greeted us at the door with a broad smile on his face, saying, "Here are the English retirees." Much to his delight we hobbled to our seats bent double.

Phil having been placed on the retirement list explained the call I had received from a retirement home for a trial day and the more recent phone call he had answered, inviting him for a free meal in a new restaurant in Cognac, with the bonus of meeting others who were retired. Such calls and gifts made us feel very assured that we could look forward to a promising retirement in the Charente, with many freebies to augment our pensions. Statistics for long life were good in the region, and we know many elderly folk over ninety, partaking in many a meal with them. The eldest person we have met is a glamourous lady of ninety-eight years old, frighteningly sprightly in stilettos, who told us she once was a model but now she is just a flirt. The effects of cognac and pineau cannot be ruled out!

By the end of February our prayers had been answered and the weeks on the calendar we had set aside for Joie de Vie were full – from the middle of April right up to the middle of October! Nineteen had booked in – serving and ex-serving Army, RAF, Navy; support services to the Forces as well – and we prayed none of them would have a reason to cancel. We had chosen two weeks of each month for Joie de Vie bookings, leaving the other two weeks in the month for friends and family. Over the next couple of weeks all those available weeks were full too.

We thought it sensible to plan just two weeks per month for Joie de Vie guests, not only to allow us a break from being on our best behaviour, but to give us time to reflect on how we might do things better and, importantly, be fully refreshed and eager for the next guests' arrival. We set high standards and wanted to present the annex and its surroundings shipshape. We also knew that whilst with us guests' personal problems weighed on our minds, and for the benefit of the next guests arriving we had to be able to meet them without prejudice and any assumption that their situation or problems would mirror the last guests'. We wanted to strive to give the best care; we wanted them to feel spoilt and loved.

CHAPTER THIRTY-ONE

"Not to us, O Lord, not to us but to your name be the glory..."

Psalm 115:1

Shrove Tuesday, the day before Ash Wednesday, can fall in February or March because the date is determined to be forty days before Easter (without counting Sundays). The expression 'Shrove Tuesday' is derived from the past tense of the English verb 'shrive' which means 'to obtain absolution from one's sins'; it is the season when Christians prepare to be shriven before the start of Lent, on Ash Wednesday, by fasting or doing things in moderation. It gives them time to focus and reflect on Jesus' last weeks, his sacrifice and death on the cross, leading up to his glorious resurrection on Easter Sunday.

In the UK, Shrove Tuesday has now become synonymous with Pancake Day because traditionally it was the day to use up the richer, fatty foods of milk, eggs and sugar before changing to a plainer diet of abstinence leading up to Easter. I am always slightly amused at the number of people who have no faith in Jesus yet observe this abstinence by giving up chocolate, alcohol, smoking or certain calorific foods and take Lent very seriously. Many Christians fast too, but it is primarily a time to get back to basics in our faith, to reflect where we have gone astray and more commonly to do something extra, such as renew contact with a friend or relative, do some volunteering, forcing ourselves to do something more than we normally do and commit to pray and read the Bible more often.

In France, Shrove Tuesday is called 'Mardi gras' – Fat Tuesday – and people still prepare crêpes as well as eating beignets de carnival, which are small sugary doughnuts. Many towns and cities have a carnival, the largest of which is held in Nice (actually the location for the first Mardi gras carnival in France) which is famous for its tremendous flower parade and exotic floats. The French love crêpes and at virtually every event there are crêpes. Generally, much to our disappointment, they are served cold; they are also much thinner and more delicate than pancakes because the mixture has many more eggs added, as well as butter and sugar. In our area you will not be surprised to learn that the recipe traditionally includes cognac, which is yummy and makes up for them being cold.

Our church, the Eglise Evangélique, celebrated the start of Lent by organising a themed service in the theatre in Cognac, Centre des Congrès la Salamandre, followed by what can only be regarded as an attempt to get into the Guinness Book of Records for the vast display of crêpes with the greatest variety of filling. We enjoyed the regular favourites but also wonderful fillings such as caramel and apple, chocolate and pear, goat's cheese and walnut, mushroom and bacon, chicken, ham and macedoine of vegetables, to name only a few. We thought the only flavour missing might be Marmite, of which the French are sadly ignorant.

I have had a love of Marmite since a small child but Phil cannot bear even to look at the jar, since his university friend assiduously dissected a Rolo (a chocolate resembling a lampshade with a top to it) and then removed all of the delicious caramel replacing it with Marmite. *Mmm...mh!* I enjoyed Marmite on my toast most mornings, except on Saturday 10th March – the opening of the fishing season. By the time I got to the shop at 9.30am, to collect our regular order of bread for my toast, I was told quite unashamedly that it had been sold as bait! Every man and his worm were apparently out tickling the trout. All I could do in the circumstances was exercise my best French shrug and trudge back to the house disconsolately.

That same day Phil stayed indoors with the Six Nations whilst I joined the walking group for a trek in the countryside, with my usual purpose of upholding Two Nations! Often we find we are the butt of much banter from the French regarding our roots, the British or the weather – most of it tongue in cheek and generally ending with someone saying, "God save the Queen." Whilst holding the fort in the countryside, I happened to comment that there was a distinct lack of wildlife that afternoon, to which the hunt members in our group declared that they weren't at all surprised as it had all been shot! What I hadn't appreciated was the fact that the fishing season had opened the day after the hunting season had closed.

In France, sixty-four species of bird and twenty-four species of mammal may be hunted within set limitations decided by the local authorities. Most hunters are only catching small game: pheasant, partridge, rabbit, hare with the occasional roe deer and while dreaming of sanglier (wild boar). Several women had husbands who had passed up the chance of a healthy walk for the pull of the line (instead of the pull of the rugby) and they were anticipating a delicious fish supper. I suggested they may like to place a tin of sardines on the table in case the catch was poor, which was met with much mirth. They agreed do that and explain it was all my idea – one step forward in diplomatic relations and two back!

A week later we had our friends from the Mill, at the end of the road, up for supper, and keeping diplomacy in mind I decided to steer clear from producing French haute-cuisine or unfussy British dishes, instead opting for a Chinese meal. Our friends viewed the table appreciably as I had placed several orchid plants on the table, which was set traditionally with bamboo placemats, little bowls and large china spoons. However, their eyes popped out of their heads when they saw the chopsticks laid at each place setting. Jean-Pierre strode to the table, picked them up and declared, "What? I can't use these!" I discretely provided a fork, but the meal was a complete success and as they watched us use chopsticks they also took up the challenge.

The troublesome sticks taught us more French vocabulary than we bargained for. The French word for 'chopstick' is 'baguette', which can be confusing as a baguette can refer to any type of stick, piece of wood, baton, beading and edging strips, picture moulding, electricity cable trunking, magic wand, drumstick, pointer (such as to point at a board or screen), filled sandwich like a sub, as well as the traditional thin shaped bread. Basically, if lost for words use 'baguette'.

On 16th April we celebrated our Thirtieth Wedding Anniversary. Where had the years gone? We had a wonderful day, got up with the larks and caught the 08:33 bus from Jarnac to Cognac, taking the rest of the morning to walk back to Jarnac across the hills by way of the vineyards and along the river Charente. It was as glorious and dry as the day we were married. We particularly enjoyed the tranquillity on the river – a vast stretch of open water with barely a ripple. Curiously we watched an inflatable boat come upstream, inside which were two boatmen attired in public works uniforms, probably from the Mairie at Jarnac. Then we noticed several large cages floating on the water, mostly attached to tree trunks growing next to the edge of the river, and each wooden cage base was filled with fresh apple and carrot.

208

We later learnt the cages were to entice and trap the pest ragondin (coypu) because they undermine the river banks with their busy subterranean lifestyle and block water courses. We were surprised to count at least twenty cages en route, needless to say all without tenants. We wished we had bothered to have a closer regard inside the inflatable boat.

We picnicked by the side of the river at Jarnac and couldn't help but reflect on the past thirty years: the ups and the downs, how we had walked in the darkness but now knew without doubt the wonderful light in knowing Jesus. We were created by God and he had given us free will to choose whether to trust him or not; how we thanked God we had chosen to trust him! We felt so at peace, in a peaceful place, knowing without doubt he had the ability to protect us at that very moment, as he had done in the past, and as he would do so in the future. And that was just our earthly life! We also had the knowledge of looking forward to eternal life.

How our days had improved beyond all measure since we had embraced a living God! I couldn't think of a faster fix for pain, anxiety, concern, fear, doubt, stress and confusion than the sure knowledge of God's grace – his grace which transformed these depressing emotions into peace, love, comfort, confidence and a limitless capacity to cope. Alcohol, drugs, addictions and binges, going on a spending spree, chocolate or whatever else one chooses to do to distract from one's problems are merely temporary fixes. The magnitude of God's grace is astoundingly different, inexhaustible, never-ending, limitless, eternal and moreover free.

EPILOGUE

During the past two years (2012-2013) our Joie de Vie project has flourished beyond our imagination. We have entertained thirty-three guests, from all three services and from support services currently working with serving or ex-serving military personnel. We have delighted in meeting each of our guests, and from each different experience we have gained so much more knowledge about combat stress, physical injuries, illnesses and the complexities of the human mind and body. What we hadn't envisaged was how much more we would discover about ourselves.

There is a verse in the Bible, "Do not forget to entertain strangers, for by so doing some people have entertained angels without knowing it." (Hebrews 13:2). Our guests have arrived as 'strangers' and very many have left as friends, which must have surprised them as much as it has surprised us. We have been amazed by the number of mutual contacts we have discovered, been humbled by our guests' honesty and openness to share their life experiences with us, and privileged to see our ministry for the Lord bear fruit. This is reason enough for us to pray for many more guests to cross the Joie de Vie threshold over the years ahead.

We have been blessed by all our guests, yet we suspect they have little idea how much they themselves have been a godsend. Running a rest and recuperation facility has made us realise how much we, too, need to take time out, relax and recuperate. God very sensibly gave us a day of rest and it is imperative we step off the treadmill. You may think you are a machine but even machines need time out to be serviced, otherwise they grind to a halt and finally break with little hope of repair. However impossible it seems, schedule in at least half a day a week for yourself. Taking time out always improves the efficiency of time in. You may even find yourself going to church to be restored and revived!

The years of suffering I endured, compared with the life I have now, are a distant memory. I have no regrets for those 'wasted' years; I have come through and learnt so much about myself. I realise now that the dire times could have been fewer if I had been a whole lot smarter and turned to Jesus a whole lot faster. I passively waited for God to heal me and nothing happened for years. Only when I decided to seek Him, read His word and turn from focusing on "Why me?" did the doors fly open – in ways I could never have conjured up! My waiting was misguided and ineffective, yet He didn't give up on me; He was waiting patiently for me to freely choose to make the first move towards him. When I fully gave myself to Him, He healed me, showed me the gifts He had created in me, and encouraged me to seek a way to use them to help others.

Phil and I live in God's Promised Land (his kingdom), in another promised land of his choosing, having crossed the water from our land of birth. We comprehend God's desire for us to bless and spoil as many people as we can: to love them unconditionally and to pass on our story. We do not know the full result of our labour. We speak naturally and honestly to our guests, our friends, our family and our acquaintances, about our life in France, of God's call on our hearts and our work for his ministry of Joie de Vie.

We do not know the result... but we pray for a reaction, hoping we have lit a spark and that person has spied the chink of the light at the end of the corridor.

We do not know, we might never know, but we are assured, really assured, that God knows.

APPENDIX

IN CHRIST ALONE MY HOPE IS FOUND[16]

In Christ alone my hope is found;
He is my light, my strength, my song;
This cornerstone, this solid ground,
Firm through the fiercest drought and storm.
What heights of love, what depths of peace,
When fears are stilled, when strivings cease!
My comforter, may all in all –
Here in the love of Christ I stand.

In Christ alone, who took on flesh,
Fullness of God in helpless babe!
This gift of love and righteousness,
Scorned by the ones He came to save.
Till on that cross as Jesus died,
The wrath of God was satisfied;
For ev'ry sin on Him was laid –
Here in the death of Christ I live.

There in the ground His body lay,
Light of the world by darkness slain;
Then bursting forth in glorious day,
Up from the grave He rose again!
And as He stands in victory,
Sin's curse has lost its grip on me;
For I am His and He is mine –
Bought with the precious blood of Christ.

---

[16] Extract taken from the song 'In Christ Alone'
by Stuart Townend & Keith Getty
Copyright © 2001 Thankyou Music*

No guilt in life, no fear in death –
This is the pow'r of Christ in me;
From life's first cry to final breath,
Jesus commands my destiny.
No pow'r of hell, no scheme of man,
Can ever pluck me from His hand;
Till He returns or calls me home –
Here in the pow'r of Christ I'll stand.

About Joie de Vie

Joie de Vie was designed with two objectives in mind: a commitment to provide a comfortable, relaxing and enjoyable holiday at minimum cost and not to exclude a guest where mobility is a problem. The self-catering accommodation suits a couple or single person. We can offer an evening meal if desired for no charge and we ask simply for a donation of 5 euros per day to help cover our costs. We are very flexible with dates and can arrange pick-up/drop off from Bordeaux / La Rochelle / Poitiers / Limoges served by low-cost airlines or the TGV connection at Angoulême. We aim to assist you in whatever way possible.

We know from experience how valuable it is to enjoy a special break away just when you are most in need of time out and relaxation. If you are currently serving in the military, retired or work closely alongside the military, please come and enjoy life among the vineyards near Cognac.